CONSCIENCE AND CHRIST

CONSCIENCE & CHRIST

SIX LECTURES
ON CHRISTIAN ETHICS

BY

HASTINGS RASHDALL

D.Litt., LL.D., D.C.L.

FELLOW AND LECTURER OF NEW COLLEGE, OXFORD
FELLOW OF THE BRITISH ACADEMY
CANON RESIDENTIARY OF HEREFORD

LONDON

DUCKWORTH & CO.

3 HENRIETTA STREET, COVENT GARDEN

KRAUS REPRINT CO.
New York
1969

First published 1916
Second Impression January 1917
Third Impression November 1924

L.C. Catalog Card Number 17-2649.

Reprinted with the permission of the original publisher
KRAUS REPRINT CO.
A U.S. Division of Kraus-Thomson Organization Limited

Printed in U.S.A.

TO

THE PRESIDENT

AND

THEOLOGICAL FACULTY

OF OBERLIN COLLEGE, OHIO

U.S.A.

ı   THESE PAGES

ARE GRATEFULLY DEDICATED

PREFACE

THE present lectures were delivered as the Haskell Lectures in the Theological Seminary of Oberlin College, Ohio, U.S.A., during the autumn of 1913. They would have been published earlier but for the war. They were delivered very much as they stand, with a few omissions. I have thought it best to add considerable notes and appendices rather than to enlarge the lectures to an extent which would in several cases have involved complete re-writing.

It may be desirable briefly to explain the design of this little work. For more than thirty years the present writer has been a University teacher of Philosophy, devoting himself especially to Moral Philosophy. He has also been to some extent a student of Theology. He has been struck by the different tone in which moral questions are dealt with by Philosophers on the one hand, and by Theologians and preachers on the other. The Moral Philosopher, if he is not one of those who explain away Morality altogether, usually holds that Morality means the following of Conscience. In theological books and sermons it is as commonly assumed that the supreme rule for a Christian should be to follow Christ. The writer believes that there is truth in both principles, but it is obvious that this position involves a problem as to the relation between the two authorities—and a problem not very often explicitly dealt with. That is the problem with which these lectures are mainly occupied.

There seems to be an especial call for some attempt at a systematic enquiry into the subject at the present moment, for a disposition has recently been manifested in more than one quarter to disparage the moral teaching of Jesus Christ. The supposed discovery that the teaching of Jesus consisted mainly in " Eschatology " has led to the adoption of an almost contemptuous attitude towards His ethical teaching on the part of writers who describe that teaching as a mere " Interimsethik " of little present value or significance ; while (strange to say) the tendency has been to some extent welcomed on the part of certain Theologians of quite a different school because they discern in it a confirmation of the position that there is nothing particularly characteristic in this part of our Lord's teaching, and that it is only in the dogmatic teaching (to be found chiefly in the Epistles and in the later Creeds) that the true essence of the Christian Religion is to be discovered. They hope therefore that they have discovered in this " eschatological " tendency of modern Criticism a new weapon against the old-fashioned " Liberal Protestantism " which is

accused of making too much of the actual teaching of
Christ and too little of the doctrine about His Person
and work. The present writer is not one of those (if
indeed there are such persons) who believe that Christianity consists solely in the ethical teaching of its
Founder, but he does believe that any true representation of Christianity must treat it as a Religion
rooted and grounded in Ethics. He does strongly hold
that any doctrine of our Lord's Person which does not
base itself primarily upon the appeal which the teaching of Jesus makes to the conscience of mankind rests
upon an extremely precarious foundation.

There are two or three points which I would especially invite the reader of these pages to bear in mind :

1. The lectures are confined to the ethical side of
Christ's teaching. I have imposed these limitations
upon myself partly because in so short a course it
was impossible to deal with the whole of our Lord's
teaching, and partly because it was only by isolating
the ethical side of that teaching that it seemed possible
to discuss with thoroughness and definiteness the
question whether or not the ethical ideal of our Lord
can still be accepted by the modern world as the expression of its highest Morality, and to ask in what relation
this ideal stands to that continuous teaching of Conscience in which, as I believe, there is no less certainly
contained a revelation—a progressive and evolving
revelation—of God. That there may seem to be something a little artificial and unnatural in so isolating the

A 2

moral teaching of One for whom Morality stood in such close and intimate relation to Religion, I am well aware ; but this seemed to be the only way in which the particular problem on which I wished to concentrate attention could be discussed without its becoming mixed up with many others.

2. The reader—particularly any Theologian into whose hands the book may fall—is asked to remember that this little book is not intended primarily as a contribution towards the solution of critical or historical problems. I should have preferred to confine myself to purely philosophical and ethical questions, but it is impossible to examine the proper attitude of the modern Conscience to the teaching of our Lord without asking what in point of fact this teaching was; and I have therefore felt bound—somewhat reluctantly—to take notice of, and to pass judgement upon, not a few critical questions, and still more often to recognize the existence of alternative critical possibilities. The critical Theologian will be the first to appreciate the fact that these questions about sources and authenticity are not yet settled with such a degree of certainty that a writer who wishes, as far as possible, to look at the matter from the point of view of Moral Philosophy can simply take over on authority some established view, and confine himself to examining the ethical teaching involved in the sayings accepted as genuine. Most critics will admit that a certain degree of probability is all that can

ever be hoped for on many of these questions. They will therefore readily forgive the writer for not expressing confident opinions on the more disputed points.

And here it may be convenient to say that as to the origin of the Synoptic Gospels I accept the now generally received two-document hypothesis. I believe, that is to say, that the writers of the first and third Gospels derive the greater part of their information from two documents : (1) The Gospel of St. Mark in a form very nearly identical with that which it has now assumed ; (2) A work (consisting principally perhaps of sayings) which used to be spoken of as " the Logia," but is now generally known as " Q." Such a document is generally believed to be the source of those sayings or discourses found in the first and third Gospels, but not found in St. Mark. Besides these each Evangelist doubtless used other sources ; in particular we may recognize an important document used by St. Luke in those passages, including some of our Lord's most characteristic parables, which are peculiar to his Gospel. Upon these matters there is practically now a consensus ; but on such difficult questions as the exact " limits " of " Q," the relation of St. Luke's source to " Q," whether St. Mark had " Q " before him or not, I have not felt myself bound to express definite opinions. I am well aware that no opinion on such matters can have much value which is not based on years of special study.

3. I am fully conscious of the incompleteness of the book. On the critical side many sayings of our Lord which are not of primary importance for ascertaining the nature and value of His ethical teaching are not noticed at all. The treatment of many questions of philosophical Ethics which incidentally arise is so brief that I should hardly have liked to let the book go forth at all but for the fact that I have already discussed many of them at considerable length in a previous work, *The Theory of Good and Evil*.[1] I trust I shall be excused for rather frequently referring the reader who is desirous of a more thorough discussion of particular points to a chapter in that work.

My obligations to many writers upon the life and teaching of our Lord and upon questions of Gospel criticism will be sufficiently obvious. The quotations from one of them are so extensive that a word of gratitude and apology may seem called for. I have been tempted to make frequent quotations from Mr. Claude Montefiore's *Synoptic Gospels* partly by their intrinsic excellence, and partly because, when questions arise as to the originality of our Lord's teaching and its relation to earlier Jewish Ethics, the verdict of one who occupies the position of Liberal Judaism is peculiarly free from the suspicion attaching to the writings of Christian Theologians. Mr. Montefiore, in spite of his reverent appreciation of our Lord's

---

[1] Also in a very brief form in a little volume on *Ethics* published in The People's Books Series.

teaching, cannot be accused of being a " Christian Apologist " ; while he is wholly free from that tendency to belittle or explain away the distinctive elements in the teaching of Jesus which is unhappily at the present moment by no means confined to ultra-" liberal " Theologians.

I have been greatly helped in the original preparation of these lectures by the Rev. J. R. Wilkinson, Rector of Winford near Bristol, and in their revision for publication by the Rev. C. W. Emmet, Vicar of West Hendred, Oxon, and by my colleague, Canon Streeter, to all of whom I owe many important suggestions. I must also gratefully acknowledge valuable assistance in the final revision of the proofs from the Rev. W. M. Browne, Chaplain to the Bishop of Hereford, and the Rev. G. L. H. Harvey, Vicar of Allensmore, Hereford.

H. RASHDALL

THE CLOSE, HEREFORD
March, 1916

CONTENTS

LECTURE I

MORAL PHILOSOPHY AND MORAL AUTHORITY

Contents

LECTURE II

ETHICS AND ESCHATOLOGY

LECTURE III

THE ETHICAL TEACHING OF JESUS CHRIST

Additional Note on the Ethical Teaching of Christ in Detail

Contents

Additional Note on Christian Ethics in the Apostolic Writings

LECTURE VI

CHRISTIAN ETHICS AND OTHER SYSTEMS

APPENDIX I

On the Love of God

APPENDIX II

On Christ's Teaching about Future Reward and Punishment

CONSCIENCE & CHRIST

LECTURE I

MORAL PHILOSOPHY AND MORAL AUTHORITY

IF you open a book of Moral Philosophy written by a philosopher of any school which does not altogether explain away moral distinctions, you find it invariably assumed that it is possible to find out what is right and what is wrong by an appeal to some power, faculty, or activity of the human mind. The Philosophers may differ as to what this faculty is, as to the method of its procedure, as to the precise meaning attached to the ideas of right and wrong and as to what particular acts are right or wrong. But if we confine ourselves to the greater philosophical writers of any period, or to any philosophical writers great or small who have written in modern times, you will invariably find this much common ground between them. In none of them will you find yourself referred to any external authority—any authoritative book or books, any body of decrees or canons emanating from any external authority whether of the past or of the present—as our only means of discovering what we ought to do.

B

Probably you will not find such authorities even mentioned at all as a source of guidance on ethical questions. On the other hand, when you take up a book of orthodox Theology or read a discussion upon some particular practical problem in a Church assembly or a religious newspaper, you are very likely to find it assumed without apology or qualification that the difference between right and wrong is to be decided wholly or mainly by the exegesis of scriptural texts, or by an appeal to Canons of Councils passed—it may be in light, or it may be in very dark, ages of the Church's history. The only difference of opinion seems to be as to what are the authoritative pronouncements to be considered, and as to their relative authority. In the older discussions—the discussions, for instance, on the deceased wife's sister question in English Convocations or episcopal utterances of forty years ago—you will find the Old Testament appealed to as well as the New. In modern times the appeal is usually to the New Testament, or possibly (in writers or speakers a little touched by modern critical views) exclusively to the teaching of our Lord Himself ; while the amount of stress laid upon past decisions of the Church will depend upon the theological school or party of the controversialist. This proposition could be illustrated not merely by discussions on questions connected with marriage, about which for obvious reasons opinion is peculiarly apt to be affected by ecclesiastical differences, but by controversies over the broadest questions of social Ethics. It is not an unknown experience even at the present day to hear a clergyman at a clerical meeting actually maintain that, if a man does not acknowledge the authority of Christ, a Christian would have no common basis of discussion with him as to such questions as strikes, wages, Socialism and the like. And even less unphilosophical Christians sometimes talk as though it were only in the positive teaching of the Christian Scriptures or the Christian Church that you can find satisfactory principles for dealing with social difficulties.

And, still more curiously, we sometimes find both attitudes illustrated by the same man under different circumstances. The Theologian may also be a Philosopher. A clergyman may be a teacher of Philosophy, and when he discourses before his class upon Moral Philosophy he will say a great deal about the authority and validity of Conscience. Indeed, the more orthodox he is as a Theologian, the more certain he is to adopt the philosophical opinions which insist most strongly upon the authority of Conscience. He will probably treat Kant's theory of the Categorical Imperative with profound respect, if he does not adopt all his opinions. He is still more likely to accept Bishop Butler's view that there is " a superior principle of reflection or conscience in every man, which distinguishes between the internal principles of his heart, as well as his external actions : which passes judgement upon himself and them; pronounces determinately some actions to be in themselves just, right, good, others to be in themselves evil, wrong, unjust: which, without being consulted, without being advised with, magisterially exerts itself and condemns him, the doer of them, accordingly."[1] You may be quite sure that you will never hear in a philosophical lecture—even if delivered by a Bishop or a lecturer in some definitely theological institution—the faintest suggestion of the theory that the only way of settling what is right and wrong is to discover a text which bears upon the subject. The most conservative Theologian, when addressing a meeting of working men on some great moral question, or when writing apologetically upon the fundamental truths of Religion against Agnosticism and Naturalism, will be sure to adopt the same tone. But let the same man get upon his legs in a Church assembly or take up his pen to write an article in a Church newspaper upon a moral question, and immediately the whole tone is altered. We hear nothing more about Conscience or the Moral Law or the Categorical Imperative, but only about the true exegesis of some text in the Gospels, or about the decrees of some Spanish Council in the eighth century or the like. Sometimes we hear such questions discussed by cultivated ecclesiastics as if the solution to be given in the twentieth century, not only by an individual Christian but by whole societies, to the gravest problems of social policy must depend

[1] Sermon II.

upon the answer which critics give to a question of various readings.

The contrast between these two methods may be illustrated by an incident in which I was personally concerned. I was requested to give evidence before the Royal Commission which has recently been investigating the question of the Divorce Laws in England. I ventured to suggest that the question was one upon which the moral consciousness had something to say. Thereupon I was severely cross-examined by eminent ecclesiastical authorities as though I were a setter forth of strange gods—and very dangerous and unorthodox gods too. The most exalted of them had enjoyed the advantage of a philosophical education, had sat at the feet of Edward Caird, had no doubt written plenty of essays upon Moral Philosophy in his student days, and would be quite capable of dealing with such problems in a way befitting a philosopher : yet he pressed me to say whether I did not think it was a very dangerous thing to proclaim that such a question was one to be settled by the moral consciousness. Another Commissioner, an acute and learned High-church lawyer, talked as if it really were the first time he had ever heard of the moral consciousness, and as if the admission that the human mind possessed any such activity would be fraught with the gravest disaster to Church and State.

Now it is pretty obvious that this division of the

mind into water-tight compartments is not a desirable attitude. It may be assumed almost off-hand that there must be something to be said for both points of view. Only very uninstructed or very prejudiced religious people will seriously deny the existence and authority of Conscience : while the most liberal and least dogmatic of Theologians are precisely those who will be most disposed to insist that the following, the imitation, the obeying of Christ represents an essential element in the Christian ideal of life.[1] If we are to recognize both the authority of Conscience and the authority of Christ, we ought surely to aim at clear views about the relations between the two. And yet, it would, I fear, be difficult to point to any work in which the problem is satisfactorily dealt with from a point of view which is at once modern and uncompromisingly Christian.

We have excellent works on Moral Philosophy on the one hand, and on Christian Ethics on the other, in some of which no doubt the true relation between the two subjects is incidentally assumed or suggested. But I do not think that the exact problem which I have in mind has often been formally discussed in recent English or American Theology. The subject certainly deserves more serious treatment than it has received. I need hardly say that in these six lectures I cannot

---

[1] At least this would have been their attitude a few years ago ; among the ultra-eschatological Theologians this would not perhaps be assumed. The attitude of such Theologians is dealt with in the next Lecture.

hope to supply this desideratum in our theological literature in any but the most inadequate way. In the little time at my disposal, I shall not aim at any great theoretical completeness, and can only hope to direct your attention to some of the problems which most pressingly demand solution, and offer a few suggestions as to the way in which they ought to be dealt with.

The question with which we are concerned is at bottom " What is the proper relation between philosophical and theological Ethics—between the subject usually called Moral Philosophy or Ethics and the subject known among Roman Catholic divines as Moral Theology, among Protestants more usually as Christian Ethics ? " Now it is clear that such a discussion must logically presuppose not merely that we know something about philosophical Ethics, but that we have adopted some particular ethical system ; for the answer to our problem may, it is clear, be profoundly affected by the particular views we adopt. It being impossible in so brief a course to enter upon any real discussion of these fundamental ethical problems, I can only tell you in the barest and baldest way the main conclusions which I shall presuppose.

I start then with the assumption that we have a power of distinguishing between right and wrong. I assume the existence and the validity of the moral consciousness, or in more popular language the existence and authority of Conscience. This moral consciousness cannot be any kind of Moral Sense or emotion or amalgam of emotions.[1] For the strongest of our moral convictions is precisely this—that the Moral Law possesses objective validity : that acts are right or wrong in themselves, independently of what I or any other individual may chance to think or feel about the matter. Our ultimate judgements are therefore to be compared rather with the axioms of mathematics or the physical laws of nature than with mere emotions. They express propositions, which, if true at all, are true for all minds whatsoever. A mere feeling—an emotional approbation of one kind of conduct or disapprobation of another—could not possibly claim any such objectivity. Mustard is not objectively nice or objectively nasty : it is simply nice to one person and nasty to another. If our prejudice against murder were a mere emotional dislike, the man who did not as a matter of fact see any harm in murder would not be in error, any more than the colour-blind man who experiences a sensation of indiscriminate grey, when the majority of us see green or red, is in error. The thing really is grey to him, red or green to the normal-sighted person. Upon that view it is senseless to discuss which view of murder is the right one : murder would simply be wrong for you and me

---

[1] I have discussed this subject fully in *The Theory of Good and Evil*, Bk. I, chap. iv *sq.*, and more recently (in reference to recent theories) in *Is Conscience an Emotion?* being the West Lectures for 1913, published by Leland Stanford University (in England: Fisher Unwin).

who are repelled by such an act, right for a man like Benvenuto Cellini who gloried in it. And this is just what the moral consciousness of most people undoubtedly refuses to admit. Our moral judgements claim to be objective—to state a matter of objective fact, something which is true not for this or that person, but for all minds whatsoever. If this claim is to be admitted, they must come from the intellectual part of our nature, whether we call it Reason or Moral Reason or anything else—not from a Moral Sense or any other emotional capacity. Objectivity, of course, does not imply infallibility. People may make mistakes about questions of right and wrong, just as they may make mistakes in doing a sum in Mathematics, or in the formulation of a scientific law, or in determining the guilt of a prisoner at the bar. What it does mean is that if A says " I ought to do this under such and such circumstances," and B says, " you ought not to do so," one or other of them must be wrong. The moral faculty has, of course, developed slowly—just like any other intellectual capacity. Not only are the moral ideas of savages different from ours in detail, but it may even be doubted whether the lowest savages can really be said to possess at all the notion of an absolute or objective right and wrong as that notion existed in the mind of a Socrates or a Kant. As applied to the lowest savage, the emotional theory of Ethics developed by such writers as Professor Westermarck and Mr. MacDougall is not perhaps so very far wrong : the merest germ of the notion of an objective " duty " is to be detected in such minds. But the existence and validity of an objective Morality is no more affected by its gradual development, or by the fact that infants and very low savages may not possess the notion at all, than the validity of mathematical axioms is affected by the fact, if it be a fact, that some savages cannot count more than ten, or that mathematically deficient minds—sometimes very brilliant minds in other ways—cannot follow the simplest geometrical reasoning.

As regards the nature and authority of the Moral Consciousness then, I agree in the main with the rationalistic School of moralists, though I should admit that emotion has a great deal more to do with our actual moral judgements in detail than moralists of the Kantian type have commonly recognized. But I must not dwell further upon that matter.

When we pass from the question of right and wrong in general to the question of the ethical criterion—that is, the question how we are to ascertain what particular actions are right or wrong—we find that writers who believe our ultimate moral judgements to be self-evident deliverances of Reason have often supposed that it is possible to determine the morality of particular actions without reference to their consequences. If I want to know whether I ought to tell a lie or not, I must (so one kind of Intuitionist would say) wait till the moment of action, and then I shall hear a commanding voice within me telling me not to tell this particular lie or (it may be—in very exceptional circumstances) to tell it. Or (according to another School) I am supposed to find written on my consciousness a general law which tells me that it is always wrong to lie—even (so Kant explicitly held) when an armed highwayman asks me the whereabouts of my best friend. I must not stay to develope the absurd consequences—as they seem to me—of accepting either of these systems. It is impossible logically to distinguish between an act and its consequences. The consequences, so far as they can be foreseen, are included in the act. And if we once admit that consequences are to be considered, there is no logical stopping at any particular point. We must consider *all* the consequences, so far as we can. The true, ideal, final solution of a moral problem must depend upon the effect of the particular act upon the well-being of the whole human race, though for obvious reasons it is not necessary as a rule to trace out those consequences so far : it is enough to know that its more immediate consequences will be better than those of any alternative course which presents itself to us, and that we have no reason to anticipate any remoter bad consequences which would outweigh the good. So far I agree with the creed commonly known as Utilitarianism. But Utilitarianism, as it is ordinarily understood, is committed to the further position that human well-being means nothing but pleasure, and

pleasure measured quantitatively. From that position I entirely dissent. The belief in duty carries with
it the further conviction that the doing of one's duty
—the good will, goodness, virtue, character—is an end-
in-itself, that it is itself a good, and the highest of all
goods. And I believe many other elements in human
life to be intrinsically valuable besides goodness and
pleasure—knowledge, intellectual activity, æsthetic
satisfaction ; affections, emotions, and desires of
many sorts. All these kinds of conscious life and
activity are normally accompanied by pleasure, but
their value is not always proportionate to their pleas-
antness. And when we do think of them in the light
of pleasures, we recognize that they differ in kind :
their value is not (as the Hedonist supposes) dependent
upon their mere duration and intensity taken together.
Human Well-being or Good includes a whole hierarchy
of goods. There is a good of the will or moral good : a
good of the intellect : a good of feeling. True good—
good in the singular—includes all these goods in
due proportion. Acts are right so far as they tend to
bring about for all mankind such a true good—the
largest amount of it that is possible and the justest
distribution of it that is possible. When we have to
choose between different goods, our aim should be to
bring about the greatest attainable good on the whole.
The Utilitarian is right, it seems to me, in aiming at
the maximum of human Well-being and a just distribution of it : he is wrong in identifying that Well-being

with maximum pleasure. The Intuitionist of the traditional type is right in holding that the ultimate moral judgement is intuitive, immediate, or, if you like, a priori : he is wrong only in treating isolated impromptu judgements upon particular cases of conduct, or, again, hard and fast exceptionless rules as to whole classes of acts, as final, irreversible, absolutely binding deliverances of the moral consciousness. The true ultimate moral judgement relates not to acts but to ends : the true moral judgement is a judgement of value. It is expressed in the form " this is good," not " this is right." The concept of good no doubt includes that of right or duty. If something is good, that means that it is always right to try to bring it into existence, except so far as it stands in the way of some greater good. On the other hand, the judgement " this act is right " always, if thought out, implies that there is some good which ought to be realized, absolutely, for its own sake, as a means to no end but itself. What the good is, it is for the moral consciousness to pronounce. The good is an ideal which the moral consciousness creates or recognizes. Such is in barest outline the ethical system which I have ventured to call " Ideal Utilitarianism."

I cannot hope, of course, in the time at my disposal to explain and justify this mode of ethical thinking to those to whom it is unfamiliar, or who have definitely adopted some other system. I have thought it best to indicate in this, I fear, rather dogmatic manner the

point of view from which I myself approach the subject ; for I shall be obliged at times to assume a particular answer to certain ethical problems.   But I
trust it will be possible for many to accept the general
view which I hope to set before you of the relation
between philosophical or (as some people might call it)
" natural " Ethics and the special Ethics of Christianity
without adopting my own particular answer to the
problem of the ethical criterion.   In most of what I
have to say it will be enough to assume merely that
you agree with me in holding that we have a natural
power of determining what is right and wrong, and
that we ought in the last resort to guide our conduct
by the ethical judgements which we derive from this
moral faculty of ours.   The problem which on such an
assumption confronts us is this : If we have this
natural power of judging between right and wrong,
where can we find room in our moral life for any
external authority—for any authoritative rules of
right and wrong such as we find in the Bible, in the
traditional laws or decisions of the Church, and especially in the commands and ethical sayings of our Lord
Himself—or (to put the problem in its most general
form) for any positive body of ethical doctrine such as
every historical Religion sets before its adherents ?   If
Conscience is to be supreme, it might seem at first sight
that to set up any such body of ethical precepts as
final and infallible, or even as entitled to any particular
respect, must be superfluous or else pernicious.   If we

already know what is right, why appeal to the authority
of any outside moral legislator ?   Might we not (it
may be asked) apply to the enactments of such an
authority the dilemma by which the Khalif Omar is
said to have justified the conflagration of the Alex-
andrian Library ?   " If these books contradict the
Koran, they are pernicious ; if they agree with it, they
are superfluous."   If the precepts of authority agree
with those of our own Consciences, they must be superfluous : if they contradict them, they must be false.

Now at this point I must remind you that the process
of deciding what ought to be done in any conjunction
of circumstances is not really so easy a process as it
might at first sight appear from the simple assertion
that human Reason gives us certain self-evident
judgements on the subject. (1) In the first place these
self-evident judgements relate, as we have seen, to the
value of ends : what are the means to the end judged
to be good, we must learn from experience. A great
deal of knowledge about plain matters of fact is required to enable an individual mind—even an adult
developed mind at an advanced period of civilization
—to give a right answer as to what ought to be done
in any particular conjunction of circumstances. Such
a judgement demands much knowledge about the consequences of actions which can only be ascertained fully
by an experience much wider than that of the average
individual. And then (2), even in pronouncing upon
the value of an end, the individual is always limited

to his own experience or to some experience which he can understand by the analogy of his own. If the question be as to the relative importance of culture and (say) athletic exercise, an individual must have some experience of both before he can decide : he need not have an actual knowledge of the particular literature or music whose value is in question, or else it would never be possible to decide upon the value of any experience till it was over, but he must have had some analogous experience. He need not wait to justify his spending time upon hearing Wagner or reading the last new poet till he has made acquaintance with their works : but he cannot decide whether music or poetry are good without knowing to some extent what music and poetry in general are like. And (3) it must be remembered that, even when the actual experiences are before him—when he knows that act A will lead to such and such a state of consciousness and act B to some other state of consciousness, and knows what these states of consciousness really are,— not everyone possesses equal powers of judging values, any more than all individuals are equally good judges of scientific truth or of historical evidence or are equally competent critics of poetry and painting.

From these considerations it follows that the great majority of individuals in the great majority of their actions cannot possibly decide for themselves about their rightness or wrongness in the way that is often assumed to be possible in the abstract discussions o moral philosophers. That would be so even if each individual were born into the world with his faculties already fully developed. Still less are children capable of giving an independent answer of their own to such problems. As a matter of fact the earliest state of the human infant is one in which he differs from a low type of animal only in having less strong and valuable guidance from his instincts and a greater capacity for future development : while, if we look to the history of the race, the civilized modern man has emerged from a savage ancestor in whom it is hard to detect any such rational reflection upon conduct as the moral philosopher presupposes, and further back from an animal in which there was certainly no such reflection. Even when we turn to the developed intelligence in its most reflective moments, we at once recognize that the behaviour of most men in most circumstances is determined by instinct, by passion, by custom and habit, or (in so far as it is based upon consciously accepted ethical principle) by rules which are not due to the independent working of their own intellect but have been handed down by social tradition and are imposed upon them by a social environment. It is unnecessary for the present purpose to ask what determines the established morality of a community in early times—how much is due to instinct, how much to the operation of natural selection, how much to the teaching of experience and conscious utilitarian calculation, how much to the influence of leading minds

c

and the traditions which they have created, how much
to emotion and how much to Reason. It is enough for
us to take note of the fact that in primitive communities
morality consists mainly in obedience to custom ; and
that in so far as custom is due to the working of the
moral Reason, it is largely the Reason of the community
rather than the deliberate reflective verdict of any
particular Conscience that expresses itself in its
morality. As civilization and moralization advance,
Morality tends to become more conscious, more reflective, and more individual. But even in the most
advanced and developed communities, the greater part
of the average individual's moral ideal is the ideal of
his community. He starts with a set of rules, ideals,
institutions, which he does not consciously question, and
the ultimate grounds of which he does not investigate.
The part which his own Conscience plays in the matter
is for the most part that of accepting and recognizing
the moral ideal of his community, or in choosing
between several social ideals which may be contending
for the mastery within the wider community, or in
applying the general principles which are so accepted
to the determination of particular cases. Only occasionally does the individual Conscience assert itself to
the extent of criticizing, rebelling against, defying on
some particular point, the accepted ethical code.

This line of thought has been carried by some
Moralists so far that they absolutely refuse to contemplate the case of an individual sitting down to

consider on general philosophical principles how he ought to act in a particular case. That is one of the characteristics of Hegelian Ethics. In Hegel himself, it has been not unjustly said, there is no moral Philosophy, but only political Philosophy. Full as he is of the idea that Morality is an expression of Reason, it is always the social and not the individual Reason that he has in view. The individual must accept the established customs, traditions, and institutions of his time as final authorities. " The wisest men of Antiquity have given judgement," Hegel tells us, " that wisdom and virtue consist in living agreeably to the ethos of one's people." And Hegel avowedly accepts this judgement of antiquity. Mr. Bradley has gone one better than Hegel, and pronounced that for a man " to wish to be better than the world is to be already on the threshold of Immorality."[1] Now it is tolerably obvious that, if this system is to be carried out thoroughly, no moral progress would be possible—unless we choose to adopt the startling position that all past progress in the ethical standard of communities has been effected by a succession of private immoralities. Moral progress has, in point of fact, only been brought about by the acts of individual men and women who have had the courage to condemn, to go beyond, and to defy the existing code of public opinion at a given time and place. It is true that the development of moral ideals is effected very gradually and imper-

[1] *Ethical Studies*, p. 180.

ceptibly. Sometimes you may not be able to point
to the particular person or persons whose thought and
action have brought it about. Sometimes the same idea
or tendency seems to seize upon a whole community at
once ; more often it takes possession of some considerable minority of persons almost at the same time,
though it triumphs only at the cost of a violent struggle
with the creed of the majority. Even in those cases
the change is really due to the working of individual
consciousnesses, however much they may act and
react upon one another, and however impossible it
may be for the historian to determine who the individuals were. But that is not always the case.
Many of the great steps and stages in moral progress
are definitely associated with the work of individual
men—actual historical characters, great rulers, great
teachers, great thinkers, reformers, prophets, men of
genius. And among these—especially at a certain
middle period of history intervening between the era
of primitive custom and that of modern civilization—
the most prominent individual workers in this great
task have been the founders or revolutionary reformers
of the great historical religions. Whatever else an
historical religion is, it always represents a certain body
of teaching about right and wrong, a body of ethical
rules, a moral ideal. And one difference between the
influence which is exercised by such great religious
teachers and other personal influences which have con-
tributed to ethical progress is just this—that it is much

more conscious and personal. These men have, of course, like other contributors to moral progress, influenced the world by introducing into the tone and traditional morality of the community changes which go on operating among those to whom even their names are unknown : but their strongest influence is dependent upon the actual knowledge of their words, their lives, their characters. And this influence is kept alive as a definite tradition in the societies which they have founded or reformed or influenced—whether in the form of sacred books or of traditional rules, customs, and institutions. To overlook or underrate the influence which has been exercised upon moral development by great personalities has been a too frequent tendency of philosophical Ethics, especially in the writers of the Hegelian School. In the ethical region —men of Science are beginning to say in the biological region also—nature takes more leaps and longer leaps than a priori evolutionary thinkers like to admit. And the form which such leaps assume in the moral region is most commonly to be found in the appearance of great personalities.

Now to a considerable extent the influence of the great personality consists simply in making people more disposed to do what their Consciences already recognize that they ought to do. It is most important, of course, to remember that men's actual morality depends upon many things besides knowledge—knowledge of what they ought to do. And we might attach very great value to the influence of Christ and of His followers and of the Society in which the memory of His sayings and His character is kept alive even if we never appealed to His authority to decide what ought to be done, but only pointed men to Him as supplying an example which makes men more willing to do what their own Consciences enjoin. To a very considerable extent the moralizing influence which Christ has exerted has been of this nature. It has stimulated and deepened the moral consciousness in general. But a recognition of this fact does not solve the particular problem with which we are immediately concerned—that is to say, the question what and what kind of authority we ought to attribute to His teaching on particular questions of conduct. We must go on to ask " how can Christ—how can any great teacher or great personality—help us to know what we ought to do in spite of the fact that we have all got Consciences to tell us ? "

The answer may, I think, be gathered from the considerations which have already been insisted upon.

(1) In the first place men's capacities for ethical judgement vary enormously; and average men have to rely to a very large extent upon the judgement of the gifted few. The prophet or great personality may be looked upon as one in whom Conscience has attained an exceptional development.

(2) The moral consciousness can only give ethical judgements upon the basis of the materials presented

to it. An ideal must be thought of before it can be approved, and to think of a new ideal of life requires genius no less than to think of a new tune or a new scientific hypothesis. The ordinary man can see to some extent—not always in a moment but in course of time—the nobleness of a new ideal which has actually been placed before him ; but he could never have thought of it for himself. The savage into whose mind the idea of unselfishness has so little entered that he finds it easier to believe that the missionary has sprung from the foam of the sea than to believe that he has not come among them to serve some purpose of his own is nevertheless found quite capable of appreciating the beauty and the nobleness of self-sacrifice when once he has been brought to believe in its existence. It wants some poetic capacity to appreciate Shakespeare, but not nearly so much as it took to be Shakespeare. It requires some moral capacity to appreciate the ideal of a moral genius, but not nearly so much as it takes to conceive that ideal.

And (3) even when the truth of a moral rule is not actually seen, it is quite justifiable to accept the decisions of a moral authority whom we judge to be more likely to be right than ourselves. We do all of us begin by accepting our parents' ideals, and then the ideal of our community. If we come to the conclusion that a particular individual or some group of men or a society within the general community is more likely to be right than we are, it is a quite reasonable and

morally justifiable course to accept and act upon the
decisions of this authority, just as we accept the decisions of experts on any other subject. Two reserva-
tions must, however, be made in laying down this
principle. (*a*) The first is that even this acceptance of a
moral authority implies some exercise of the individual's
own moral judgement : for it implies that he knows
the meaning of right and wrong in general, even if he
accepts another's verdict upon some particular question as to what is right or wrong. This notion of right
and wrong in general no external authority could
possibly teach him except by calling into activity the
latent powers of his own soul. And (*b*), while on details
the wisest of men will always show their wisdom by
trusting the judgement of those who are likely to know
best, yet when we come to the fundamental principles
of conduct, to act in obedience to authority must be
regarded as a lower kind of Morality—one only to be
recommended as a step towards the cultivation of an
independent ethical judgement. We could hardly
imagine a man believing that he ought not needlessly
to injure his neighbour on authority. The man who
could not see that much would hardly be a moral
being at all. It is not so inconceivable that one who
was indisposed to treat a man of another race as his
neighbour might be prepared to do so in obedience to
an authority which he revered.

On these principles there is ample room for the
exercise of great influence over the moulding of moral

ideals by ethical authorities of various kinds—living teachers, the recorded sayings of teachers in the past, traditional systems, organized societies.   And if we could find any human being of supreme ethical insight, we should have on these principles a sufficient reason for placing him in a supreme position among our ethical authorities.   Indeed, it might seem that, if only we could be sufficiently sure that his insight was of such a unique character, we might have a sufficient warrant for the most absolute surrender of ourselves to his authority.   And this is precisely the position which much traditional Theology would assign—sometimes to the Bible as a whole, sometimes to the New Testament only, sometimes to the Bible and the Church (in whatever relation they may be supposed to stand to each other), sometimes to Christ alone.   I will confine myself for the present to the authority of Jesus Christ Himself.

And here, when we approach the central question, " What kind of ethical authority are we prepared to recognize in Jesus ? " everything turns upon the grounds upon which we suppose that He is supremely likely to be right in his ethical judgements.   The old way of defending the authority of Christ was something of this kind.   First it was established by historical evidence that Jesus said certain things, and that He worked certain miracles.   The miracles were held to prove that what He said must be true.   Then it was either directly inferred that all His ethical teaching must be divinely inspired, and therefore fully and eternally true ; or else the same conclusion was indirectly inferred from the premiss that He taught the doctrine of His own Divinity. Now even supposing that both the miracles and the sayings could be sufficiently attested by historical evidence, and supposing it were certain that the events commonly called miracles were in the fullest sense violations of the laws of nature, it is an immense leap from the fact that a human being was able at some point to suspend the laws of nature to infer that all that he said was true. Moses, according to the traditional conception, worked miracles : yet Christians have always believed that certain parts of his teaching were contradicted and set aside by Christ, and therefore could never have been altogether true. Elijah is said in the Old Testament miraculously to have brought down fire from heaven to consume the captains and their fifties ; yet this very miracle was treated as an indication of an ethical temper deserving of severe condemnation by One whom Christians have accepted as a higher authority than Elijah. If we make the inference indirectly—through the supposed fact that Jesus claimed to be God—the inference to His ethical infallibility might be better justified. Even then we should really be making a good many other assumptions, though they might be reasonable assumptions. But fortunately we are dispensed from the necessity of answering so abstract a question. A critical study of the Gospels makes it certain that Jesus never did claim to be actually God. The doctrine of Christ's Divinity rests rather upon the sense of His unique religious value entertained by His followers than upon any direct claim of His own. It is due to the reflective consciousness of the Church and not to the actual teaching of Jesus.[1] That He claimed to be the Son of God or the Messiah, to speak with authority, to have a divine message to deliver, is true. But the other prophets had claimed to have a divine message and that with obvious bona fides, and yet we do not regard all their words as final and infallible revelations of moral truth. If it is admitted that revelation or inspiration admits of degrees, a mere claim to be an inspired revealer, or even to be the promised Messiah of Jewish expectation, will not prove ethical infallibility.

But the supreme difficulty in the way of this old Paleyan conception of Christianity as a body of supernaturally guaranteed truth attested by historical evidence, lies in the doubtfulness of the miracles themselves—the doubt, as to some of the events, whether they actually occurred, and as to others whether they cannot be accounted for without supposing any actual violation of the laws of nature, however much they may imply unusual and abnormal degrees of that control of physical processes by mental influence which in lower degrees is a matter of everyday experience.

[1] This of course implies that we do not regard the fourth Gospel as a record of the *ipsissima verba* of our Lord—a conclusion which would now be admitted even by scholarly defenders of its Johannine authorship.

Even those who believe in the Gospel miracles in the most uncompromising manner as actual violations of physical law do not usually at the present day rest their proof of Christ's Divinity chiefly upon the miracles. They believe in the miracles because they already believe in the Divinity rather than believe in the Divinity because they believe in the miracles. And in their proof of the Divinity they rely very largely indeed upon the impression made upon the Conscience by our Lord's moral teaching and character. They see a supreme revelation of God in His character and teaching because they can conceive none higher or more capable of satisfying the demands of their own moral consciousness. And therefore it would be absolutely suicidal to invite us to accept the moral teaching merely on the strength of the miracles, or on the strength of any claims which are proved by the miracles. To argue that Jesus was divine because His moral teaching appeals to us as supremely true, and then to contend that His teaching must be true because He was divine, is to argue in a circle. If we once allow the self-evidencing truth of His moral teaching to occupy a prominent place in the argument for His Divinity, we are trusting to the validity of our own moral consciousness ; and when we have done this, we can no longer profess ourselves willing to accept any and every moral precept of Christ, without any criticism of its contents, on the strength of the historical evidence that He uttered the words.

And this consideration sets strict limits to the extent
to which a Christian can be asked to accept a precept
in blind obedience to Christ, regarded as an external
moral Legislator or an external Revealer of truth
otherwise inaccessible to the human mind. We can
accept the revelation only because, and in so far as,
it appeals to the moral consciousness as true : it is
because it does make such an appeal to us that we
believe it to be a revelation. That holds, I should
contend, of other than the ethical aspects of the
Christian revelation, but with those other sides of
Christ's teaching we are not immediately concerned.
It holds still more clearly with regard to His ethical
teaching. No doubt it will remain possible to treat
Christ's deliverances on particular points with profound reverence : it may even be quite reasonable for
an individual to accept Christ's verdict on particular
questions, and to act upon it even when he fails
on the fullest reflection to see the ground of that verdict. That is the principle on which we accept the
judgement of the expert on any subject. We defer to
him beyond the limits within which we can see clearly
because we have tested his insight, and seen it to be
superior to our own, within the limits within which we
can judge for ourselves. But there must be a point
beyond which such blind submission cannot go : we
submit without judging in a detail just because we
have judged and approved the ideal as a whole. If the
collisions between our own moral judgement and his

were too frequent or too fundamental, that would under-
mine all the grounds which we have for trusting his
judgement. And then, when we do accept the validity
of authority against our private judgement, it will not
commonly be a case of the individual's solitary judgement being pitted against that of the authority to
which he defers. The judgement of the solitary
teacher—be it Christ or some other great ethical
teacher—will commonly be supported by that of the
community generally, or some large section of it. If
it were not merely our own individual judgement but
that of our whole community, including its best and
wisest, that were in collision with the judgement of the
great teacher, then we could hardly contend that the
ipse dixit of any authority, however justly venerated,
ought to prevail against the voice of such a collective
Conscience.

The conclusion to which all I have said points is
that the kind of authority which we can attribute to
the teaching even of Christ Himself, and the limits of
that authority, must be determined by the impression
which His teaching actually makes upon the moral
consciousness of the present. And therefore we cannot
in the old-fashioned way first examine the credentials
of the Master's authority ; and then, having done so
and found them satisfactory, profess ourselves willing
to accept and act upon His precepts blindly, no matter
what the actual character of the acts commanded.
We cannot pronounce on the authority justly to be

claimed by the teaching of Jesus till we have examined what that teaching is, and asked how far it appeals to our moral consciousness. In the following lectures I shall contend that the authority which Christ's ideal of life can still justly claim is based upon the fact that it does, in its essential principles, appeal to and satisfy the demands of our moral consciousness in the present. But meanwhile I will add one or two further remarks on this general question of submission to authority in Ethics.

(1) Whatever professions may have sometimes been made to the contrary, submission to authority in matters of conduct has never been absolute. There has been, of course, *much*—often too much—submission to authority in such matters. Without a certain amount of it no community could hold together for a year ; in its excess such submission has been responsible for some of the greatest crimes in history. All the great religious persecutions have been justified by the precepts of the Old Testament or of the Koran. But with good men this submission has always had limits. In his famous controversy with Mr. Gladstone Cardinal Newman frankly admitted that, if a collision arose between a Pope who should command him to be disloyal to his Sovereign and the Conscience which bade him obey that Sovereign, he would put Conscience above an authority which he theoretically regarded as infallible in all matters of faith and morals. Enlightened divines still frequently talk as

though they would be prepared to obey a dictum of
Christ, no matter what they themselves thought of
its morality. Some of them are even willing to obey
Him (as I shall point out hereafter) on the strength of
a conjectural emendation of His recorded language—a
deference to Criticism which they do not always display
in other directions. But let us suppose not merely that
Criticism had detected an adventitious gloss in a particular text, but that a first-century MS. of the second
Gospel were discovered from which it appeared that
the true text of the passage about Divorce was this :
" thou shalt not put away thy wife in case of adultery
but thou mayest take two others," can we suppose
that any one of those Anglican ecclesiastics who are
so irreconcilably opposed to the remarriage of the
innocent divorcee on the strength of a saying of Christ
would be prepared to act upon the recommendation ?
Of course they would not. It is open to them to say
that what they believe to have been the actual command of Christ appeals to their conscience, or at least
is not opposed to its dictates, whereas the hypothetical
injunction would not make that appeal. But on that
view it is really because they approve that they obey.
Whether they approve or disapprove, they are equally
sitting in judgement. These divines could not condemn
others for rejecting on a particular point a dictum of
Christ which should not commend itself to the modern
Conscience. Whether there are any dicta of Christ
Himself which fail to appeal to the modern Conscience,

I shall examine in future lectures. It is enough to insist that no one really makes his submission even to the teaching of our Lord Himself absolute and un-limited except in so far as the actual injunctions of that authority commend themselves to his conscience. As a rule, of course (where people are naturally in-clined to disagree with some authoritative command), an open collision is avoided by interpreting the com-mand of their authority in a way which does not contradict the deliverances of the present-day Con-science. Such interpretations always have been, and always will be discovered, in these cases.

(2) And, secondly, it is important to insist that our Lord Himself does not claim any such absolute sub-mission to Himself as to a merely external authority. He always addresses Himself to Conscience. He assumes that His hearers, too, have some of that power of judging about questions of right and wrong which He possessed Himself in a supreme degree. I shall return to this point hereafter. Meanwhile it will be sufficient to remind you that, even when He appealed to the works which are commonly called miraculous, He appealed not so much to the power exhibited by the works (which He admitted might quite conceivably come from Satan), but to their goodness. It was the merciful character of His healings which showed that they came from God, and that would be no evidence at all if we had no power of judging for ourselves that mercy is more divine than malice. His language about

D

the sin against the Holy Ghost—whatever were the exact words He used and whatever their precise meaning —implies at least that His Pharisee opponents were struggling against their own conviction that His teaching came from God—a conviction which could only be based on the witness of Conscience. " The lamp of the body is the eye : if therefore thine eye be single, thy whole body shall be full of light. But if thine eye be evil, thy whole body shall be full of darkness. If therefore the light that is in thee be darkness, how great is the darkness."[1] There we have an explicit testimony to Jesus' belief in a light which, in greater or less measure, lighteth every man : and it was that light to which He appealed as the supreme sanction for His claims. But it is not so much upon any detailed passage that I would rely as upon the spirit of His whole teaching. Habitually He assumes that, though men did require to have the truth about Morality set before them, though it had never been set before them so fully as He felt Himself able to reveal it, yet when it was set before them, they were capable of recognizing its truth. " Why even of yourselves judge ye not what is right? "[2] The words occur incidentally in a somewhat obscure passage, but they only recognize a power of moral judgement which is implied in the whole of our Lord's best-authenticated teaching. He did not ask men to obey his precepts except in so far as their

---

[1] Matt. vi. 22 (=Luke xi. 34, 35).
[2] Luke xii. 57.

Consciences bore independent witness to their truth. Doubtless He thought of that inner light in other men as coming from the same heavenly Father who had in an exceptional way spoken in the Old Testament Scriptures and was speaking also in Him : but it was a voice within, not a merely external voice, to which He appealed in confirmation of the claim which He made upon their allegiance.[1]

[1] This side of our Lord's teaching is very much developed in the fourth Gospel. More directly than any of the Synoptists the Evangelist appeals to the " works " in attestation of Christ's claim, but after all the appeal to the works comes second : " Or else believe me for the very works' sake " (xiv. 11).

LECTURE II

ETHICS AND ESCHATOLOGY

IN my last lecture I endeavoured to show you that it is impossible to determine the kind of authority which may reasonably be claimed for the ethical teaching of our Lord in advance—before we have examined the teaching itself. For, in His own view, that teaching was assuredly not regarded as the promulgation of a moral code by an external authority, to be accepted in consequence of some already established claim to Messiahship[1] or Divinity—without examination, without interior assent, without spontaneous acceptance. It was put forth as an appeal to Conscience. Still more certainly the authority which it possesses for us at the present day must depend upon its own intrinsic character. In the view alike of His own immediate disciples and of the reflecting Theologians of later ages, the claim of the Teacher to be something more than one among many inspired teachers or prophets has been based—to a very large extent at least—upon the appeal which the teaching

---

[1] It is most probable, I think, that this claim was not definitely made till towards the close of His Ministry, and it is doubtful how far it was made in public at all.

and the character have actually made to the moral
consciousness, upon the response which they have awak-
ened and still awaken in the human heart. I should
like to have gone on at once to examine what the
ethical teaching of Jesus actually was in detail, and
then to invite you to consider what authority it can
justly claim for the modern world. Ten years ago I
should probably have adopted that course. But in
the present state of theological thought we are liable
to be met with a preliminary objection which it will,
I think, be well to deal with in advance. We are
liable to be told that the teaching of Jesus was not
primarily ethical at all. It was primarily eschatological. Its main content was simply this: the
Messianic Judgement, long foretold by prophet and
apocalyptic writer, was at last on the very point of
coming—a sudden, catastrophic, in the fullest sense
supernatural, appearance of the Messiah upon the
clouds of heaven—a violent and abrupt winding up of
the present world-order, followed by the establishment of the Messianic Kingdom in an outward and
visible form whether upon a very much altered earth
or in a Heaven beyond the skies. Any ethical teaching
which the Teacher uttered was merely incidental to
this His central message: and that teaching is almost
destitute of any special value or significance for the
modern world just because it is so intimately bound
up with ideas about the Universe which we cannot
share, and with anticipations as to the future which the

course of events has already shown to be delusive.[1] I should very much have preferred to pass over these questions in silence. I have no claim to speak as a specialist upon this subject—a subject which involves for its adequate discussion intimate acquaintance not only with the difficult and complicated Synoptic problem but with all the apocalyptic literature of later Judaism and early Christianity. Nor do I believe that these questions have in reality any very close connexion with our proper subject ; but I fear that to brush them aside and proceed to examine the ethical teaching of the Gospels without touching upon them would expose the lecturer to the suggestion that his whole point of view was out of date, and that everything he had said must in consequence be consigned to the limbo of obsolete apologetics. I must therefore at least make a short statement as to the attitude of my own mind towards the problem, though a thorough discussion of it will be impossible. I must be content with giving you conclusions with no more than the merest outline of the reasons which lead me to them.

All students of Theology—and most of those who,

---

[1] "The truth is, it is not Jesus as historically known, but Jesus as spiritually arisen within men, who is significant for our time and can help it. Not the historical Jesus, but the spirit which goes forth from Him," etc. (Schweitzer, *The Quest of the Historical Jesus*, E. T., p. 399). There is a sense of course in which one might accept such statements, but if this "spirit" really "goes forth from Him," i.e. the historical Jesus, there must be something in common between the two, and this something must be capable of being distinguished from its eschatological surroundings.

without being professed students of Theology, take
some interest in the course of theological thought and
enquiry—are aware of the great change which has
taken place in the prevailing attitude towards what
are called the eschatological sayings of the Gospels—
that is to say, the predictions alleged to have been
uttered by our Lord about His own future coming
again, about the Judgement which that coming would
inaugurate, and that supernatural winding up of the
existing order of things which is popularly spoken of
as the end of the world. Conservative Theology has
never of course doubted that these sayings were
actually uttered : and, as regards the central event,
it has been disposed to understand them very literally.
The Master is reported to have said that He would
come again seated on the clouds of heaven. Conservative and orthodox Theology has always assumed
that that prediction would be literally fulfilled. All
that is said in the Gospels as to the second coming of
Christ, as to the Judgement, and the physical catas-
trophes which should precede, accompany, or follow
that Judgement have been understood with almost
equal literalness, or at all events in the most uncompromisingly supernatural sense. On the other hand, the
passages which seemed to speak of these events as
impending in the very near future—before the disciples
had gone over the cities of Israel or in the lifetime of
those who listened to Jesus—were explained either by
understanding the " coming " (so far as those particular

passages were concerned) in some spiritual sense or by referring them to that approaching destruction of Jerusalem which was regarded as a sort of preliminary anticipation or first instalment of the final Judgement. When we come to the nature of the Kingdom, there has been much diversity of opinion. Some passages were understood as referring to the establishment of the Kingdom by the missionary work of the Apostles on this earth ; and the main difference of opinion among orthodox thinkers has been as to how far they were to be understood in a spiritual sense of a Kingdom of Christ in the hearts of the individual believer or in the invisible aggregate of believers, or how far the Kingdom might be identified frankly and without more ado with the visible, organized, hierarchically governed Church. But there were other passages in which the establishment of the Kingdom was so closely connected with a judgement of a supernatural character that the Kingdom had there to be understood as a new order of things to be established—after the judgement—whether on this earth or (from the time when " Millenarianism " came to be looked upon as heretical) more usually " in heaven."

The tendency of " liberal " thought until recently has been towards a more complete spiritualization of this eschatological teaching. Theologians like Frederick Denison Maurice and his followers were inclined to explain in a spiritual sense the whole idea of the " coming " and " the Kingdom." The Kingdom meant for them a gradual remoulding of human society in accordance with the ideas of Christ. The coming was to be gradual, though it might include catastrophic episodes—startling historical events which constituted peculiarly signal exhibitions of that divine judgement of the world which was always going on for those who had spiritual eyes to see it. In particular passages there might be a reference to the destruction of Jerusalem as one of the first and most significant of the epochs or stages in the continuous world-judgement; while others might be understood as a dramatic embodiment of that judgement of God upon individual souls which gradually takes place as each one dies and stands before what was metaphorically described as the judgement seat of God. Maurice belonged to that school of pre-critical Liberalism which was peculiarly English. Such men knew little of the critical work of their German contemporaries, and there was practically no such thing as higher criticism in English Universities or among English theological writers. English liberalizing writers were content for the most part to accept the recorded words of Christ as substantially authentic, and to limit their criticism of the traditional Biblicism to the substitution of a moderate and a spiritual for a mechanical or verbal theory of Inspiration. More advanced Liberals were disposed to deny that the more intractable eschatological sayings were really uttered by our Lord, and to put down the apocalyptic imagery and colouring, when it could not with any plausibility be spiritualized, to the influence upon the minds of the Apostles and the Evangelists of narrow Jewish ideas, the existence of which in other minds than that of Jesus they had no desire to conceal.

During the last few years there has been a much closer study of the Synoptic problem on the one hand and of the apocalyptic literature on the other—of Daniel and the Revelation of St. John within the Canon and of that group of extra-canonical writings— some of them only recently edited—of which the Book of Enoch is the best-known representative. And the result is that Theologians have for the most part become convinced that the apocalyptic and eschatological element in the teaching of Jesus cannot be so easily disposed of. The tendency of the older Liberalism was to spiritualize as much as possible, and either to explain away or to reject what was non-spiritual. Now a precisely opposite disposition prevails. The more "advanced," the more liberal, the more emancipated a Theologian claims to be, the more probable is it that he will insist on regarding as authentic, and on explaining in the most literal sense, every saying of Christ that could possibly be understood as having an eschatological significance. It is just the prima facie more spiritual, more ethical sayings that are explained away or rejected as ecclesiastical insertions. By the fashionable school of German Eschatologists which has culminated in Schweitzer, and by the Catholic Modernists of the Loisy type, the older Liberalism is now accused of having made of Jesus a German liberal Protestant. The historical reality, we are told, was very different. In the view of Jesus Himself—according to Schweitzer and his stricter followers [1]—His whole message was primarily Eschatology. He conceived of Himself not as Messiah in some new, spiritualized, transfigured sense but in the literal sense of Jewish Apocalyptic. And he accepted that rôle with all its consequences and all its concomitants. He expected a catastrophic judgement in the near future. He faced—some of them say He courted—death in order to hurry on the miraculous interposition which He expected to follow or to prevent it. His hopes were disappointed : His cry of agony on the Cross was the cry of one who had expected a supernatural deliverance, and found it not. He really felt Himself forsaken of God. All His teaching about the Kingdom refers to the expected future personal reign of Himself, the Messiah, after the Judgement at which He was Himself to preside. It was to be a Kingdom of a very material, though a very supernatural, kind—to be set up suddenly and catastrophically. He had no thought of a gradual permeation of Jewish society by His teaching —still less of a conversion of the Gentile world to His principles. His moral and religious teaching, what

---

[1] Loisy is less extreme in his Eschatology. He doubts many sayings which Schweitzer accepts, and he has more respect for the ethical teaching of Christ.

there was of it, was not much in advance of the higher rabbinic teaching of His time. His ethical precepts consisted merely of very simple instructions for the behaviour of His followers during the few months which He expected to intervene before the Judgement. It was a mere " Interimsethik "—as the phrase is— of little value, or even interest, for us at the present day who know His Messianic ideas to be a delusion and anticipate no catastrophic judgement or sudden "end of the world." [1]

What are we to say to these new ideas ?

(1) In the first place as to the critical basis. I have no time to enter upon a discussion of particular passages, but I must confess that I am still very sceptical as to the more definite sayings—the sayings which profess to indicate the exact time of the coming Judgement. Not one of them belongs to what is perhaps the best attested stratum of Synoptic tradition. Not one certainly belongs to the source now known as Q—that is to say, to the original document which underlies the sayings common to Matthew and Luke. If we put aside the apocalyptic discourse[2] of which I shall speak in a moment, not one of them which occurs

---

[1] Of course I do not deny that these ideas are often expressed with considerable qualifications in the writings of the ultra-eschatologists (and with considerable exaggeration in their more private utterances); but, in proportion as such writers qualify their statements, they do not differ from the theologians whom they criticize. Cf. Schweitzer, *The Quest of the Historical Jesus*, p. 239, pp. 399–401.

[2] Mark xiii. with its parallels.

in Mark is found also unaltered in the other two Gospels.[1] And they are not consistent with one another. In one passage our Lord is represented as saying that His disciples would not have gone over the cities of Israel till the Son of Man should be come (this is found in Matthew only) :[2] at another He says that only some of those who stood by should witness the coming, implying that the time would not be in the very near future.[3] In the long series of predictions contained in the thirteenth chapter of St. Mark and largely amplified in the other two Synoptists, He speaks of a number of false Christs as destined to come first, which means of course that He was to disappear in some way from the earth, and that there was thus to be a considerable interval before the coming again, although all three Synoptists here make Him say that this generation should not pass away till all these things came to pass. And all these passages are inconsistent

---

[1] Unless the prediction that He would drink no more of the fruit of the vine till He should drink it new in His Father's Kingdom (Mark xiv. 25=Matt. xxvi. 29=Luke xxii. 18) be regarded as an exception, and be understood in an extremely literal sense. There is again the passage : " Ye shall not see me henceforth till ye shall say, Blessed is he that cometh in the name of the Lord " (Matt. xxiii. 39 : Luke xiii. 35). But this passage seems to imply a disappearance and a reappearance after an interval of some duration, rather than any immediate manifestation of the Kingdom.

[2] Matt. x. 23. The extreme improbability that Jesus should have spoken thus is pointed out by Loisy (*Evan. Syn.* I, p. 866). See note on page 46.

[3] Mark ix. 1 : Matt. xvi. 28 : Luke ix. 27. Luke has simply " see the Kingdom of God." This is probably, it must be confessed, a correction of Mark.

with the express declaration that He Himself did not
know the date of the Judgement, but only the Father.[1]
This last is one of the five " pillar-texts " which
Schmiedel treats as the most certain of all the sayings
of Jesus, because the least likely to be invented by a
disciple or by the unconscious growth of tradition.
All the others may quite conceivably be attempts made
by successive generations of Christian teachers at once
to adjourn the date of the Coming and to reassure the
waning hopes of Christ's followers.[2]   The thirteenth
chapter of St. Mark is obviously, according to some
even of the more eschatological critics, a Jewish-
Christian Apocalypse variously amplified and touched

---

[1] Matt. xxiv. 36 : Mark xiii. 32.   Luke no doubt omits the saying
as derogatory to the omniscience of Jesus.   It may be suggested
that this means merely "He did not know the *exact* date," but
to say that the Judgement should come before a tour of Palestine
could be completed was surely to claim a very exact knowledge,
hardly less so to say it would come within some forty years.

[2] The saying most difficult to account for, " Ye shall not have
gone over the cities of Israel till the Son of man be come," is found
only in Matthew (x. 23).   Sayings found in Matthew alone are the
most doubtful of all the words put into our Lord's mouth, especially
when they can be explained as " ecclesiastical additions." Schweitzer
treats this as an actual saying which was meant literally.   Jesus
was disappointed when the disciples returned, and the kingdom
had not come.   But the context should be remembered : " When
they persecute you in this city, flee ye into the next, for verily I
say unto you ye shall not," etc.   The disciples were in little danger
of persecution at this time.   The situation presupposed by this
verse, as by much else in Matthew's version of this discourse, is
that of the disciples during their later Palestinian mission.   The
Evangelist evidently means the whole mission of the Church to
be understood as a continuation of the first and original mission
of the Twelve during the earthly life of their Master.   The date
contemplated is therefore much the same as that implied by " This
generation shall not pass away."

up in the different Synoptists by a succession of hands.
It may contain genuine sayings of Christ, but it cannot
be treated as conclusive evidence as to the way
in which Christ Himself spoke of His "coming."
Even the earliest version in Mark assumes that a not
inconsiderable time will elapse between the departure
of Jesus and His return. If we accepted it as genuine, it
would positively disprove the notion that Jesus looked
for a quite immediate Parousia. The succession of
false Christs could not be expected while Jesus was
still with His disciples or in any very short period after
His departure. With regard to the declaration before
the High Priest it may plausibly be argued that critical
probability is in favour of the Matthew-Mark version,
according to which our Lord says: "Henceforth ye
shall see the Son of Man sitting at the right hand of
power and coming with the clouds of heaven," though
Luke's account has simply "from now shall the Son
of Man be seated at the right hand of the power of
God."[1] But what are the probabilities of the exact
words of Jesus at the Judgement-seat being accurately
preserved by any tradition whatever? It seems that
none of His disciples was present. How infinitely
greater were the probabilities of Luther's words before
the diet of Worms being correctly remembered. Luther
spoke in an orderly assembly of hundreds or thousands,
among whom many were attached followers. Some of
these were princes or great personages, occupying

[1] Mark xiv. 62 (=Matt. xxvi. 64); Luke xxii. 69.

prominent places, and all were hanging upon his words. Yet very different versions of his words were in circulation a few years after his death, and the famous " Here I stand, I can do no other," which has become classical, is now shown to be opposed to the testimony of an eye-witness who wrote very shortly after the event.[1]

I look then with great suspicion upon all the passages which profess to fix the date of the Judgement, and I have also grave doubts as to the share which Jesus personally claims for Himself in the judgement of which He speaks.[2] It is doubtful whether He ever spoke of Himself as the actual Judge. I think I could give you critical grounds for these doubts if I had time to go through the passages seriatim. But

[1] See Lindsay, *Hist. of the Reformation*, I, p. 291. " It is most likely," says Dr. Lindsay, " that in the excitement men carried away only a general impression and not an exact recollection of the last words of Luther."

[2] That Jesus claimed to be Himself the Judge in the coming Judgement can be established only by three parables reported in St. Matthew—the parables of the Talents, the Sheep and the Goats, the Tares. Only the first is in Luke also. In this (Matt. xxv. 19) we are told that it is only " after a long time " that the Lord will return to reckon with the servants. Either therefore we must give up saying that Jesus expected a Parousia as immediate as is contended for by Schweitzer and his uncompromising followers, or the parable cannot be treated as in its present form an accurate representation of His words. The Lukan version—the parable of the ten pounds—is said to have been uttered " because he was nigh to Jerusalem, and because they thought that the Kingdom of God should immediately appear " (Luke xix. 11) ; and even apart from this comment, the intention to discourage the notion of an immediate Parousia is sufficiently evident. It is therefore quite possible that in the original parable the function of the Messiah was less distinctly that of a Judge. The parable of the Sheep and the Goats is found in Matthew only (xxv. 31). It is based on Enoch (cap. lxii.), where (1), though the Messiah judges, it is not

I do not deny that there is a residuum of truth in these eschatological ideas. Nothing is more certain than that the burden of Christ's earliest Gospel was that "the Kingdom of God is at hand." And by the coming of the Kingdom we cannot suppose Him to have meant anything so vague as a gradual leavening of Society by His own teaching. In the light of the current apocalyptic conceptions and of His own parables, I think we must admit that Jesus did expect a coming of a sudden, catastrophic kind in the very near future. I also admit the probability that before the end—it is not probable that that was so from the first —He had made up His mind that He was Himself that promised Messiah ; and He therefore may very

until "the Lord of Spirits seated him on the throne of His (i.e. God's) glory," (2) the "elect One" is not called "The King." The King is God. Perhaps this was so in the original parable.

The third passage in which the Messiah is represented as judging the world Himself is in the parable of the Tares (or rather in the explanation of it), in which "the Son of Man shall send forth His angels," etc. (Matt. xiii. 41). This is found in Matthew only, and the explanations of parables are less trustworthy than the parables themselves. If the saying as a whole be genuine, it is quite conceivable that the rôle which is here discharged by the Messiah was in Jesus' words attributed to the Father, or, as in verse 49 of the same chapter, to the angels ("the angels shall come forth," etc.). And after all this Matthean parable (like the last) strongly suggests the circumstances of the early Church. The absence of passages definitely implying a judgement by Jesus Himself in Mark and (with one exception) in Luke is very significant. The words about coming in the clouds of heaven at the trial, if genuine, do not imply Judgement *by* the Messiah : it is more probable that Jesus should have spoken of Himself as sitting on the right hand of the divine Judge, than that He should claim to *be* the actual Judge. Luke xiii. 25, xxi. 36 hardly imply more than Assessorship, even if they are unaltered.

E

well have applied to Himself some of the current
apocalyptic imagery—how much we cannot be sure.
If he were indeed the Messiah, as His sense of close
communion with God and His consciousness of a divine
mission suggested to Him, it would follow that His
heavenly Father would in some signal way manifest
His Son to the world, visibly interpose in His favour,
and set up the long-promised Kingdom in some visible
and conspicuous form. Jesus probably applied to the
coming of the Kingdom—whatever He may have said
about His own personal rôle in it—the accepted
Messianic symbols, and no doubt we cannot explain
such imagery in a wholly " spiritual " sense, if by that
is meant the entire absence of anything miraculous or
supernatural in the manner of its setting up. But
not all the sayings can with probability be attributed
to our Lord, nor need we take all this imagery (when
it is well attested) with the deadly literalness which
the extreme Eschatologists demand. In view of the
ethical and spiritual tone which pervades His teaching
as a whole, it is unlikely that He thought of the
Messianic banquet as a banquet at which literal bread
would be eaten or literal wine drunk—the more so as
this was denied by some of the rabbis.[1] We know

[1] " The world to come is neither eating nor drinking, nor
increasing and multiplying, nor giving and receiving, nor jealousy,
nor hatred, nor strife ; but the righteous sit with crowns on their
heads, and enjoy the light of the Shechinah " (b. Ber. 17a, quoted
by Herford, *Pharisaism*, p. 274). Why should Jesus have been
less "spiritual" than the Rabbis, even if it be assumed that He
cannot have been more so ?

that He thought there would be no marrying or giving in marriage in that Kingdom. And, if He did apply to Himself the traditional picture of the coming with the clouds of heaven (which is by no means certain), we need not suppose that He who certainly spiritualized so much of the old prophetic teaching necessarily conceived that the exact mode of supernatural manifestation had been revealed to Him.[1]

But (2) it is simply not true that the Kingdom of Heaven is *always* represented as something to be set up in the future by a sudden and catastrophic event. Side by side with the passages in which this is the case, there are, as has been well pointed out by Prof. von Dobschütz in his admirable little book on *The Eschatology of Jesus*, other passages in which the Kingdom is as definitely spoken of as already present, or as destined to spread here upon earth in a moral, spiritual, gradual way. " If I by the finger of God, cast out devils, then is the Kingdom of God come upon you " — is already come ($\H{\epsilon}\phi\theta\alpha\sigma\epsilon\nu$).[2] This passage is found in Matthew and Luke, and doubtless

---

[1] I doubt whether our Lord promised the disciples that they should sit on twelve thrones judging the twelve tribes of Israel (Matt. xix. 28=Luke xxii. 30, not in Mark). How could He who made such a promise have declared that to sit on His right hand and on His left was not His to give? (Mark x. 40=Matt. xx. 23, omitted by Luke as derogatory to the Apostles). Whether genuine or not, the "thrones" may have been suggested by *Testaments of the Twelve Patriarchs* (Judah xxv. 1).

[2] Luke xi. 20. An attempt is made on the analogy of modern Greek to make this mean "is just coming." Such a conjecture might serve once, but the extreme eschatological position involves explaining away so much.

forms part of the oldest Gospel source which used to be known as the Logia, and which it is now customary to speak of as Q. So is the passage : " from that time the gospel of the kingdom of God is preached, and every man entereth violently into it."[1] Another passage is not quite so well attested, being found in Luke only, but there is no reason for rejecting it. "The Kingdom of God cometh not with observation : neither shall they say, Lo here or Lo there ! for behold the Kingdom of God is within you."[2] And, in the light of these two or three pretty clear cases, there is no reason why we should not interpret in their obvious and natural sense those passages which can only by a forced and tortuous exegesis be squeezed into conformity with a purely futurist and catastrophic conception— the parables of the grain of mustard-seed,[3] of the

---

[1] Luke xvi. 16. In Matt. xi. 12 the words are somewhat different, but the essential part is the same : " The Kingdom of Heaven suffereth violence and men of violence take it by force." It would be out of place to discuss the meaning of this difficult passage.

[2] Luke xvii. 20, 21. (ἐντὸς ὑμῶν). If we accept the translation " among you," that will not affect the argument. (Luke probably meant "within"; the meaning of the original Aramaic is more doubtful, cf. below, p. 55 *note*.) Canon Streeter gives good reasons for attributing this saying to Q (*Oxford Studies in the Synoptic Problem*, p. 201). It may have been omitted simply because it was not understood. Matt. xxi. 31 (" the publicans and the harlots go into the Kingdom of God before you "), cited by Prof. von Dobschütz, may be got rid of by the suggestion that in the original Aramaic the tense used was the imperfect, which admits of being translated either in present or future.

[3] Matt. xiii. 31 ; Mark iv. 31 ; Luke xiii. 19. The stress may (as is contended by some) be on the contrast between the smallness of the beginning and the greatness of the culmination, but still the transition from the one to the other is by a process, not by a catas-

leaven,[1] of the wheat and the tares,[2] of the seed growing secretly.[3] All such passages may be much more naturally understood of the rapid spread of Christ's teaching —not, indeed, in the Gentile world or in a distant future, but now, during His earthly life among His own people, before His very eyes. So again, while our Lord sometimes speaks of " entering " the Kingdom, He elsewhere speaks of receiving the Kingdom of God " as a little child "[4]—which lends itself naturally to the present and spiritual interpretation. He who receives the good news of the Kingdom, and prepares himself for its coming in the right spirit, is already in a sense within the Kingdom, or the Kingdom may be said to be already in him.[5] The transition from the one aspect of the Kingdom to the other is not a difficult or a violent one. Jesus certainly started with the conception of the Kingdom as something future. But

trophe. It is suggested that the idea of development is modern, but after all the ancients were quite familiar with the fact that trees grow gradually.

[1] Matt. xiii. 33 ; Luke xiii. 21.

[2] Matt. xiii. 24. This parable may no doubt be coloured by a reference to the state of the Church in the Evangelist's day.

[3] Mark iv. 26.

[4] Mark x. 15; Luke xviii. 17. Matthew (xviii. 3) has "Except ye turn and become as little children." The words that follow (" he shall in no wise enter into the kingdom ") show that the *full* coming of the Kingdom is future.

[5] So the scribe who answered discreetly was not far from the Kingdom. If the Kingdom was nothing but a future event, his distance from it could not be affected by his moral condition. It is implied that had he a little more completely lived up to the spirit of his answer, he would be already within the Kingdom. But as this occurs only in Mark xii. 34, it may possibly be regarded as an addition of the Evangelist's.

when He saw before Him the spiritual effects of His
teaching, He may well have been impelled to exclaim
" The Kingdom is already come." " You need not
wait till the distant future for it," He suggests: " whenever the teaching about the Kingdom bears fruit in
human society, in men's hearts and in their lives,
wherever men are living as they will live who shall
hereafter live in the Kingdom that is to be, the Kingdom is theirs already : the essentials of the Kingdom
are already present." In such passages we get what
Prof. von Dobschütz has called a " transmuted
Eschatology "[1]—the old eschatological or apocalyptic

[1] The transition from the idea of the kingdom as something
future to the kingdom as something present is far easier than
it is sometimes assumed to be, and there are precedents for such
a transition in Jewish literature. The original meaning of the
Hebrew and Aramaic terms translated kingdom of God is simply,
we are told, " Sovereignty of God," though it does seem to imply
also the social system in which that sovereignty is exercised.
" The sovereignty of God belongs, in the first instance, to the
current age, and is as yet fully acknowledged only in Israel. The
future will, however, bring a fuller development" (Dalman, *The
Words of Jesus*, I, p. 98). " ' The sovereignty of God ' is for Jesus
invariably an eschatological entity, of which the present can be
predicated only because ' the end ' is already approaching " (l.c.
p. 135). " There was already in existence, prior to the time of
Jesus, a tendency which laid little stress on the Jewish national
element in the hope for the future. This aspect of the future
hope Jesus thrust still further into the background, placing the
purely religious element decisively in the foreground, and He
thereby extended the conception of the ' sovereignty of God ' so
as to include within it the blessings mediated by this sovereignty.
For Him the sovereignty of God meant the divine power, which,
from the present onwards with continuous progress, effectuates the
renovation of the world, but also the renovated world into whose
domain mankind will one day enter, which is even now being offered,
and therefore can be appropriated and received as a blessing " (l.c.
p. 137). " It is indubitable that He developed His own ideas in

language applied or reinterpreted in a present, a moral and a spiritual, sense.

And the very possibility of this transmutation implies something further. It implies not merely that the Kingdom is not wholly future, but that even the Kingdom that is future is at bottom—in its inmost essence—a moral and spiritual conception. The Messianic idea and its spiritual significance lay so near to each other in the mind of Jesus that He probably passed from one aspect of the Kingdom to the other quite naturally and almost unconsciously.[1]

(3) And this brings me to a third point which it is important to insist upon as against those extreme Eschatologists who can see in our Lord's teaching nothing but a piece of tawdry apocalyptic romance of no more present spiritual significance than the expectation of Nero's reappearance, or the vision in the book

regard to the sovereignty of God in conscious opposition to the Zealot movement " (l.c. p. 138). From this point of view there is no difficulty whatever in supposing that He might have said " The kingdom of God is among you," or even " within you." Dalman appears to have no doubt that He said one or the other : he inclines to the view that the original Aramaic meant " within." The whole treatment of the subject by Dalman is most instructive.

[1] On the basis of Matt. xiii. 52 we might argue that Jesus was not quite unaware that in His mind and His teaching the conception of the Kingdom had undergone a " transmutation." " Therefore every scribe which hath been made a disciple to the kingdom of heaven is like unto a man that is a householder, which bringeth forth out of his treasure things new and old." If the saying be genuine, it betrays a consciousness that the old Messianic language was being invested with a new meaning. But the passage, or the turn given to it, may possibly be due to the Evangelist, though personally I see no reason why it should be so. Luke may have omitted it because he could not understand it.

of Enoch about the stars which became bulls and the cows which gave birth to elephants.

The conception of the Kingdom throughout—whether it is looked upon as future or as present, as to come gradually or to come suddenly—is at bottom ethical and spiritual. Doubtless the environment, the accidents, the setting of the jewel are apocalyptic. No doubt our Lord expected that the Kingdom was to be established in a supernatural manner, just as all believers in Immortality think of that immortal life as involving a divine action which goes beyond anything of which natural law as at present known to Science can tell us. True, the belief in Immortality does not necessarily involve a breach of natural law, and the eschatological conception does : but that difference does not make the one conception spiritual and the other not. The essence of the Kingdom of Heaven, as Jesus thought of it, was that it was a state of closer union between God and man, a state of things in which God's will was to be perfectly fulfilled.

How shall I establish this position in a way that will convince those who do not see that it is implied in all His sayings about it ? The best proof that can be offered is perhaps the purely spiritual character of the means by which it is to be entered. The proclamation " Repent " is as undoubtedly part of the earliest message of Jesus as " the Kingdom is at hand." And all through His teaching it is insisted that nothing can secure admission to the Kingdom but goodness. Not

descent from Abraham, not circumcision, not the
observance of the ceremonial law, not the sacrifices or
any other external rite, not (as was sometimes taught
by the Jews of a later day[1]) the Day of Atonement
and its ritual could procure forgiveness of sins,
deliverance at the Judgement, and admission to the
Kingdom. About these not one word is said in any
part of our Lord's teaching. Admission to the Kingdom depends upon righteousness and upon nothing
else. " Not every one that saith unto me Lord, Lord,
shall enter into the Kingdom of heaven, but he that
doeth the will of my Father which is in heaven."[2]
It is the righteous and they alone who will shine forth
as the Sun in the Kingdom of their Father. All the
parables of the Kingdom, whatever other aspects of
it they emphasize, imply this—that repentance and
righteousness, moral regeneration, lives devoted to
the good of their fellows, were the sole means of
entering it.[3]

---

[1] This was not the only view. See Herford, *Pharisaism*, pp. 210–
215.

[2] Matt. vii. 21 = Luke vi. 46–8. " Except your righteousness
shall exceed the righteousness of the scribes and Pharisees, ye shall
in no case enter into the Kingdom of heaven " is in Matthew only
(Matt. v. 20), and therefore perhaps not in Q.

[3] If we could rely on it implicitly, we might especially point to
the parable of the marriage-feast (Matt. xxii. 11 ; cf. Luke xiv. 16).
It is arbitrary and extravagant to interpret the wedding-garment
by " election " (as is done by Schweitzer), and to quote it in proof
of the fact that Jesus was a " predestinarian " ; though after all
to be a predestinarian is not necessarily to be unethical. But
the passage about the wedding-garment is in Matthew only. It is
curious how uncritical an " Eschatologist " can become when he
finds anything to suit his purpose.

No doubt Jesus thought of the Kingdom as something more than an ethical condition : it was a state of reward : it included, it may be assumed, happiness and freedom from the cares and sufferings of human life as we know it : and to be excluded from the Kingdom meant punishment and suffering—of what kind it is unnecessary now to ask. If this is to be unethical, almost all teachers who have believed in Immortality have been unethical,—Plato and Kant and nearly all the most spiritual teachers of philosophical Ethics no less than all the prophets of all the Religions. Even with a negative Eschatology such as Gautama's, freedom from pain is part of the promised reward.[1] In the teaching of Jesus this reward is symbolized by the ordinary apocalyptic image of the Messianic banquet. The rejected gnash their teeth with shame, and remain in the darkness outside the brilliantly lighted banqueting hall. But there is in His teaching singularly little insistence upon the joys of the Kingdom—still less is there anything about carnal joys except what is implied in the imagery of the banquet. A Kingdom which is entered by righteousness and nothing else must surely be conceived of as a Kingdom of righteousness : that much is after all implied in the old prophetic conception of the King-

---

[1] Jesus never taught that the good deed was to be done only for the sake of the reward. The Pharisees, says Mr. Herford, " were emphatic in teaching that the ' Mitzvah ' [good deed] was not to be done for the sake of the reward, as if to obtain thereby some payment of what was due " (*Pharisaism*, p. 275).

dom, and even in that of the more spiritual Apocalyptists.[1] The bare fact that Jesus taught that a Messianic Kingdom was to be set up involves no disparagement of Ethics. Unless to promise a future reward for righteousness is to be unethical, there is no antagonism, as seems to be assumed in some quarters, between Ethics and Eschatology. In the preaching of Jesus the announcement that the Kingdom was to come and the ethical appeal went together. But to be eschatological is not necessarily to be unethical. Everything depends upon the question where the emphasis is laid. According to the ultra-eschatological School, all the emphasis was upon the Eschatology. I believe the exact opposite to be the case. In the teaching of Jesus all the emphasis was on the Ethics, and upon Religion of an intensely ethical type.

It is scarcely possible to emphasize Ethics more than to urge men to devote their whole energies to winning an entrance into the Kingdom of God, and then to tell them that the only way of entering it is to be righteous. And there is hardly anything said about the Kingdom—if we put aside the " little Apocalypse "—except in close connexion with exhortations to

---

[1] This is well put by Mr. Montefiore who has assuredly no bias in favour of Christian orthodoxy. " The essential feature of the ordinary conception of the Messiah was that of a *righteous* King ruling over a righteous people ; the Messianic era was indeed one of prosperity, but far more was it one of peace and goodness and the knowledge of God. So far as it was this, why should not Jesus have wished to be the Jewish Messiah ? " (*Syn. Gospels*, p. xcvii). Of course Mr. Montefiore would admit that out of the various and conflicting Messianic ideals, Jesus picked the most spiritual.

righteousness. By the simple process of counting verses, it can be shown that the teaching is mostly religious or ethical. And what the Gospels do not contain is as significant as what they do contain. Compare our Lord's sayings with the book of Daniel, or the Apocalypse of St. John, or with any of the other avowedly eschatological and apocalyptic 'writings. These are not entirely wanting in ethical elements, but the ethical parts are small in bulk compared with those which deal with the details of the awful calamities coming on the earth, of the historical or physical disasters which would precede or follow it, of the rewards in store for those who should be saved from the approaching judgement. There is nothing therefore in the mere fact that our Lord believed that the Kingdom of God would be set up in the near future, and in a catastrophic manner, which proves that Ethics formed an unimportant or subordinate part of His teaching ; or that that teaching possesses no value for us. If this is to be shown, it must be shown from the actual character of His teaching. What the character of that teaching was, we shall examine in our next lecture.

But, it may be asked by some, " Does not the mere fact that Jesus expected the coming of the Kingdom and a general winding up of the present physical and social order within a few months or a few years by itself imply that His teaching cannot be suitable to the moral needs of our times—that it must be merely an ' Interimsethik ' — a mere temporary makeshift, a provisional code for a strictly transitional state of things ? " I submit that this is not to be assumed a priori. Why should we spend our time otherwise because we are going to die, or to pass into some new stage of existence, in six months than we should do if we were to know we had twenty years of life before us ? " To live this day as if my last "—has not this been at all times a familiar prayer among religious people and a commonplace of religious exhortation ? No doubt, when we come to details, the probable duration of life does become important. A wise man who knows that he has only a year or so to live does not set himself down to write a Lexicon or a Universal History. Objects of pursuit that are really vain and unimportant may seem doubly so in prospect of an early death : but not the things that are best worth doing. And the same principle will apply to the duration of Society as to the duration of the individual life. Here the difference in detail might be greater. A good man who knew he was to die in six months' time would go on ploughing his field because he knows that, even if he will not be able to reap the harvest and eat the bread, others will do so. He might well devote himself to the founding of enterprises which others will carry on. But, if he thought the world was coming to an end, or that human Society as at present constituted was to be wound up, in five years' time, he would not begin to build a Cathedral or to found a new University. Still, these are matters of detail, not of principle. In point of fact the moral teaching of Jesus contains very little detail. It deals almost entirely with general principles. The imperative need for repentance, the supreme importance of pure motive, the swallowing up of all the commandments in the command to love God and our neighbour —these are its main ideas. There is no reason why commands like these should not be equally valuable for a society which believes itself destined to endure till the sun waxes cold, and for a society which believes that some world-transforming catastrophe is close at hand. There is no a priori reason for treating the Ethics of Jesus as useless to a modern society, because He entertained certain eschatological expectations. Once more, if we want to discover whether it is an " Interimsethik " or not, we must examine the teaching itself, and say how it appeals to us.

And here let me remark that in answering this question we are no longer obliged to adopt a meek and deferential attitude towards the experts in Synoptic criticism or in Apocalyptic literature. When it is a question of spiritual values, such persons have no particular claim to be heard. To say what is the present value of our Lord's teaching is the business of the Philosopher or of the Moralist ; and even they of course have after all no data to go upon but the deliverances of their own moral consciousness. Here it is ethical or spiritual insight which counts rather than

critical learning or acumen, though a certain amount
of philosophical training and acquaintance with the
general history of thought may be considered not
altogether irrelevant. And I will venture the further
remark that in this matter the extremer eschatological critics have shown no superiority to the
old-fashioned Liberal Protestant Theologians whom
they affect to despise.

I proceed then to ask how far the eschatological
expectations of Jesus—whether those which I admit
He entertained or those more detailed expectations
which He may have entertained if we suppose all the
eschatological utterances attributed to Him to be
genuine—have actually coloured His ethical teaching,
and diminished the value of it for ourselves. There
is, I believe, only one way in which the character of
our Lord's ethical teaching may have been affected by
His belief in the coming end. In the face of the approaching Judgement all other occupations, interests,
aims in life seemed *comparatively* unimportant beside
that of announcing that the Judgement was at hand
and calling upon men to prepare themselves for it. And
therefore He did sometimes emphasize the unimportance of worldly goods, and encourage His disciples to take no thought for the morrow to an extent
which would require some correction before it could
be literally applied to the case of those who do not
believe that the world is just coming to an end. The
essential principle even of such sayings does, however,

remain eternally true. " Seek ye first the Kingdom of God and His righteousness." The Kingdom
of God first, all else afterwards. If we refuse to accept
that principle, it will be because we do not care
for righteousness as much as Christ, not because our
eschatological ideas are different from His. Here,
as elsewhere, we must distinguish between eternal
principles and particular applications. It is true that
to some men He did address the invitation, as the
supreme thing to be done for the moment, to leave
their ordinary occupations and join His missionary
band. He did not, it would appear, impose that
task upon all His hearers : the call which He addressed
to the Twelve and to some others was a call (as M. Paul
Sabatier has remarked) not to a new religion, but to a
new apostolate. The call was addressed to those
whom He judged fit for it. And, as we look back upon
the work of Jesus and His Apostles in the light of
history, was He after all so very much mistaken as to
the supreme importance of this task ? He was engaged, according to the Eschatologists, in trying to
save a small section of one Jewish generation from a
terrible calamity which awaited the unrepentant in a
few months or a few years' time, after which the
effects of His preaching would end. In the light of
history we see that He was really sowing the seeds
of a vast spiritual revolution, founding a new religion
instead of regenerating an old one—a religion which
was to convert the whole Roman Empire within some

few centuries, which has now after nearly two thousand years spread to the remotest corners of the world, and has so far proved itself to be the only one of the ancient historical religions which can hold its own in the light of modern Science and modern Culture. Surely the task of preaching what Jesus called the Kingdom of God really *was* the most important task to which any human being could then and there have addressed himself. Doubtless the task was conceived by Himself and His followers under the limitations of Jewish thought : but that did not affect its essential importance. If Jesus was not the Messiah as Jewish thought conceived Him, it was only because He was so much more : if the ideal of a Messianic Kingdom, as He and His disciples expected it, was not to be realized, the Kingdom that they really did set up was something much greater than they contemplated. Like all the world's greatest spiritual builders, they builded much better than they knew. Jesus was not wrong then in the advice which He gave to the best men of His own generation. With all our fuller knowledge and larger experience, we could not wish that He should have taught, or that they should have acted, differently.

But what of the application of that call to ourselves ? No doubt in order to apply it to the conditions of modern life, we must to some extent translate the conception of the Kingdom into terms of modern life. For us the light of Science and the course of History have dispelled the dream of a speedy return of Jesus

F

upon the clouds of Heaven. But how far need that
modify our conception of the Kingdom ? It is necessary that we should face this question, because so
much of Christ's ethical teaching was conveyed under
the form of parables about the Kingdom. If we cannot make the Kingdom mean something modern, there
is a large part of Jesus' teaching which will mean
nothing at all for us. I have endeavoured to show you
that, though the original conception was that of a
future, catastrophic Kingdom, Jesus did also in all
probability speak of a Kingdom which should come
gradually, which was actually coming gradually in
a quiet, unobtrusive, uncatastrophic development, as
individual souls listened to His message, and as a little
society formed around Him in which God's will was
being already done. If this meaning of the Kingdom was for Him, in a sense, a secondary meaning, it
is clear that to us it must be the primary one. The
Kingdom of God, after all, means only the reign of
God. To bring about a reign of God in human society
is surely the true conception of the supreme end of
human life. And then there is a sense in which the
futurist interpretation of the Kingdom will always be
the right one. Of course, if we think that the idea of
a future life better than the present was a baseless
or even a demoralizing dream, then, indeed, we should
have arrived at an ethical ideal which would be
fundamentally irreconcilable with the deepest ideas
of Jesus. But if we share the hope of Immortality,

then it makes little difference, from an ethical and religious point of view, whether the entrance upon this future life was to be effected by a sudden catastrophe or by the departure of individual souls from the present scene and their reawakening in some other state.

And there is no real incompatibility between these two aspects of the Kingdom of God—the present ethical aspect of it, and the future or "transcendental" aspect. The late Father Tyrrell in one of his last books, *Christianity at the Cross-roads*, adopted a curious attitude towards this eschatological question which has attained a certain popularity in England. He agrees with the extreme Eschatologists that the teaching of Jesus was Eschatology and very little else, and that the eschatological hopes which He cherished are a delusion. But, instead of drawing the inference "Christianity cannot be the Religion of the Modern World," he infers on the contrary that the Christianity of the modern world must be equally eschatological. For him the Christian idea of the Kingdom of God has absolutely nothing in common with that hope of a gradual improvement in the social and spiritual condition of Humanity in which Protestant Liberal Theology has been disposed to find its deepest meaning. Tyrrell pours ridicule upon the modern idea of indefinite progress, moral advance, social improvement. His view of the present condition of the world is profoundly pessimistic, and he treats the hope of any

serious improvement in it as absolutely baseless. The
only hope for the future that there is must be concentrated upon another world than this. The essence
of Christianity must always lie in the dream of a new
heaven and a new earth. By the vulgar, it seems to be
suggested, that expectation will always be accepted
in some rather literal and materialistic sense : more
cultivated Christians will treat it as a symbol of a
somewhat vague hope for a better world beyond the
grave which will supply a sort of spiritual anodyne for
the irremediable badness of life, even if it is actually
doomed to eventual disappointment.[1]

I venture to think that this attempt to combine a
pessimistic contempt for the present life with
optimistic hopes for the future is profoundly illogical
and self-contradictory. For upon what in the last resort
are our hopes of Immortality founded ? For those at
least who are not prepared to base them entirely upon
the historical evidence for a bodily Resurrection of
Christ, it must rest chiefly upon our conception of the
character of God. It is no doubt just because the
present life does not seem good enough to be the sole
end of creation for a just and a loving God that we
feel constrained to regard it as the educational preparation for—or the introductory stage of—something
better. To deny altogether the existence of real evil

---

[1] A much more sober and intelligible account of Father Tyrrell's
position is given in the last of his *Essays on Faith and Immortality*.
There is much in this volume with which I feel great sympathy.

in this life does no doubt destroy all logical basis for the belief in Immortality, unless indeed the position be taken that the sole real evil in this present life is its brevity and its sudden termination. And as a matter of fact most of those philosophers who do take an optimistic view of the present, or explain away the existence of real evil under cover of a belief in a super-moral Absolute, are avowed disbelievers in anything like a personal Immortality. We may admit the radical incompatibility between such Optimism as this and the religion founded by Jesus. Christianity treats the evil in the world as real evil. But because we admit the existence of some evil in the world, that is no reason why we should believe that the evil is dominant, and always destined to remain so. If we get rid of the popular notion of Omnipotence as a power to do anything or any combination of things which we take it into our heads to imagine, we must regard God as really contending against a real evil, and ourselves as called upon to become in the most literal sense fellow-workers with Him. But this is scarcely a possible position for those who hold that all their efforts are by some divine decree or some impersonal fate doomed to utter disappointment so far as the present life is concerned, though there is a bare off-chance of some better life beyond the grave. The very same considerations which make us hopeful for the future of the individual soul hereafter should forbid our alto-gether despairing of the present life. A Theology which

bids men love and serve one another because God works
with them cannot despair of a brighter future—though
not necessarily an actual extinction of evil and of
struggle—for Humanity on earth. And therefore for
us, as for Jesus, there is no essential incompatibility
between that sense of the Kingdom of Heaven in
which it means the hope of a better world beyond for
the individuals who pass away from this life and that
sense of it in which it means a better social state to
be gradually set up on this earth by the progressive
penetration of human society with the principles
which Jesus taught. The Kingdom of God must be
for us an ideal to be realized in part here, more completely hereafter. The fact that we no longer anticipate
the sudden winding up of the imperfect Kingdom and
the sudden appearance of a perfect one by a catastrophic world-judgement is, ethically speaking, an
unimportant detail. We can accept Jesus' fundamental idea that the supreme object of human life
should be the promotion of the Kingdom in the sense
of an ideal social state. That conception already
implicitly involves the notion which, we shall see, is
developed in the actual teaching of Jesus—that the
duty of mutual love is the best summary of human
duty. The conception of the Kingdom of God may
be regarded as expressing fundamentally the same
idea as Kant's notion of the Categorical Imperative,
with this additional advantage—that it expresses not
merely the bare " form " of the Moral Law, but also,

when it is read in the light of the rest of Christ's teaching, the most essential element in its true content.[1]

Of course it is a priori conceivable that, though there is no necessary incompatibility between eschatological hopes and an Ethic of eternal significance, the teaching of Jesus might have been so far affected in detail by these eschatological notions as to render it incapable of becoming the concrete expression of the moral ideal for a modern civilized community or rather for a universal, world-wide, " absolute " Religion. I shall endeavour in future lectures to establish the two following propositions : (1) that even in detail this was not to any considerable degree the case—that the teaching of Jesus was not affected by His eschatological expectations even to the same extent for instance as that of St. Paul, whose advice about marriage really was dominated and seriously distorted by this expectation ; (2) that this was so just because the teaching of Jesus was so much confined to fundamental, eternal, truly ethical principles that in point of fact there can hardly be said to be any detailed injunctions. The details are mere illustrations—often paradoxical illustrations—which have, indeed, a certain colouring which is local and temporary, but this colouring can

---

[1] No doubt Kant's conception of Kingdom of Ends does to some extent supply the desired content, and the conception is of course only a philosophical interpretation of Christ's " Kingdom of God " with the disadvantage that it leaves out the religious aspect of the Kingdom.

easily be distinguished from the principle which they illustrate. Once again, everything depends upon what conclusions we arrive at as to the actual, concrete character of the teaching. All I have aimed at in this lecture is to show you that there is nothing in the eschatological teaching of Jesus—even if we accept the views of the extremer Eschatologists as to the merely critical and historical questions—which would necessarily affect the value of His ethical, and more generally of His spiritual, teaching. The subject must be approached with an open mind. It would be as absurd to reject or to disparage the ethical ideal of Jesus a priori because He entertained eschatological hopes which we cannot share, as it would be to reject a priori the metaphysical conceptions of Plato because we have outgrown his physics, or to scrap-heap all the metaphysical systems which came before the Darwinian revolution in Biology. The parallel is not, indeed, adequate ; for Ethics can much more easily be separated from Apocalyptic Eschatology than a metaphysical conception of the Universe can be abstracted from its author's conceptions of natural law. There is no reason then why the Ethic of Jesus should not be an Ethic of universal, paramount, and eternal value because He may have thought that the physical Universe was on the eve of a vast catastrophe.

It may be suggested that, though the eschatological ideas do not affect the truth of the moral ideal, they do most materially affect our conception of Christ's

Person, and so the authority of His teaching. We are not now directly concerned with the doctrine of Christ's Person or even with the theological aspect of His teaching. That is not my subject. But I am unwilling to have suggested a difficulty which it is quite reasonable for religious minds to feel without saying a word which may tend to meet it. In the first place I have endeavoured to suggest that the extent to which Jesus shared the eschatological ideas of His time has been exaggerated, and that some of the more definite eschatological sayings are probably distorted or coloured by the ideas of His immediate disciples or of the early Church. But we shall do well to prepare ourselves for the possibility that the more advanced Eschatologists are right on the purely critical questions, or at least that some quite Christian minds may think them to be right, and to ask ourselves what we should say if it could be shown that all the eschatological sayings were uttered and were meant in a sense not very different from that of current expectation. I should venture to ask whether even such an admission would demand more than a slight extension of that doctrine of the limited knowledge of Christ which has now, I suppose, been accepted by all serious Theologians and by most thoughtful Christians. We have most of us come to recognize that the theory of the unique Divine Sonship of Jesus is not incompatible with the admission that He knew no more about the date and authorship of Old Testament

books or the causation of mental disease than other
men of His time. Need our Christology be much more
affected by the discovery that He also shared their
conceptions as to the way and the time in which God
would judge the world, and set up the Messianic
Kingdom ? We gather from one of the most generally accepted [1] of His own sayings that He did not
claim to know the exact date of the Parousia :
need it affect the fullness of His spiritual insight that
He knew—perhaps would have admitted that He
knew—almost as little about its mode ? The fact
that He accepted traditional language and even
traditional ideas on the subject which were in point
of fact mistakes, is no reason why the God who reveals
Himself in some mode and in some measure through
every human conscience, who dwells to some extent
in every human soul, should not have made His fullest
revelation of Himself in one conscience, one character,
one life.

If what we want in a doctrine of Christ's Divinity is
a supernatural guarantee for an externally communi-
cated moral code, then, indeed, our conception of
that doctrine will be profoundly modified by the discovery that He could make mistakes. If, on the
other hand, belief in His Divinity is based upon the
appeal which His teaching and His character make

---

[1] Some doubt the genuineness of "neither the Son," but this
omission does not affect the disclaimer of such knowledge for
Himself.

to heart and Conscience, the force of that appeal will be in no way weakened by the discovery that it has survived so many changes in men's conceptions of the material Universe. That the ethical ideal presented us by the teaching of Christ does still appeal to us in its essential principles as the highest that we know is the thesis which I shall endeavour to establish in the following lectures.[1]

[1] The following passages from Mr. Montefiore seem to me to go to the root of the matter in spite of his not being willing to assign to Jesus that absolutely supreme and unique position which Christians claim for Him : " We may reasonably argue that Jesus, as a great and original religious and ethical thinker, could hardly not have allowed his religious and ethical views to affect his conception of the Messiah. It is not right to call his ethical doctrine a mere ' Interimsethik.' Righteousness was to be the keynote of the new Kingdom, as well as the passport of admission within its gates. . . .

" And among those virtues upon which he laid stress may we not safely assume that the virtue of self-sacrifice, of service for the sake of others, was undoubtedly one ? Is it not reasonable then to suppose that he looked upon his own life as a service, and that this thought may even have developed into the idea that he might have to die in order to complete his service ? Death would not be the end; death was to no man the end; certainly not to the righteous ; least of all to the Messiah. Was the glory and was the triumph perhaps only to come *after* the life of service had been ended by a death of sacrifice ? If the principle of non-resistance was adopted by him in his ethics for daily life, it is not unnatural that it should have been adopted by him as regards his own special life and his position as Messiah. Hence we see how it may have come about that his conception of the Messiah may have been modified. The Messiah was no more the conqueror and the warrior-prince : what destruction there was to do would be done by God. The Messiah would, indeed, rule in the perfected Kingdom, but this rule was hardly looked upon in the ordinary way, and the stress was not habitually laid upon it. The stress was rather often laid upon the Messiah's work in the present and the near future, a work of service, even of lowly service, and a work which was, perhaps, to culminate in death. This, then, may have been the special development made by Jesus to the conception of the Messiah ; and such a view would fit in with the supposition that Jesus identified the Messiah with the mysterious Man (Daniel vii. 13) who was to be sent by God at the great crisis to superintend the final consummation, and that he believed that this Man was himself—himself as he was to be in his glory, rather than himself as he then was" (*Syn. Gospels*, I, 53–4).

" The real greatness of Jesus consisted in that side of his teaching which was independent of these old watchwords and battle-cries. Though the more original and beautiful parts of his teaching are, as it were, set in the framework of the conception of the coming Messianic era, and were partly produced by this dominant idea, they are yet independent of the framework, and they can be detached from it and can survive it" (*l.c.*, I, 58).

For a further discussion of the subject from a Christian point I may refer to *The Eschatological Question in the Gospels* by the Rev. C. W. Emmet, and an excellent article by the same writer on " Is the Teaching of Jesus an Interimsethik ? " in *The Expositor* (Nov., 1912); also to *The Eschatology of Jesus* by Dr. Latimer Jackson. No recent writer has done more to reduce the eschatological element in Christ's teaching to its proper place than Prof. B. W. Bacon (of Yale) in *The Beginnings of the Gospel Story*. On the critical side of the question see Canon Streeter's Appendix to *Oxford Studies in the Synoptic Problem*. His general conclusion is that " in the series Q, Mark, Matthew, there is a steady development in the direction of emphasizing, making more definite, and even creating, sayings of our Lord of the catastrophic Apocalyptic type, and of thrusting more and more into the background the sayings of a contrary tenor " (p. 433). This is, of course, quite consistent with the possibility that St. Luke may have somewhat attenuated the eschatological element.

LECTURE III

THE ETHICAL TEACHING OF JESUS CHRIST

IN my last two lectures I have tried to remove some a priori objections to the principle—usually accepted alike by the most orthodox and the most liberal forms of Christianity—that the ethical teaching of an historical person who lived nineteen hundred years ago can still be regarded as representing in its essentials the highest ideal of the modern world. I admitted—or rather strongly contended—that the authority which can rightly be claimed for the historical Christ must base itself upon the fact that the moral consciousness of the present still recognizes its truth, and finds its highest aspirations satisfied by the picture which the Gospels present us of His character and His teaching. I tried to show that, in spite of the difference between His circumstances and ours—in spite of the eschatological medium, so to speak, through which His teaching was given—there was no a priori reason why such a teacher should not have taught an ethical ideal which, in its fundamental principles, later ages might recognize as eternally true. To-day I want to enquire what in its fundamental principles this ideal actually is, and whether it does as a matter of fact commend

77

itself to the moral consciousness of the modern world
at its highest.   It is needless to say that the Christian
Ethic is not presented to us in the New Testament
as a philosophical system.[1]   But that does not make
it incapable of being reduced to a system which may
harmonize with the results of the deepest philosophical
reflection.   By reflection on the actual practice of
great Artists we may build up Canons of Criticism, a
system of Æsthetics, a Philosophy of taste : but the
Artist himself, as a rule, has no such system.   The
poet may teach profound truths which the speculative
philosopher may subsequently reduce to something like
a philosophy of life : but in the poet's mind they are
not, as a rule, reduced to a philosophy.   And so the
greatest moral teachers of mankind have not, usually,
been speculative philosophers.   That was eminently the
case with Jesus Christ and His first disciples.   It is
true that an instinct of reverence is apt to blind us to
the immense amount of real, hard thinking which was
implied in the religious and moral teaching of Jesus :
the greatness, the originality of Jesus was intellectual

---

[1] On the other hand it is a great deal too much to say with
Mr. Selwyn (*The Teaching of Christ*, p. 79) that " there is no Christian ethic, but only a Christian spirit."   If the Christian spirit (in
matters of character and conduct) is capable of articulate expression, that expression will be an Ethic, which can be to some extent
analysed and systematized by the philosopher.   If it is not capable
of such expression, it would be useless to go to the Gospels to discover that spirit.   A Christianity which is not capable of articulate
expression can have no connexion with History.   This may be said
with the fullest allowance for the inadequacy of all formulæ *fully*
to embody an ethical ideal.

as well as moral. But still His teaching—His religious and His ethical teaching alike—was not presented in the form either of a theological system or of
a speculative philosophy. It came to Him by way
of intuition : it was presented to His hearers in the
form of aphorism or of parable. It was homely
practical teaching addressed for the most part to people
of little culture or education, or with a culture which
was popular, intensely national, and closely connected
with Religion. In the present lecture I want to examine the actual teaching of Jesus in the form in
which He presented it to His own mind and to that
of His hearers.

It must be remembered that the teaching of Jesus
Christ presupposes a morality of a very advanced
and developed order. I must not now stay to compare the ethical teaching of the Jewish prophets with
that of the other great ethical and religious systems
of the world. I shall have something to say upon
that subject hereafter. It must suffice for the present
to remark that, if we compare the teaching of the
later Judaism with the Ethics of ancient Greece and
Rome, there can be no doubt that it represents, on the
whole, a higher level than any teaching known to the
West, at least till the time of Zeno and the Stoics.
In many respects the ideal of developed Judaism
represents a higher moral standard even than that of
the two great Hellenic thinkers—Socrates and Plato—
whom we may fairly recognize as belonging, like the

Jewish seers, to the goodly fellowship of the Prophets. It was enormously superior to the intensely narrow, civic, aristocratic morality of Aristotle. It was strong just where the Greek philosophers were weakest. The political and the intellectual development of Greece were no doubt greatly in advance of anything known in Israel. All those virtues which had to do with political activity and with the intellectual life were better understood by Socrates and Plato than by Amos or Isaiah : and, of course, the high intellectual development carried with it emancipation from some superstitions in matters of conduct. But in Religion, and in those matters of personal morality which are apt to be most affected by the state of religious feeling and religious belief, the Greeks of Aristotle's time were mere children compared with the Jews. The principle of Justice, in its simpler and most elementary form constitutes, indeed, a common ground between the civic morality of Socrates and the religious morality of Judaism. But in two great matters the Jews were enormously in advance of the Greeks—in the matter of Chastity and in the matter of Charity.

Whether we look to the teaching of the philosophers or to the average practice, there can be little doubt about the superiority of the Jews on the side of sexual Morality. Polygamy was, indeed, allowed among the Jews, though before the time of our Lord it had become rare and exceptional ; and the position of women was perhaps slightly more honourable and more secure in parts at least of the Greek world than among the Jews. But the great principle which confines sexual relations to lawful marriage was hardly propounded even by Moralists among the Greeks : it was fully acknowledged among the later Jews. The ordinary Greek morality on this matter was simply that extra-matrimonial intercourse must be with non-citizen women; for that such intercourse was profoundly degrading to the woman, the general feeling of mankind has almost universally recognized. But there was no sense of the intrinsic rights of Humanity as such which could protect the non-citizen woman from that degradation, or make it appear wrong for the man to subject her to it. I need do no more than allude to those still darker vices which, if they were not exactly approved by the highest pagan morality, were condemned with a lightness which is itself the best evidence of their commonness even in the most cultivated, refined, and aristocratic Greek circles. And the higher moral teachers of the time did little to preach a sounder morality on these matters. On the other hand, the Jewish Law and the Jewish prophets are full of denunciations of sexual transgression of all kinds.[1] And not only the prophets. In some respects what is called the Wisdom literature—

---

[1] As to Adultery, see Lev. xx. 10 ; xix. 20–22. (It is doubtful whether the penalty of death was actually carried out.) As to Fornication, Lev. xix. 29 ; Deut. xxiii. 17, 18 ; Jer. v. 7 ; Amos ii. 7 ; Hos. iv. 14. Cf. also Gen. xiii. 13, xix. 5–7 ; Deut. xxiii. 17, 18 ; 1 Kings xv. 12, etc.

G

the Book of Proverbs in the Canon, and the Books
of Wisdom and Ecclesiasticus now relegated to the
Apocrypha—represent perhaps on the whole a lower
level of religious insight and religious enthusiasm than
the great prophetic teachers of the later Monarchy and
the Exile ; but at all events in this they show the
same superiority to the contemporary Greek morality
—that they are full of zeal for social Purity.[1]

In the other great matter to which I have alluded
the superiority of the Jews is still more marked. It
is a commonplace to say that the Greeks in the time
of Aristotle had very little notion of the rights of man
as such. Aristocrat and democrat might differ as to
who should be citizens, but they were agreed that the
citizens should not be the whole population : for the
rights of the barbarian or the alien Greek, the slave
or the freedman, the Athenian democrat had only
a little more tenderness than the aristocratic Aristotle,
who tells us frankly that " the work of the artisan or
the labourer has nothing to do with Virtue," and that
therefore it is best that such persons should be altogether excluded from citizenship—from civil rights as
well as political rights. Even as regards citizens, the
Greek conception of one's duty towards one's neighbour was for the most part limited to the idea of public

---

[1] Prov. ii. 16–19, v. 3–6, vii. 5–27 ; Ecclus. ix. 3–9, xli. 20 ;
Wisdom iv. 6, xiv. 24, 26. The letter of the law only forbade an
Israelite woman to be a prostitute (Deut. xxiii. 17). This seems to
have led to the multiplication of foreign prostitutes. Hence the
denunciation of the " strange woman " in the Book of Proverbs.

service (in that matter they have still much to teach modern Christians) and to the idea of Justice, that is to say, respect for the property and other legal or customary rights of individuals.   There was little or no feeling that there is a duty of positive service or mutual helpfulness owed by one individual to another, even within the ranks of the citizen-class beyond the limited circle of one's own family or friends.

Still less was there any idea of a special claim on the part of the weak, the oppressed, the sick, the suffering, the poor.   The duties of Philanthropy, of Almsgiving, of Mercy are simply non-existent in the elaborate enumeration of virtues and duties given us by Aristotle ; and in the far higher, more spiritual, more cosmopolitan teaching of Socrates and Plato there is almost as little inculcation of these virtues, if there is less that is shocking to modern Christian sentiment in their way of treating the ignorant and the humbly born.   With all his magnificent conscientiousness, his scrupulosity about matters of conduct, and his sense of public duty, it never seems to have occurred even to Socrates to ask himself whether it might not be morally binding on Society or on individuals to think about the kind of life that was being led by his poor fellow-citizen in the next street or by the slave in his own household.   To Plato the sick were simply objects of dislike.   The economic problems of our great cities were hardly known in their modern form : but still the orphan, the widow, the unfortunate have always been with us : yet (so far as we can discover) in the time of Aristotle nobody troubled their heads about them, either speculatively or practically. Even high-class citizen women were not thought to matter very much, though, of course, the Greek idea of their position was far removed from the ordinary Oriental conception of woman as the mere toy and plaything of man. The ethical teaching of the Socratic School reaches its highest level in the scenes connected with the trial and death of Socrates. Socrates died a martyr to truth and to civic duty : yet in the Phaedo Socrates drives his wife and children from the room with something like brutality that his last moments might be spent in undisturbed philosophical converse with his male friends.

What a contrast to all this is presented by the teaching of the Jewish prophets! Amos lived three centuries and a half before Socrates. He is full of denunciation against the cruelty and oppression of the poor, whether practised by the enemies of Israel or by its own rulers and rich men. " For three transgressions of Israel, yea, for four, I will not turn away the punishment thereof ; because they have sold the righteous for silver and the needy for a pair of shoes : that pant after the dust of the earth on the head of the poor, and turn aside the way of the meek."[1] Isaiah lived some three centuries before Socrates. Doubtless Socrates had a strong sense of Justice ; but it would be difficult to find in any teaching attributed to him

[1] Amos ii. 6, 7.

much special tenderness for the poor or unfortunate—
any equivalent of Isaiah's " seek judgement, relieve
the oppressed, judge the fatherless, plead for the
widow."[1] The prophet who is commonly known as
the later Isaiah lived more than a century before
Plato. The Hellenic philosopher would have sym-
pathized keenly enough with the Jewish prophet's
denunciation of superstitious confidence in sacrifices
and fasts ; but it would never have occurred to him,
in enforcing the idea that the true fast was repentance
and righteousness, to make his conduct to inferiors
the test of a man's moral position. " Is not this the
fast that I have chosen ? to loose the bonds of wickedness, to undo the bands of the yoke, and to let the
oppressed go free, and that ye break every yoke ? Is
it not to deal thy bread to the hungry, and that thou
bring the poor that are cast out to thy house ? when
thou seest the naked, that thou cover him ; and that
thou hide not thyself from thine own flesh ? "[2] In the
teaching of the Jewish prophets Mercy is always
closely associated with Justice in descriptions alike
of the character of God and of the character which He
requires in men. Neither Mercy nor any equivalent
of it appears in Aristotle's very detailed list of virtues ;
the nearest he gets to it is in the Equity which is only
a higher form of Justice.

In the interval between the great prophetic era and

---

[1] Isa. i. 17.

[2] Isa. lviii. 6, 7, often assigned to a later " Trito-Isaiah."

the birth of Christ a twofold change had come over the ethical ideas of the Jews. At scarcely any other period in the development of any nation have progress and retrogression been so strangely mixed. On the one hand the place of the prophet was taken by the scribe. The customs about sacrifice and ritual and religious observance which had originally been handed down by oral tradition were now reduced to writing, supplemented by highly sacerdotal additions, and combined with earlier documents, in the books which we call the Pentateuch. The letter of the Law came to be surrounded with superstitious reverence. And yet the Mosaic Law, as it was embodied in the Penta- teuch, became in the hands of the Pharisaic scribes only the basis of a vast superstructure of comment, amplification, and Casuistry. The Law contained a general command to rest upon the Sabbath : the Pharisees developed this command into a prohibition of the most ordinary, necessary, and even beneficent occupations of life. It was unlawful on the Sabbath to pluck ears of corn because that was equivalent to reaping, or to rub them in the hand because that was threshing, or to walk more than 2000 cubits—less than three-quarters of a mile—because Moses had commanded the Jews in the wilderness to remain in their places on the Sabbath-day. And so on. The dietetic regulations and the rules about avoiding con- tact with a dead body, which the Jews had no doubt inherited from primitive systems of Totemism and

Taboo, were insisted upon with a punctiliousness which shut off the Jews from all ordinary intercourse with Gentile neighbours.   It was the fear of incurring ceremonial pollution which drove the Pharisees to insist so much upon the washing of hands before eating, upon the washing of cups and pots and the like,[1] and this carried with it unwillingness to sit at table with Gentiles.   Even sound moral principles were degraded and narrowed by being made to rest upon the positive written rules of an authoritative book, instead of being treated as the injunctions of a Conscience which believed itself to derive its inspiration directly from a living God : while an immense host of petty observances of no real moral importance were placed side by side with the eternal laws of Justice and Benevolence, and this had the inevitable result of practically throwing them into the shade and at times of contravening them.   Men were taught (if we may accept our Lord's saying as sufficient evidence of the fact) how to avoid supporting their parents by taking a vow not to give them anything,[2] how

[1] Mark vii. 4.   But we are told that this is an exaggeration.

[2] According to Mr. Herford (*Pharisaism*, p. 159) " If a man make a vow upon a matter between himself and his parents, i.e. one which, if he kept it, will occasion injury or loss to them, then he is to be released from it on the ground of honour to his parents.   The commentators on the Mishnah all agree in this interpretation, and there is no doubt as to the intention of the Mishnah.   Moreover, there is no indication that there ever had been a different opinion, as if the statement now made in the Mishnah had taken the place of an earlier statement.   There is no evidence that the Pharisees ever held or taught the doctrine attributed to them by Jesus, while it is contradicted in the most definite manner by the declara-

to cheat their neighbours by taking oaths which had no binding force, how to neglect the duties of Charity and Mercy under pretence of observing the Sabbath, and so on.

All this represented serious moral retrogression. Legalism took the place of Morality. Many qualifications might be required if we were dealing with the question of rabbinical Morality in detail. No doubt it is possible to quote from the Rabbis passages in which the comparative unimportance of ceremonial as compared with moral transgression is insisted upon ; but still the existence of an extreme overestimate of the letter of the ceremonial Law is hardly denied by any student of the Talmud : the pages of

---

tions of their own legal authorities." When Mr. Herford says " There is no evidence," he seems to overlook the evidence of the Gospels themselves. It is difficult to understand how the saying of Jesus is to be accounted for if the other view had absolutely no supporters. It may well be that it was at no time the accepted view. The Talmud was of course not put into its present form till centuries later ; and, however much we may be disposed to trust the attribution of particular sayings to the Rabbis of an earlier period, it is unreasonable to suppose that all their opinions were preserved. This was one which later Rabbis might well wish to have forgotten. As Mr. Montefiore remarks, " It is not at all improbable that so vast an innovation as the annulment of vows met with opposition at first " (*The Synoptic Gospels*, I, p. 166). According to the same writer " ' Corban ' does not mean that the property was dedicated to the use of the Temple. The word is used as a mere oath. When I say, ' Corban, if you shall ever eat anything that is mine,' that does not mean that my eatables are dedicated to the use of the Temple, in which case neither I nor you might eat them, but merely that, so far as you are concerned, they are ' dedicated ' ; you may never eat what is mine. I should sin in letting you eat any of my food, so long as the vow stands, and you, if you ate, would sin also. The Temple does not come in " (*l.c.*, p. 164).

the Gospels would be sufficient evidence of the fact, even if we had no other : for, though Christian compilers may have exaggerated this side of Judaism, they could not have invented it. The antagonism to Judaism to which such representations would have to be ascribed, if nr t justified by the facts, could not have existed but f(r the bitter conflict between Jews and Jewish Christians on this matter of the ceremonial Law.

And yet the enormous change which took place during this somewhat obscure period in the mental history of Judaism was not all retrogression. After all the Law did contain the most essential principles of Justice and neighbourly conduct, though it contained much besides. Reverence for the Law was, after all, reverence for Morality, though sometimes the moral precepts which it enshrined were spoiled by the company in which they found themselves. I must not now speak of the religious changes which took place during this period further than to notice that they were, in part at least, changes which made for righteousness. There was a growth in the consciousness of Jehovah's goodwill not merely to Israel collectively, but to the individual Israelite. And that carried with it the belief in individual responsibility. In the teaching of Ezekiel the belief in a mere collective or family responsibility (" the fathers have eaten sour grapes, and the children's teeth are set on edge ") was superseded by the idea of a divine Justice which took account of individual acts : " the soul that sinneth, it shall die."[1]   During the Exile and the Dispersion, worship was spiritualized ; the Synagogue for a time took the place of the Temple, and continued side by side with it after the Return : the Scribe—the expounder of the Law, the teacher of righteousness, the preacher of Religion—became more important than the sacrificing Priest.   Prayer and reading and meditation—spiritual modes of worship which could be practised anywhere—overshadowed in importance the sacrificial ritual of Jerusalem.   And all this did carry with it a deeper feeling of the importance of personal conduct, a deeper sense of sin, a more anxious conscientiousness.   All these things imply a moral advance, and paved the way for the spiritual revolution which transformed Judaism into Christianity.   It may be that on the whole the progress of this age was far greater than the retrogression.[2]

And if we look to the details of the Moral Law, there too we see advance.   If we compare the prophets with the apocryphal books of later Judaism—both those accepted as deutero-canonical and those which

---

[1] Ezek. xviii. 3, 4.

[2] " It is high time to put away altogether, as one of the exploded errors of history, the notion that Ezra, by the exaltation of the Torah to the supreme place in Jewish religion, set that religion upon the down-grade.   I believe it to be nearer the truth to say that after Moses and Isaiah (or perhaps Jeremiah) Ezra is the third greatest man in the Old Testament " (Herford, *Pharisaism*, p. 74). This may be so; still, we need not look beyond the Book of Ezra itself to see that the religiousness of Ezra and his age had its deficiencies.

have never found their way into any Canon—there
can be no doubt that this latest age of Judaism was
an age of ethical progress. There is less of ethical
inspiration, far less of religious inspiration ; but if
we tried to compile a code of duties out of the Old
Testament, and then compiled a similar code from the
Apocrypha, the latter would come considerably nearer
to a modern and a Christian formulation of the whole
duty of man. The prophetic insistence upon personal
and upon social Morality becomes more detailed and
more exacting. The general inculcation of beneficence
to individuals is translated into definite precepts
about the relief of the sick,[1] of widows and orphans, of
the poor and helpless ; systematic almsgiving[2] becomes
a recognized duty. If we would judge this period
aright, we must remember the enormous capacity of
the human mind for inconsistency. The very same
teachers who spoiled Judaism by their legalism, their
ceremonialism, their casuistry, were quite capable of
appreciating the best elements of Old Testament
teaching and even of improving upon them. Doubtless there were different schools and tendencies even
among the teachers of the same period. The Greek-

[1] " Also to the poor man stretch out thy hand, that thy blessing
may be perfected " (Ecclus. vii. 32). " Be not slow to visit a sick
man " (*ib.*, 35).

[2] " As thy substance is, give alms of it according to thine abund-
ance : if thou have little, be not afraid to give alms according to
that little " (Tobit iv. 8). There is of course a superstitious side to
this insistence upon Almsgiving, e.g. " Almsgiving will make an
atonement for sins " (Ecclus. iii. 30).

Jewish writer of Wisdom and the Hebrew writer of Ecclesiasticus were on the whole perhaps more liberal and more enlightened than many of the Rabbis whose teachings survive in the Talmud. Among the Rabbis themselves the School of Hillel may have been more liberal than the School of Shammai, and so on. And there is one writing of this period which stands absolutely alone in its close approach to the teaching of Jesus. In the prominence which it gives to the love of God and one's neighbour, in its inculcation of forgiveness—even to enemies—in its insistence upon purity of heart and intention, the " Testaments of the Twelve Patriarchs " may be taken as representing the highest ideal that the world ever knew before the coming of Christ. And it is a work which, it is highly probable, Jesus had actually read.[1] There are many different moral levels among the Jewish writers of this period. And yet it is probable that it was very often the same men who taught the things which excited

[1] The date of the original work is fixed by Dr. Charles as between 109 and 105 B.C. The Jewish additions belong chiefly to the period 70–40 B.C. There are Christian interpolations which long caused the whole work to be assigned to a Christian writer. Here are a few of its noblest precepts which are not interpolations : " Love ye one another from the heart ; and, if a man sin against thee, speak peaceably to him, and in thy soul hold not guile ; and if he repent and confess, forgive him " (Gad. vi. 3) : Issachar (vii. 6) is made to say, " I loved the Lord ; likewise also every man with all my heart." There is no trace of a limitation of this love to fellow-countrymen, and the Messiah whose advent is announced is to be the Saviour of the Gentiles as well as Jews. The emphasis on sexual purity is very marked, while there is no disparagement of marriage, e.g. " He that hath a pure mind in love, looketh not after a woman with a view to fornication ; for he hath no defilement in his heart,

our Lord's scathing denunciations and who uttered the sayings upon which His own early spiritual life must have been fed and nurtured. There is much of the highest moral teaching and the most spiritual religious teaching in the sayings of the Rabbis who lived before and during the ministry of Christ. And yet only a strong anti-Christian bias can suppose that Jesus is adequately accounted for by the ethical teaching of Hillel. Wellhausen has remarked in a famous passage that learned Jews are fond of pointing out that all the moral precepts of Jesus can be found in the Talmud. " Yes," he replies, " all and much more." [1]   And it is, as he goes on to point out, just in the absence of that much more that the superiority of Jesus lies. The pure wheat of Morality was to be found in the teaching of the Rabbis, but the tares were there too, and the wheat was in danger of being choked by the tares. The work of Jesus consisted to a very great extent in separating what was true and eternally valuable in the

because the spirit of God resteth upon him " (Benj. viii. 2). Some of the contrasts drawn in the text between the ordinary Jewish morality and the teaching of Christ do not apply to this remarkable writing. Prof. Burkitt, however, tells me that in his opinion the translator was a Christian, and that the translation may have been slightly, perhaps only slightly, influenced by Christian ideas.

[1] Cf. " Jewish scholars think that all that Jesus has said is to be found also in the Talmud. Yes, all and much more. How is it that He was the first to discover something true and eternal in the waste of legal learning ? Why has no one else done so ? And is it certain, when a saying of Jesus is attributed to the Rabbi Hillel, that in such cases the Talmud is right ? Can nothing from the Gospels have been introduced into the Talmud, and be sailing there under false colours ? That the Talmud depends upon pure

traditions of His people from the lower and inconsistent elements which in practice largely neutralized their effect.

All this may seem to be a long preface to a lecture which is to deal with the moral teaching of Jesus, but it is impossible to understand the unique position which that teaching occupies in the moral history of the world unless we realize exactly what were the defects in the current moral ideas of contemporary Judaism, and what was the transformation which it wanted to turn it into an adequate basis for the world's future moral development. Three great changes were introduced by our Lord into the current moral ideas of His time. They are briefly these : (1) The separation of the genuinely ethical and permanently valuable elements in the teaching of the Jewish Law from the ceremonial and transitory elements ; (2) the correction of the current legalism by a more inward morality which condemned the uncharitable or unclean thought or intention as well as the completed act : (3) the definite proclamation of the

oral tradition is a pure superstition : it is largely based upon literature." (*Israelitische und jüdische Geschichte*, p. 317, note). Of course I cannot venture to express any opinion as to the probabilities of a Christian influence upon the Talmud. On this point Mr. Montefiore says, " The religious value of the teaching of the Synoptic Gospels for the modern Jew is not to be measured by the presence or absence of parallels to the various sayings of Jesus in the later Rabbinical literature. I do not merely refer to the fact that almost all the parallels are later in date. . . . When Talmud and Gospels are compared, the originality is almost always on the side of the Gospels " (*Syn. Gospels*, p. civ.) Wellhausen's " all " is probably an exaggeration.

principle that the neighbour to whom the Jew owed duties was not merely his fellow-countrymen, but his fellow-man.   Let me dwell upon each of these great moral revolutions in detail.

(1) The question of the attitude of our Lord towards the Jewish Law has been a matter of much dispute. Here I must content myself with suggesting conclusions without much discussion or argument.   In the first place our Lord clearly drew a sharp distinction between the injunctions contained in the books attributed to Moses and the Pharisaic amplifications of them.   Sharing the ordinary ideas of His contemporaries about the authorship and origin of these books, He acknowledged their divine authority.   To the Pharisaic glosses He attached no authority whatever.   Consequently He defended His disciples against charges of Sabbath-breaking either by walking through the cornfields or by rubbing the ears of corn ;   He healed on the Sabbath and laid down the far-reaching principles, " It is lawful to do good on the Sabbath-day " [1] and " the Sabbath was made for man and not man for the Sabbath." [2]   He had no scruples about eating with unwashen hands.   He took no account of the fasts which the Pharisees had invented in addition to the Day of Atonement, the only day of fasting prescribed by the Law.   He threw to the winds all

[1] Matt. xii. 12.

[2] Mark ii. 27.   In the saying " The Son of man is Lord also of the Sabbath " it is possible that the " Son of man "=man, humanity.

the immoral Casuistry by which the Scribes not merely added to the burden of the Law, but violated its most essential commands, such as the duty of honouring father and mother and of not taking God's name in vain. Secondly, within the Law itself He practically, if not avowedly, distinguished between the ethical parts of it and merely ritual or ceremonial regulations. He did not perhaps assert in so many words that He had come not to destroy the Law and the prophets, but to fulfil them, or that not one jot or one tittle should pass from the Law.[1] These sayings may belong to the attempt of the first Evangelist or of his source to extract out of isolated sayings of Jesus a systematic exposition of the Master's attitude towards the Law; but in any case the first of them does represent a true statement of what that attitude was, if (with the Evangelist) we mean by this "fulfilling" that He had come to bring out the true, ethical meaning of the Law and the prophets, to complete what was lacking in them, to develope their true principles and push them to their logical conse-

---

[1] Matt. v. 17, 18 ; Luke xvi. 17. So Loisy who suggests that St. Paul is the man destined by Judæo-Christian opinion to be "least in the Kingdom of Heaven." The second of these sayings, but not the first, certainly belongs to Q. The whole of the preface to the enunciation of the new law in St. Matthew (v. 17–19 or perhaps 17–20) is of rather doubtful genuineness. If on the strength of its appearing in Luke xvi. 17 we accept the saying about not one jot or tittle passing from the Law, it must have been said in a different and irrecoverable context. If Jesus said it, He must have done so at a period when His antagonism to Jewish legalism was not fully developed. The verse is omitted by the Sinaitic-Syriac version.

quences. And, when He proceeds to give illustrations of what He means by this fulfilment, or completion, of the law, it is to the laws against adultery, against murder, against false swearing, and the like that He applies the principle. There is not a word about the ceremonial law. The first at least of our Evangelists[1] is anxious to make the most of all utterances which imply profound respect for the Law : yet we nowhere find even the first Gospel representing our Lord as insisting upon the importance of sacrifice, of avoiding ceremonial pollution, of abstaining from unclean meats, or upon the efficacy of the Day of Atonement and its ceremonies, which was a prominent element in the teaching of many Rabbis. The strongest recognitions of the obligation for Jews of complying with the ritual requirements of the Mosaic Law are found only in that most Judaic of the Gospels, and must be looked upon with some suspicion. The injunction to the leper to show himself to the Priest and offer the gift that Moses commanded is, indeed, found in all three Synoptists.[2] Two Gospels give the injunction which follows our Lord's scathing words about the tithing of mint and anyse and cummin, while the weightier matters of the Law were neglected : " These ye ought to have done, and not to have left the other

---

[1] Or one of the sources which he used. The last Edition of the first Gospel was certainly universalistic, but he must have used a source—possibly some later edition of Q—which was more decidedly Jewish-Christian. Some have suggested that the original Q was a work of this character.

[2] Matt. viii. 4 ; Mark i. 44 ; Luke v. 14.

H

undone,"[1] but they are omitted in St. Luke by the Codex Bezæ (D), and may well have come in from Matthew. The strongest of all is the explicit statement —peculiar to the first Gospel—" The Scribes and the Pharisees sit on Moses' seat : all things therefore whatsoever they bid you, these do and observe: but do not ye after their works, for they say and do not. Yea, they bind heavy burdens, and grievous to be borne, and lay them on men's shoulders : but they themselves will not move them with their finger."[2] Taken literally these words seem inconsistent with our Lord's actual teaching and practice on other occasions : He certainly did refuse to observe, or enjoin the observance of, the Sabbath in the Pharisaic way, or the washing of hands, and many other things which the Scribes and Pharisees bade men do. The absence of such words in Luke suggests that they are a gloss of the Evangelist or some later redactor, a traditional amplification of the Master's actual words. But, even if they are genuine, the significance of what Jesus does *not* say in Matthew—the total absence of any insistence upon specific ceremonial rules—is none the less marked.

To some small extent our interpretation of Christ's attitude towards the Law may be affected by our estimate of the relative trustworthiness of the different Evangelists in such passages as these—upon the

[1] Matt. xxiii. 23 ; Luke xi. 42
[2] Matt. xxiii. 2, 3.

question whether we look upon the more legalistic passages of Matthew as Judaistic additions or upon the omission of such sayings in Luke as universalizing excisions. To my own mind the evidence in most cases favours the former alternative. But, however we decide such questions, there is not much room for serious doubt on His general position. We are not entitled to say that Christ ever actually encouraged the non-observance of precepts obviously and fairly deducible from the commands of Scripture : or that He ever explicitly drew a distinction between ceremonial precepts which were not, and moral precepts which were, of eternal obligation. He assumed as a matter of course that Jews would go on observing their national law, and He probably never doubted that in some sense the law of Moses was of divine origin. At the same time it is to be observed that He never sanctions extreme views of biblical inspiration. It is to Moses, not directly to God, that He refers the injunctions of the Pentateuch : He says vaguely, " it was said to the men of old time," not " God said." He did not doubt that Moses was divinely commissioned, or that the Scriptures were divinely inspired ; but that is a different thing from laying it down that the whole Old Testament was written by the finger of God. When the sons of thunder, in accordance with Old Testament precedent, desired to call down fire from heaven to consume the Samaritan village which rejected their Master, no reverence for the Old

Testament or for Elias prevented His rebuking them.[1]

The truth seems to be that by a sort of instinct of spiritual insight the mind of Jesus fastened upon the spiritual and ethical import of the Jewish Scriptures, and ignored all the rest. In principle the negative side of St. Paul's teaching about the Law is already contained in the teaching of Christ. Whenever the Law stood in the way of a higher law, He disregarded it boldly. He healed on the Sabbath,[2] which was certainly " work " of a kind, defended His disciples for plucking the ears of corn and rubbing them in their hands, and laid down a principle which goes further than St. Paul went by saying that, even in its application to Jews, the Sabbath was made for man and not man for the Sabbath.[3] Most important of all is the explicit depreciation of the whole system of clean and unclean meats which was the main foundation

[1] Luke ix. 55. The words " As Elias did " are omitted in the best MSS. The words " Ye know not what spirit ye are of " (though omitted in some MSS.) are better attested than the words which follow : " For the Son of man came not to destroy men's lives but to save them."

[2] Mark iii. 1–6 ; Matt. xii. 9–14 ; Luke vi. 6–11. It is important to remember that this event marks the beginning of the designs upon our Lord's life by Herod Antipas and the representatives of official Religion. Cf. also Luke xiv. 1–6.

[3] Mark ii. 23–28 ; Matt. xii. 1–8 ; Luke vi. 1–5. There was a rabbinic saying, " The Sabbath is yours, and you are not for the Sabbath " (quoted by Holtzmann and Loisy). In Luke vi. 5 D adds the well-known story that the Lord said to a man picking sticks on the Sabbath, " Man, if thou knowest what thou doest, blessed art thou ; but if thou knowest not, thou art accursed and a transgressor of the law."

of that social barrier between Jew and Gentile eventually broken down by the influence of St. Paul and the development of a Catholic Church. " Perceive ye not that whatsoever from without goeth into the man, it cannot defile him. . . . That which proceedeth out of the man, that defileth the man. For from within, out of the heart of men evil thoughts proceed, fornications, thefts, murders, adulteries, covetings, wickednesses, deceit, lasciviousness, an evil eye, railing, pride, foolishness : all these evil things proceed from within, and defile the man."[1] St. Mark is assuredly right in adding by way of comment that in these words our Lord was virtually repealing the whole system : " this He said making all meats clean." What our Lord would have actually advised if one of His disciples had proposed to eat unclean meats, we cannot say : but He denied altogether the absolute moral validity of the command to abstain from them. In principle that carries with it the abrogation of the whole ceremonial law as a matter of eternal, intrinsic obligation or divine command.

(2) Our Lord deepened, transcended, spiritualized the strictly moral requirements of the Law.

At the present day the principle that Morality lies

---

[1] Mark vii. 18–22 ; Matt. xv. 18–20. The explanation contained in Matt. xv. 15–20, and in a more condensed form in Mark, is looked upon with suspicion by some critics, but that gives us no reason to doubt the saying itself (Matt. xv. 11). And it is supported by the general tone of Christ's teaching. Loisy may well remark : " L'émancipation de Paul, beaucoup plus apparent, n'était pas plus réelle " (*Evan. Syn.* I, p. 569).

in the intention, that a man who intends to kill is no less guilty because a pistol missed fire, while the accidental homicide is not guilty at all, seems so obviously reasonable that we are inclined to forget that this was not always recognized.　Primitive Law and primitive Morality alike dealt almost entirely with acts, very little with motives ; they knew nothing of the guilt of unfulfilled intention or even of the absolute innocence of involuntary blood-shedding.[1] As Morality advanced, people came no doubt to realize more completely the importance of motive and intention ; but it may be doubted whether by the wisest of the ancients the principle was ever understood with the fullness and definiteness and distinctness which it attained in the moral conscious- ness of Him of whose deeper thoughts the Sermon on the Mount contains the most concentrated dis- closure.　Matthew Arnold was right in making the " inwardness " of true Morality one at least of the characteristic thoughts of Jesus.[2]

We have seen reason to believe that, if the first Evangelist has actually formulated for himself the principle that Jesus came to fulfil ($\pi\lambda\eta\rho\hat{\omega}\sigma\alpha\iota$) the Law and the Prophets, i.e. to develope the eternal

[1] The Jewish law protected the accidental homicide, but only if he could reach a city of refuge (Deut. xix. Cf. Numbers xxxv. 22).

[2] Aristotle makes the value of morality consist chiefly in the $\pi\rho o\alpha\acute{\iota}\rho\epsilon\sigma\iota s$, but $\tau\acute{\epsilon}\lambda\epsilon\iota\alpha$ $\mathring{\alpha}\rho\epsilon\tau\grave{\eta}$ implies both intention and act ; and he is wholly incapable of conceiving that a man may be liberal who has little or nothing to give.　The saying of the widow's mite is quite beyond his ken.

principles implied but not adequately expressed in
the Mosaic Law, he had a right conception of the
Master's actual attitude towards that Law. The
old Law dealt only with acts: the new righteousness
required a love of goodness, a love of one's neighbour,
a passionate desire to fulfil the will of God in the
inmost depths of the heart. That principle is illustrated by a succession of detailed applications. The
old Law had forbidden murder : the new Law forbade
malicious thoughts or evil intentions. The angry
thought, prevented from taking effect by a prudential
regard for consequences, may be as bad as murder.
So with regard to the seventh Commandment, the old
Law had forbidden adultery, which later Jewish
interpretation had made to include fornication. To
Christ the lascivious thought was evil in itself ; the
lascivious thought prevented from turning into act
by fear of vengeance or legal penalty was as bad as
adultery. The essential principle of the seventh
Commandment was that man was intended for permanent union with one woman. Hence Jesus forbade
the polygamy which the letter of the Law allowed :
though polygamy was by this time so uncommon
among religious Jews that the prohibition of it would
not, it is probable, have struck His hearers as specially
startling. Not so His peremptory prohibition of
Divorce. The Jewish Law allowed the husband to
divorce his wife for mere disinclination, and divorce,
of course, to a Jew carried with it liberty to marry

again. Some of the later Jewish teachers had discouraged divorce,[1] but none of them had positively
condemned it. Our Lord peremptorily forbade divorce
to either party, or the remarriage of a divorced person. In the text of Matthew (v. 32 ; xix. 9) an exception is added, " except for fornication."[2] The absence
of this exception from the text of Mark and Luke[3]
makes it almost certain that it was absent from the
common source and from the original utterance of
Jesus. It is not so certain that the exception would
have been repudiated by Jesus Himself. He was
laying down principles. The true principle was
permanent monogamous marriage. In a society living
up to Christ's principle there would be no divorce for
adultery because there would be no adultery. What
was to be done when the true ideal of marriage was
violated by one of the parties, Jesus (so far as we
know) did not consider. If we have no right to say
positively that He would have recognized the exception which the Church of the Evangelist's day—the
Judaeo-Christian Church of the end of the first century—evidently did recognize, we may at least be
sure that it was divorce for lesser causes than this,
divorce at the caprice of the husband, that he had
primarily in view. This, it must be remembered, was

---

[1] " I hate putting away, saith the Lord " (Mal. ii. 16).

[2] Matthew also adds to the question, " for every cause " (xix. 3).
These words may be genuine ; at all events they represent the real
question at issue. They strongly support the view taken in the
text.

[3] Mark x. 11 ; Luke xvi. 18.   Cf. 1 Cor. vii. 10, 39.

the sole question at issue between the rival Jewish Schools—the question about which the new Teacher was invited to adjudicate. Hillel allowed divorce for many causes besides adultery : Shammai allowed it for adultery alone. Both parties admitted that divorce was lawful in the case of adultery. What our Lord meant, in all probability, was to pronounce in favour of Shammai.[1]

In any case the actual attitude of Roman Catholicism and High Anglicanism on this subject is indefensible. Orthodoxy cannot refuse to admit the authority of the actual text of any one Gospel, and the text of Matthew distinctly allows the divorce *a vinculo matrimonii*. We cannot condemn the practice of half Christendom on the strength of what is after all only a conjectural, and not absolutely certain, emendation of our Lord's recorded utterance.[2] Moreover, if the letter

[1] This is the interpretation put upon the passage by Mr. Montefiore (I, 240). It is often assumed that the words which follow in Mark x. 12 can hardly be part of the original saying. Divorce was not allowed to women by Jewish law in any case, though there had been cases of high-born Jewish women leaving their husbands and marrying another, e.g. that of Herodias. Prof. Burkitt (*The Gospel History and its Transmission*, p. 100) has made the interesting suggestion that this was the case which our Lord had in view. He was carrying on the protest of the Baptist against this flagrant case of immorality. Possibly Prof. Burkitt is right. However the matter is decided, we have another illustration of the impossibility of basing modern morality purely upon authority—even upon the authority of Christ. We simply do not know with any approach to historical certainty whether our Lord allowed divorce for adultery at all, either to the husband only or to both parties.

[2] This is the position adopted by the Bishop of Oxford in *The Question of Divorce*. There was for a long time great uncertainty in the attitude of the Church on the subject, and the whole Eastern

of Christ's teaching is to be insisted on, the Western divorce *a mensâ et thoro* is forbidden as much as actual dissolution of marriage. The difficulty which we experience in determining what our Lord actually taught on this matter, impressively illustrates the absolute impossibility of basing detailed rules for the guidance of modern life upon isolated sayings of Christ. That the ideal is permanent monogamous marriage is undoubtedly the principle which Jesus taught ; and that ideal still appeals to all the higher ethical feeling of our time. By what detailed enactments the ideal may be best promoted, which is the less of two evils when that ideal has been violated and made impossible, is a question which must be settled by the moral consciousness, the experience, the practical judgement of the present. That principle has been freely adopted by the Christian Church in other cases. Our Lord's prohibition of Divorce, even if the exception is removed, is not more peremptory, as far as the letter goes, than His prohibition of oaths, of self-defence, or of going to law.

It is a significant fact that St. Paul, in spite of his strong view of the permanence of marriage, did not feel forbidden by his Master's words to permit divorce in one case not expressly mentioned by Him—in the

Church still allows divorce for adultery and the re-marriage of the innocent party, as do the Protestant Churches of the Continent. I cannot understand how Mr. Selwyn can say (*The Teaching of Christ*, p. 106) that "the Church has always interpreted our Lord's teaching about divorce as though this exception did not exist."

case of a heathen partner anxious to repudiate a newly converted Christian spouse : and in this case even the strict Western Church allows the repudiated Christian to re-marry.

The same principle is then applied to the case of swearing. Our Lord brushes aside the casuistical distinctions between oaths which were more binding and oaths which were less binding, or not binding at all. Among those who wished to follow the ideal law of God, yea would be yea, and nay nay. The rule of Veracity would be observed habitually : lying would be avoided as much as perjury. Our Lord was here probably thinking not so much either of judicial oaths or of cursing and swearing in ordinary conversation (though He would, of course, have condemned the irreverent appeal to the name of God), as of attempts to cheat one's neighbour by taking oaths to repay a debt, or the like, on which the other would rely—oaths which the casuistically learned swearer secretly knows not to be binding, and does not intend to observe.[1] In the matter of judicial oaths Christian States and Churches have followed a perfectly sound principle. Undoubtedly in an ideal society there would be no distinction between swearing and affirming ; a man's word would be " as good as his oath." But as long as there are persons superstitious enough to shrink from perjury though willing to lie, it is the less of two evils that formal oaths should be adminis-

---

[1] This point seems generally to have been overlooked.

tered to witnesses in Courts of Justice and on other
solemn occasions.

We need not linger on our Lord's other detailed
applications of His principle. They lead up to the
emphatic enunciation of universal undiscriminating
love to one's neighbour, even to one's enemy. " All
things therefore whatever ye would that men should
do unto you, even so do unto them," as it is elsewhere
expressed. If it be the Evangelist who adds the
words, " for this is the law and the prophets," he is
only bringing out the very deepest and most characteristic thought of his Master. The law of God which
was of universal obligation was the law of universal
love, the law which regards every other human being
as of equal intrinsic importance to oneself, as equally
entitled to have his true good promoted by every other
rational being. The most certain thing about the
teaching of Jesus is that He did teach this doctrine of
universal love. Anyone who admits that He did so, and
that He taught nothing inconsistent therewith, and who
also regards this teaching as the fundamental truth of
Morality, is already a disciple of Jesus, in a very distinctive and definite sense.

(3) The third great modification of average Jewish
Morality which was called for in the time of Jesus
was an extension of the meaning which was to be given
to the precept " Thou shalt love thy neighbour as
thyself." In putting that rule side by side with the
law of love to God and making these two into the first

and greatest commandments of the Law, Jesus was
only quoting the most ritualistic and least spiritual
book among the Old Testament Scriptures—the book
of Leviticus. The two great deficiencies in the application of this law by its Pharisaic expositors were these.
The first was that they taught much which was really
inconsistent with that rule, and which (as we have
seen) was in principle brushed aside by the teaching
of Jesus. By the love of God it is probable that the
author of Leviticus would have by no means understood
simply the love and service of men whose good God
wills, but also the observance of a host of ceremonial
regulations, some of which were thought to be well-
pleasing to God, but which were not at all for the
good of man. That this was not the case with Jesus
we have already seen. The second defect was that
by one's neighbour was understood simply—at the
very most—the Jewish fellow-countryman.[1] In the
Law itself, in the Prophets, in the teaching of the
Rabbis, much was said about the considerate treatment of strangers ; but the most liberal of them would
have shrunk from the assertion that a Gentile was in the
sight of God as important as a Jew, and was entitled to
the same treatment at the hands of his Jewish brother.

Did the teaching of Jesus actually affirm this
principle ? I believe that we can confidently assert
that it did. There would, indeed, be no doubt about

[1] The very question of the Scribe to our Lord shows that there
were different interpretations of it current at the time. See
Appendix I (below p. 286).

our answer, if we could rely with absolute confidence upon the genuineness of all the universalistic sayings of our present Synoptists—such as the declaration that many shall come from the East and West, and from the North and South and shall sit down in the Kingdom of God.[1] But such sayings may be doubted or interpreted in some non-universalistic sense. I think it must, indeed, be admitted that our Lord Himself considered His own mission to be to His own people. " I am not sent but unto the lost sheep of the house of Israel."[2] But this does not imply that, if and when a Jew was brought into contact with a Gentile, he was not to treat him as a brother, or that He would have had any doubts about the truth that "in every nation he that feareth God and worketh righteousness is acceptable to Him." We need not rely upon passages which a somewhat over-suspicious criticism may doubt. That our Lord's teaching was in principle universalistic is implied in the modifications of current Jewish Ethics which have already been insisted on. The whole tone and tenor of His teaching implied that a man's standing in the sight of God did not depend upon

---

[1] Matt. viii. 11 ; Luke xiii. 29. It is a curious fact that in Matthew the passage is certainly universalistic, being addressed to the Centurion, while in Luke it is just possible to suppose that it is only the Jews of the Dispersion that are referred to.

[2] Matt. xv. 24. Cf. x. 6. Luke's omission, being accounted for by his Universalism, is not conclusive against the genuineness of the saying, and yet it may be due to the first Evangelist's view of the Messiah's original mission. We cannot rely upon Mark xiii. 10, xiv. 9, or Matt. xxviii. 19, because these imply a long period before the Parousia.

descent from Abraham, upon circumcision, upon the observance of the distinction between clean and unclean meats, but upon the state of his heart, upon the degree of his love, upon the extent to which he did the will of God. If righteousness was the sole condition of admission to the Kingdom of Heaven, it followed necessarily and as a matter of course that a Gentile could enter it. If Gentiles might become subjects of the Kingdom of God without observing the distinction between clean and unclean meats, it was obvious that they must be treated as brothers. And this was, I believe, no mere implication of Christ's teaching discovered afterwards by St. Paul and the Christian Church. He could hardly have failed to be aware that no less than this was involved in it ; though it did not often (no doubt) fall within the purpose of His mission (as He conceived it) to dwell much upon it. He who associated so habitually and so lovingly with publicans and sinners—lax observers of the Law when they observed it at all—could hardly have regarded Gentiles as less the children of God than they. In proof of this view of our Lord's teaching I will not insist much on the exceptional occasions when He was brought into contact with individual Gentiles — on His healing of the Syro-Phœnician woman[1] or His approval of the Centurion's faith[2]—

---

[1] The saying above-quoted about His mission being to the house of Israel occurs in two contexts, and this may suggest doubts as to the incident, about which see below, p. 176.

[2] Matt. viii. 10 ; Luke vii. 9.

but rather upon the general tone and temper of the teaching which finds its most perfect expression in the parable of the Good Samaritan (Luke x. 30 *sq.*). The Samaritans were at least as much outside the pale of average Pharisaic charity as the Gentiles. A Jewish teacher who explicitly taught that a Samaritan might be neighbour to a Jew and spiritually superior to a Priest and a Levite, has parted company with Jewish Particularism.

If anyone is disposed to accept the conjecture that in the parable of the Good Samaritan, the Samaritan has taken the place of a story in which the barbarity of Priest and Levite is contrasted with the humanity of the simple Israelite,[1] we may appeal to the passage in the Sermon on the Mount upon love

---

[1] "As to the good Samaritan there is much reason to suppose (though no Christian commentator is likely to admit it) that he comes from a verbal alteration of the original story" (*Syn. Gospels*, I, p. lxvi.). M. Halèvy has given plausible reasons for supposing that the personages of the parable were originally Priest, Levite, and simple Israelite, and Mr. Montefiore (*ib.*, II, pp. 935–7) has accepted his theory. The grounds are briefly: (1) the improbability of a Samaritan travelling between Jerusalem and Jericho, (2) the strangeness of the collocation "Priest, Levite, Samaritan." These grounds (for a full statement of which I must refer to Mr. Montefiore's note) do not seem to me very convincing, and even if we suppose that an old Jewish story has been adapted to a new purpose, I cannot see why the adapter may not as probably have been Jesus Himself as St. Luke, but the theory prevents our treating this piece of evidence as conclusive. The parable of the two sons is often regarded as meaning "Jew and Gentile" (Matt. xxi. 28: cf. the parable of the Banquet), but those who so interpret it are disposed to regard it as an "ecclesiastical addition" of Matthew. Even if it is so, the attitude of the Jewish Church towards Gentile Christianity can hardly be explained except by the inherent universalism of the Master's teaching.

to enemies. Any Jew who was disposed to accept the traditional rule of popular Ethics, " Thou shalt love thy neighbour and hate thine enemy," would certainly have extended the principle to national as well as to personal enemies. Christ invited His disciples to love their enemies and pray for those that despitefully used them " that ye may be sons of your Father which is in heaven : for he maketh his sun to rise on the evil and the good."[1] A God who loves the bad will certainly love Gentiles, and if the followers of Jesus were to be like Him, they must obviously be no less comprehensive in their philanthropy.

I submit then in conclusion that in laying down the principle of human Brotherhood, in its fullest possible extent and with a complete absence of inconsistent additions and qualifications, our Lord has laid down the fundamental principles of all true Morality as it is recognized by the moral consciousness of the present day at its highest. Whether side by side with these principles there are other elements in the moral teaching of Christ which fail to commend themselves to the moral consciousness of to-day, I shall consider in my next lecture. Meanwhile, I leave with you the suggestion that the claim of Christ's religion to the position of a universal religion rests to a large extent

---

[1] Matt. v. 45 ; Luke vi. 35. Matthew concludes with the injunction : " Ye therefore shall be perfect, as your heavenly Father is perfect." If this version be genuine, we must suppose the words to mean " all-embracing, universal, undiscriminating in your charity " rather than " faultless " or " sinless." But Luke's " merciful " is perhaps nearer to the original.

I

upon the fact that it is the religion which has most completely and consistently insisted upon this principle. How congenial is that ethical teaching with the most characteristic idea of Christ's teaching on its strictly religious side—the Fatherhood of God—I must here content myself with merely pointing out. The Ethic which makes the duty of Universal Love its first and chief commandment necessarily involves, for a teacher in whom Religion or Morality are inseparably connected, the idea of a God who Himself loves equally all the souls whose life is derived from Him.

But before I conclude, a word must be said as to the form in which the moral teaching of Christ is presented to us. It is difficult to reduce that teaching, as I have attempted to do, to formal propositions, and then to point out its complete harmony with the conclusions of modern Moral Philosophy, without doing an injustice to the most characteristic features of the Gospel records. Such an argument may be suspected of proving too much. If all that can be said is that there is no inconsistency between the teaching of Christ and that which may be found in some modern text-book of Morality, the objection may occur, " What does it matter what we teach and preach—the Gospel or some modern Education Committee's text-book of Morality, assuming that such a work does in some way teach the duty of loving one's neighbour as oneself ? "

Fully to answer the objection would demand an elaborate discussion upon many questions which hardly belong to our immediate subject. I must be content with indicating a few of the heads under which such an answer would fall.

(1) In his inaugural lecture as Professor of Poetry at Oxford, Dr. Andrew Bradley pointed out the inseparability in poetry of form and matter : in poetry we cannot treat the poet's meaning as one thing, and the poet's language as a quite distinct and separable way of expressing his meaning. The same principle holds of the teaching of great moral teachers —and pre-eminently of Christ. The impressiveness, convincingness, and efficacy of His teaching largely disappear when the form which He gave to it is taken away. You *can* reduce the teaching of the Sermon on the Mount to a dry philosophical form, and its truth is unaffected by the process ; but when you do so, you have lost the peculiar force and charm of the sayings which have caused that discourse to be accepted as the classical summary of human duty by so many of those who have altogether repudiated the Theology with which it is associated[1]. You *can* teach the forgivingness of God and the duty of forgiving one's brethren without the parable of the Prodigal Son, the duty of Humanity without the parable of the Good Samaritan, the value of the

---

[1] It is said that the late Professor Tyndall was in the habit of reading it through once a fortnight.

individual soul without the parable of the hundred sheep ; but if you do so, you do not teach them so well. Certainly a Morality might be Christian Morality, which was taught without a single reference to the personality of Christ or to the words of the Gospel. But it must not be assumed that such a teaching of Christian Morality would be an effective substitute for a knowledge of the historic Christ and of the Gospel pages. The moral supremacy of Christ cannot be fairly appreciated apart from the form in which His teaching is presented to us.

(2) The value and impressiveness of any moral teacher's work cannot be adequately estimated by isolated sayings. A moral ideal is a connected whole, and this whole is best presented by the picture of a character and a life.[1] Even the ideal considered as so much precept can hardly be appreciated apart from the character of the teacher. Still less can the moral effect of the teaching be separated from the impression made by the teacher's life. The ethical importance of Christ and of the religion which He founded is based not merely upon the intrinsic value of His teaching, but upon the picture of a life which seems to be in complete harmony with that teaching. I have con-

---

[1] " Jewish Apologists have a habit of breaking up the Gospels into fragments. They are somewhat inclined to do the same with their own literature. But a great book is more than its own sentences taken singly or disjointedly. A great personality is more than the record of its teaching, and the teaching is more than the bits of it taken one by one. It must be viewed as a whole." Montefiore, *Syn. Gospels*, I, p. civ.

tended strongly that we cannot defend the supremacy which the Christian religion claims for the moral teaching of Christ except by contending that it actually satisfies the moral consciousness of the present. But, it must be recognized that the full extent of the appeal depends on the character and the life and not merely upon isolated sayings. The influence of a Person is stronger than that of an idea. This is a very important point to be borne in mind in estimating the moral healthiness of a religious system which places the teaching of an historical Person who lived in the remote past in the forefront of its ethical ideal.

(3) One of the most characteristic features of the Christian Ethic is the closeness of the connexion in which it stands to Religion, as it is the distinctive characteristic of Christian Theology that, more unreservedly than any other historical religion, it exhibits the complete identification of Religion and Morality. There has necessarily therefore been something unnatural and one-sided about an attempt to exhibit Christian Morality in isolation from Theology. An adequate defence of Christian Ethics would involve an attempt to show that it is morally healthy and desirable that Ethics should be taught in this close connexion with Religion. And this represents a new subject upon which I can hardly enter now.[1] I believe

---

[1] I have discussed it pretty fully—so far as I could do so without entering in detail into the special theology of the Christian Religion —in *The Theory of Good and Evil*, Bk. III, chaps. i. and ii.

that it could be shown that the idea of an objective moral obligation is not only consistent with, but naturally leads up to and even logically demands, if the fullest meaning is to be given to the term objectivity, the belief that Morality consists in obedience to the will of a perfectly righteous God. At the very least it may be said that it is thus interpreted that the idea of an objective duty comes home most powerfully to ordinary minds, and that it is most likely to influence life. And this is the form in which the idea of an absolute right and wrong is set forth in the teaching of Jesus. In His ideal of life complete devotion to the will of God is bound up with the conviction that God is perfectly and intrinsically good, and consequently wills nothing but the true and highest good of His creatures. In the whole range of Theology there is no principle so important as this. If Jesus was the first to teach that principle in its full purity, if He taught it with a purity, a force and a consistency to which no other Religion—uninfluenced by His teaching—affords any parallel, we have already discovered a sufficient answer—an answer of enormous force—to the question why we of the twentieth century should still consider ourselves disciples of Christ, and of none other in the same sense and to the same degree. We have found sufficient reason for saying with the disciple of the fourth Gospel : " Lord, to whom shall we go ? thou hast the words of eternal life."

ADDITIONAL NOTE ON THE ETHICAL TEACHING
OF CHRIST IN DETAIL

THE central truth of Christ's Morality was His promulgation of the duty of universal love. But the teaching of
Christ would not have exercised the influence that it has
exercised, it would not have constituted the epoch in the
ethical development of the race that it has actually constituted, if His teaching had consisted in nothing but the bare
enunciation of the formula " Thou shalt love thy neighbour as thyself." Nor would the merely negative merit of
excluding inconsistent additions or contradictions of the
doctrine have been sufficient to account for the effects of
that teaching. Ethical teaching that is really to come
home to men's consciences must have some body, some
fullness of content, some wealth and forcefulness of illustration : there must be more than a bare enunciation of formal
principles : the principles must be developed. There must
be concrete deductions and applications. Corollaries and
consequences must be pointed out. Contradictory and
inconsistent principles must not merely be excluded : they
must be denounced and exposed. And all these things are
pre-eminently characteristic of the teaching of Jesus.
Nothing is more remarkable in it than the way it combines
very great universality in the enunciation of fundamental
principles with great concreteness of illustrative detail and
application. An entirely incorrect impression will be formed
of it—of its originality, its importance and its distinctiveness—if it is supposed to consist in nothing but the

enunciation of the abstract law of universal Benevolence in a way that will commend itself to philosophers anxious to discover the fundamental principle of all Morality. It does enunciate that law with more clearness and consistency than had ever been done before: but there is much in it besides. And therefore it is important that we should try to enumerate and summarize the leading features of Christ's ethical teaching in somewhat greater detail than has been possible in the preceding lecture. Our limits demand that the summary should be very brief, and that little shall be attempted in the way of explaining or vindicating the teaching or applying it to modern conditions. Such a reply to objections as is possible will be reserved for the next lecture.

(1) *Love to enemies.* The principle of love to enemies is so absolutely involved in the principle of love to Humanity in general that it may be treated as simply a reassertion of the principle itself. If Humanity as such is to be loved, if its good is to be promoted, if every individual human being possesses an intrinsic worth, that principle cannot cease to be true because the man is an enemy. That does not imply that there is not much in some men which may properly be hated as Jesus hated the hypocrisy of some Pharisees and the covetousness of others. Such men are to be loved because they are capable of better things. The enunciation of this principle holds a prominent place in the sermon on the Mount.[1]

(2) *Forgiveness of injuries.* The duty of forgiveness is another implication of the same principle. This was an extremely characteristic feature in the teaching of Jesus: " Whensoever ye stand praying, forgive, if ye have aught against anyone; that your Father also which is in heaven

---

[1] Matt. v. 43–48; Luke vi. 27–35.

may forgive you your trespasses."[1]   " Leave there thy gift before the altar, and go thy way : first be reconciled to thy brother and then come and offer thy gift."[2]   " If thy brother sin, rebuke him ; and if he repent, forgive him. And if he sin against thee seven times in the day, and seven times turn again to thee, saying, I repent, thou shalt forgive him."[3] The principle is asserted even in the shorter version of the prayer which our Lord is said to have bequeathed to His disciples. It is illustrated by the attitude of Jesus to the adulterous woman where it is carried to the point of actual disobedience to the letter of the Mosaic law, providing that such should be stoned—a law which it is doubtful whether later Judaism ever enforced even when it possessed the political power to enforce it. It has been enshrined for ever in the parable of the Prodigal Son.[4] Primarily that parable was intended no doubt to teach the forgivingness of God, but in Christ's teaching the divine forgiveness and the duty of human forgiveness were indissolubly associated. It is right to add that in His insistence on

---

[1] Mark xi. 25.

[2] Matt. v. 24.

[3] Luke xvii. 3, 4 ; Matt. xviii. 21, 22, where it is further illustrated by the parable of the unmerciful servant (*ib.* 23–35). Luke's version is simpler than Matthew's more elaborate question and answer with the more emphatic " until seventy times seven."

[4] We need not suppose that either our Lord or the Evangelist meant the Prodigal Son to be a type of the Gentile world, though the principle of the parable undoubtedly carries with it in germ the justification of St. Paul's mission to the Gentiles. The latter portion of the parable—about the jealousy of the elder brother— may more reasonably be treated as a later attempt to vindicate Gentile Christians against Jews or Judaizing Christians : but there is no necessity for the supposition. The parable fits the case simply because it asserts the eternal principle upon which the mission to the Gentiles was founded (Luke xv. 11–32).

forgiveness our Lord was only pressing a point very
familiar to the highest rabbinical morality of Christ's day,
though doubtless there were some things in that teaching
—as in much later Christian teaching—which were quite
inconsistent with it.

(3) *Self-sacrifice.* Jesus insisted much upon the importance of self-sacrifice. It is obvious that, if we are really to
do what is best for our neighbours and not for ourselves
alone, this must involve—in the actual conditions of any
human society—much sacrifice of self. But the necessity
has not always been recognized—even in theory. Jesus
pushed His insistence upon it to the point of making it the
characteristic note of discipleship to Himself — the
characteristic requirement for admission to the Kingdom.
This principle was so fully grasped by the very earliest
disciples that it is difficult to say which of the sayings
attributed to Jesus represents the earliest form of His
teaching. It may well be thought that the saying about
taking up the Cross and following Him was formulated
by those who knew by what form of death He had died,
even if we suppose that His anticipations of a violent death
had amounted to inward certainty. This portion of the
saying is probably a traditional expansion in the light of
subsequent events, though it is barely possible that the
cross may have become the recognized phrase for a shameful death before it became the consecrated symbol of self-
sacrifice through the death of Christ.[1] But the rest of the
famous saying there is no reason to doubt, " If any man
would come after me, let him deny himself."[2] So again,

---

[1] See passages from classical and rabbinic literature quoted by
Archdeacon Allen on Matt. x. 38. Luke gives the saying a metaphorical application to ordinary life by adding the word " daily "
(ix. 23).

[2] Mark viii. 34 ; Matt. xvi. 24–26.

" Whosoever shall seek to gain his life shall lose it, but whosoever shall lose his life shall preserve it." [1]

On this subject I will quote the words of Mr. Montefiore, who has so nobly resisted the temptation—necessarily strong to a Jewish interpreter—to minimize the originality of Jesus. " Then come the two simple Greek words ἀπαρνησάσθω ἑαυτὸν, ' let him deny himself.' Here again we have what is practically a new conception. Self-denial was not unknown before Christ ; but the clear conception of it and the ideal which it suggests *were*, I think, new, [2] and they in their turn have exercised an immense influence upon men's thoughts, aspirations and actions. More restricted, but not less intense, has been the effect of the next words : ' let him take up his cross.' The true follower of the Master, in proportion to the perfection of his discipleship, must endure and renounce, suffer and die " (*The Synoptic Gospels*, I, 211).

(4) *The Danger of Riches.* The particular kind of self-sacrifice to which Jesus called His first disciples was determined by the needs of His mission. The hardships imposed upon His disciples were especially those involved in preaching the Kingdom of Heaven—the more so as it eventually became clear to Him that in all probability the accomplishment of that mission would involve death for Himself, and imminent peril of death for His immediate followers. On those whom He called to this work of preaching He laid the specific requirement that they should abandon—at least for the time—their homes and occupa-

---

[1] Luke xvii. 33. It may be that the primary meaning of gaining the soul or the life is " to be saved at the Messianic Judgement "; but none the less the ethical principle is laid down that self-sacrifice is demanded for entrance to the Kingdom. As to our Lord's teaching about reward, see below, p. 290 *sq*.

[2] The Buddhistic ideal of Self-renunciation was different, see below (p. 266).

tions and lead the life of itinerant missionaries.[1] Some who were rich He advised that they should sell all they had and give to the poor.[2] His teaching was full of the dangers of riches. Luke's version of the Beatitude, " Blessed are ye poor," is probably nearer the original idea than Matthew's " poor in spirit,"[3] though we are told that the Aramaic word will cover both meanings—" poor " and " poor in spirit." " It is easier for a camel to go through the eye of a needle than for a rich man to enter into the Kingdom of God."[4] That is a saying which, just because of its paradoxical character, is among those least likely to have been invented, whatever we may think of the attenuated explanation in Matthew—" how hardly shall they who trust in riches." The principle is strikingly illustrated by the parables of the rich fool and of Dives and Lazarus.[5] The difficulties involved in these passages I shall consider in the next lecture.

(5) *Humility.* Closely connected with the inculcation of self-sacrifice is the insistence on Humility.[6] The duty of Humility—properly understood—is indeed only an application of the doctrine of Love. In Aristotle's picture of the " high-souled man " the feature which revolts us is not that " he thinks much of himself being worthy," though Jesus might have suggested the doubt whether he was altogether so worthy as he thought himself, but rather

---

[1] Matt. x. 1–15. It is probable that the Commission to the Seventy in Luke is a variant of the Commission to the Twelve in Matthew. The details of both these discourses have probably been more or less coloured by the later experiences of the first Christian missionaries.

[2] Matt. xix. 21.

[3] Luke vi. 20 ; Matt. v. 3.

[4] Matt. xix. 24 ; Mark x. 25 ; Luke xviii. 25.

[5] Luke xii. 16 ; xvi. 19. Cf. also Matt. vi. 19–34.

[6] Matt. xviii. 1–4 ; Matt. xix. 13–14, etc.

his intolerable arrogance and contempt for others.[1] By the man who really loves his neighbour as himself, the excellences of others will be as highly esteemed as his own ; their sins and deficiencies will be to him a subject of genuine pity and regret, not of ostentatious self-congratulation and haughty isolation. That Jesus recognized this connexion between Humility and Love, is, I think, clear from His whole treatment of the subject. " He that is greatest among you, let him be as the younger, and he that is chief as he that doth serve."[2] True greatness consists in social service : there is one kind of ambition which He does not deny to His disciples— the ambition to serve much. The oft-repeated exhortation to become as little children refers,[3] I think, not primarily to the simplicity, guilelessness and other real or supposed virtues of childhood, but rather to the insignificance of children—with possibly a suggestion that those who wish to enter the Kingdom should, as children have to do in poor families, be much engaged in the service of others.[4] These sayings are invitations to self-subordination and social service rather than to simplicity or child-likeness of character. In condemning grasping, self-assertive, pushful ambition, Jesus was only carrying on one of the characteristic features of later Jewish morality.

---

[1] " The high-souled man justly despises " (others). " He is ashamed of receiving a benefit," for that implies inferiority. " Towards those in power or prosperity he is haughty, but to the lesser people condescending " (μέτριος), etc. (Nic. Eth. iv. 3).

[2] Luke xxii. 26.

[3] Matt. xix. 13–14 = Mark x. 14 = Luke xviii. 16 (" of such is the Kingdom of Heaven ").

[4] So in the Middle Ages the child habitually waited at table, and even the sons of the rich were brought up as pages in the households of Bishops or great secular Lords.

One reason for humility recognized by our Lord is that it is a necessary outcome of love to one's neighbour. But another ground on which Jesus could not have approved Aristotle's " high-souled man " is His strong sense of human imperfection, of the need for self-condemnation, repentance, and humility in the sight of God. " None is good, save one, even God."[1] The true moral ideal is so high that no one can self-complacently suppose that he has attained it. Of Humility on this side the noblest expression is the parable of the Pharisee and the tax-gatherer.[2] The same principle underlies the condemnation of censorious condemnation of others which is contained in the maxim " Judge not " and the saying about the mote and the beam.[3]

(6) *The Christian Good.* The duty of love means the duty of promoting the true good of Humanity, and in its practical applications it will vary enormously according to the interpretation which is given to that true good. In the teaching of Jesus the importance of the spiritual—of conduct, of character, of motive, is everywhere insisted upon, while at the same time there is no ascetic disparagement of ordinary human happiness. Happiness is not despised, but the chief good which the Christian lover will seek to realize for the loved is to make him also a lover —a lover of God, a lover of all that is good, a lover of his fellow-men. This principle has perhaps been sufficiently insisted upon in our analysis of the sermon on the Mount, but I should like here to quote a fine passage from Professor Royce's recent book on the *Problem of Christianity.* Professor Royce has mastered, as it seems to me, the true essence of Christ's own moral teaching in a way

---

[1] Mark x. 18 = Luke xviii. 19.
[2] Luke xviii. 9–14.
[3] Matt. vii. 1, 2 (=Luke vi. 37) ; Matt. vii. 3 (=Luke vi. 41).

which hardly any professed Philosopher has ever done before :—

" But now let us return to the relation of love to the services that one is to offer to one's neighbor. What can the lover—in so far as Jesus describes his task— what can he do for his fellow-man ?

" To this question it is, indeed, possible to give one answer which clearly defines a duty to the neighbor ; and this duty is emphasized throughout the teaching of Jesus. This duty is the requirement to use all fitting means—example, precept, kindliness, non-resistance, heroism, patience, courage, strenuousness—all means that tend to make the neighbor himself one of the lovers. The first duty of love is to produce love, to nourish it, to extend the Kingdom of Heaven by teaching love to all men. And *this* service to one's neighbor is a clearly definable service. And so far the love of the neighbor involves no unsolved problems."[1]

(7) *Purity.* One special application of the last principle —the superiority of the spiritual to the carnal—upon which Jesus insisted much was on the side of sexual Morality. The licentious thought was condemned no less than the licentious act ;[2] and He went beyond the letter of the Jewish law in condemning divorce, which was still common though some Rabbis condemned it, and by implication polygamy, which was practically unknown among the Jews of that time.[3]

It may be desirable to say a word about the connexion between Christ's central doctrine of Love and His principles of sexual Morality—all the more so because this is one of

[1] I, 85. I should like to quote the whole chapter. I must add that in other directions Professor Royce's interpretation of Christianity seems to me seriously defective.　　　　[2] Matt. v. 28.

[3] Matt. xix. 3–10, etc. (see above, pp. 104–5).

the few cases in which intellectual doubt as to the basis of a moral duty is probably a very frequent cause of moral transgression. What then is the true answer to the question " Why is fornication wrong ? " The duty of abstaining from fornication springs, I believe, from these two principles taken together—the duty of love, which includes respect, for every human being, and the superiority of the spiritual to the carnal. Extra-matrimonial intercourse is degrading to the woman. That it is intrinsically degrading to the woman to be used for the satisfaction of the lusts of a man, and not with a view to a permanent union in which she is to be treated as the equal companion of the man and the mother of his children, is one of those truths which are intuitively perceived. All judgements as to the nature of the good are of this character : they must be apprehended by our judgements of value. That the vast majority of men do thus judge is made plain enough by the attitude which the most licentious man of the world would instantly assume towards the seducer of a sister or a daughter, and by his contempt for immoral women. If a man accepts the principle that every human being is equally to be treated as an object of love, entitled to his or her share in whatever is truly good, entitled to be treated as a " brother or a sister " or (in more philosophical language) as an end-in-himself, then he cannot justify the treatment of another woman in a way which would arouse his utmost indignation if any woman he really cared for were so treated by another. And the obligation to treat every other woman as he would wish his sister to be treated is not altered by the fact that weakness or poverty or vanity or sinful inclination may make her a willing victim. The man who accepts Christ's principle is bound to promote the true good of every other, not to gratify all his actual desires. It may be added that in a vast number of cases the wrong inflicted on the woman is not merely the moral degradation but the first step on the road to ruin in every sense of the word.[1]

(8) *Repentance.* The very idea of an absolute duty—implied in all the teaching of our Lord—carries with it the duty of repentance where there has been a violation of duty. Or to put it otherwise, our Lord taught that sin is the worst of evils, and a recognition of that truth necessarily brings with it sorrow for sin—both for positive external wrong-doing and for any failure in love. Obvious as these deductions are, they have not always been actually drawn in practice. There is nothing about repentance in Aristotle, not very much in Plato ; more no doubt in the teaching of the Stoics, though the proud self-sufficiency of that school hardly favours a penitential attitude of mind. The insistence upon the necessity of repentance, and upon the closely connected doctrine that God will forgive wherever there is sincere repentance, was one of the great points upon which the Jewish prophetic teaching most clearly goes beyond the moral level of the ancient world. And here the doctrine of the Rabbis was quite faithful to the best traditions of Judaism,[2] though there are many things about the necessity of ritual expiation on the great day of the Atonement and otherwise which are hopelessly inconsistent with this doctrine. In the teaching of Jesus the necessity for repentance was absolutely central.

[1] Those sexual immoralities to which these considerations do not apply are equally condemned by our immediate judgements of value, and here we are able to appeal to a very general consensus. There are some pleasures which do not form part of true human good, and everyone is bound to promote his own true good as well as that of others.

[2] " Nothing can be proved by more abundant and overwhelming evidence than that the conception of God as forgiving from free grace was a fundamental and familiar feature of the Pharisaic religion, just as it still remains so " (Montefiore, *Syn. Gospels*, I, 79).

K

Even those who most one-sidedly insist upon the eschatological character of Christ's teaching admit that the
necessity of repentance for entrance into the Kingdom was
from first to last as prominent a feature of His message as
the proclamation that the Kingdom was at hand.[1] The
noblest expression of this necessity is the parable of the
Pharisee and the Publican with its emphatic declaration
that the repentant sinner was justified rather than the
self-complacent observer of the Law.[2]

The modern depreciation of repentance is a note either
of superficiality or of cant. Professor Oliver Lodge's much-
discussed declaration that the modern man has no time to
think of his sins is really one of the most unwise things
that was ever uttered by an able and religious-minded man.
If a man's will is not wholly directed towards the good, he
must hate and condemn himself in so far as his will is bad ;
and he cannot do that unless he knows himself, unless he
reflects on his bad actions and sorrows over them and the
character which they reveal, and deliberately resolves to
turn from them. If the man believes in a perfectly righteous
Being whose Will is identical with the law of his Conscience
(so far as that Conscience sees truly)—a Being from whom
he has alienated himself by his transgressions—his sorrow
will be deepened, and will assume the form of a desire for
reconciliation with that Being, which will most naturally
express itself in confession and prayer for forgiveness,
restitution, change of will. Repentance is only the reverse
side of the turning towards good. It is not complete, it
cannot exist, without effort after amendment. And this is
a truth which is everywhere taught by Jesus. It is implied
in the parable of the Prodigal Son[3] whose willingness to
become as one of his father's hired servants was already an

---

[1] Mark i. 15 = Matt. iv. 17.
[2] Luke xviii. 9–14.　　　　　[3] Luke xv. 11–32.

act of amendment. It is the especial point of the parable of the two sons. The son who " afterwards repented and went " had begun to do the will of his father.[1]

(9) *The duty of making others better.* The necessity of repentance was a prominent feature of rabbinic teaching. That was also to some extent the case with another implication of the doctrine that the most valuable element in the good life is goodness itself, *i.e.* the duty of promoting that good in others, and of encouraging repentance in those who lack it. The prophets had both by example and precept set forth the importance of making other men righteous, and so had the Rabbis. But it may be doubted whether by any of them this duty had been emphasized as it is emphasized in the teaching of Jesus. When once it is recognized that the Kingdom whose advent was foretold was an ethical and spiritual Kingdom, a new heaven and a new earth wherein was to dwell righteousness, the eschatological character of the teaching only adds additional emphasis to this supreme duty—the promotion for others of a good wherein righteousness is the most important element. From this point of view all the parables of the Kingdom, whatever subordinate aspects of it they are intended to teach, become so many emphatic assertions of this duty.

The specially characteristic application of this principle which we find in Jesus is His insistence on the duty and blessedness of bringing sinners to repentance. The importance of righteousness is a common note of all high moral teaching, but it has often been accompanied by much contempt of sinners and a disposition to avoid them. Christ pitied the sinner and sought to move him to repentance. And this is no more than a logical deduction from these three principles—the duty of love, the doctrine that

[1] Matt. xxi. 29.

sin is the worst of evils, the possibility of repentance and amendment even for the worst. The teaching of Jesus is full of this idea. It will be enough to refer to the parable of the lost sheep and the memorable paradox "I say unto you that even so there shall be joy in heaven over one sinner that repenteth, more than over ninety and nine just persons who need no repentance."[1] The truth that repentance is never impossible — and that when there is a full repentance, no punishment is called for or will be demanded by God—is illustrated by the parable of the labourers. " I will give unto this last even as unto thee."[2] The whole life of Jesus, His association with the " tax-gatherers and sinners " whom the correct religious world despised, was an illustration of it—a side of His teaching sometimes forgotten by the extreme "Eschatologists " who complain that our Lord taught no Ethics of permanent value. If they think that the ethical principle which underlies such a mission to the morally lost is suitable only for an " Interimsethik," that is their doctrine, not the Christ's. On this subject Mr. Montefiore remarks : " So far as we can tell, this pity for the sinner was a new note in religious history " (*Syn. Gospels*, II, 574).

(10) *The sin of casting stumbling-blocks.* The heinousness of the sin involved in putting a stumbling-block in the way of others, particularly of the little ones, the

---

[1] Luke xv. 7 ; Matt. xviii. 13 (Luke adds the parable of the lost piece of silver, xv. 8). The thought can only be understood literally if it be assumed that the righteousness of the ninety and nine was merely external righteousness or at least an easy righteousness helped by favourable circumstances, which implied less goodwill than the repentance of the sinner. But this is too prosaic a way to treat the parable. Matthew perhaps did not like this disparagement of the righteous which he found in his source (Q) and omitted it.

[2] Matt. xx. 12–14.

simple and the weak, is only a particular application—
a negative application—of the duty of helping others to
avoid sin.[1] And this leads on to the more general principle
—the intrinsic value of the lowliest soul, for all are capable
of goodness, however narrow their sphere of action and
however small their intellectual capacities. " See that ye
despise not one of these little ones ; for I say unto you that
in heaven their angels do always behold the face of my
Father which is in heaven."[2]

(11) *The danger of hypocrisy.* Much of the moral teaching of Jesus is concerned not so much with the enforcement
of particular duties as with the importance of goodness in
general—the good will itself. This carried with it a special
emphasis on the wickedness of hypocrisy[3]—the besetting
sin of religious people in a community in which piety was
at a premium, a passport to social recognition and importance. This is the principle which underlay His denunciation
of the Scribes and Pharisees. Here again those who
complain of the "interim" character of Christ's injunctions seem unable to distinguish between the immediate and the permanent application of His sayings.
Scribes and Pharisees are always with us, though in the
modern world hypocrisy may often assume forms strangely
different from those common in first-century Palestine—
especially the form of an " inverted hypocrisy " which sets
up claims to a greater emancipation from moral restraint
than the pretender really believes in or is prepared to put
into practice. Much contemporary literature is steeped in
this kind of hypocrisy. The interim for which, according
to some, Christ's Ethic was suited, has certainly not come
to an end yet.

[1] Matt. xviii. 6, 7 ; Mark ix. 42 ; Luke xvii. 1, 2.
[2] Matt. xviii. 10.
[3] Matt. vi. 1–6, 16–18.

LECTURE IV

OBJECTIONS TO THE MORAL TEACHING
OF CHRIST

I PROPOSE in the present lecture to consider some of the objections which are most commonly made to the moral teaching of Jesus. We have seen that the fundamental principle of Christian Ethics, as laid down in the teaching of Jesus Himself, resolves itself into the general principle of impartial love towards all mankind.[1] I have already pointed out that nothing is more characteristic of Jesus than the generality or universality of His teaching, and that it is this characteristic which makes it possible for the teaching of One who lived in a petty, not very advanced community of the ancient world, to be accepted as the basis of a universal morality and a universal religion.

At the same time it is essential to recognize that our Lord did not actually limit Himself to the teaching

[1] The word "impartial" carries with it the implication that Benevolence is to be combined with Justice. Justice requires that each individual should be treated according to his real value. That every soul of man has real value was a prominent feature of the teaching of Jesus. The relations between Justice and Benevolence are fully dealt with in my *Theory of Good and Evil*, Bk. I, chap. viii.

of this one fundamental principle. No ethical teaching that did limit itself to abstract generalities of this kind could possibly have produced a powerful influence on human souls and human lives. The moral teacher must be concrete : he must go into details of conduct. No teaching was ever more concrete than that of Christ. In a sense no teaching was more detailed or more practical. The parable of the good Samaritan embodies a principle, but at the same time it suggests an immediately practicable and very definite duty. Much of Christ's teaching—indeed much of the teaching which has most influenced the world—relates not to detailed questions about the content of duty, questions as to what particular things are right and wrong, but to the supreme importance of goodness in general. And the teaching of universal love would have been very cold and unpersuasive apart from the particular applications and interpretations which He gave to it. Indeed, the doctrine of universal love or universal Benevolence may lead in practice to totally different kinds of conduct according to the way in which it is interpreted. For what does Love mean ? It means surely desiring to promote the true good of another person, treating that other person's good as an end of no less intrinsic importance than one's own good. The precept, therefore, " promote thy neighbour's good " gives us no information until we know wherein consists this true good of one's neighbour. And again the practical rules of conduct to which this

principle leads will become very different according to
the view we take as to the means by which this true
good is to be promoted. It is chiefly to the detailed
rules of conduct—to the conception which our Lord's
teaching exhibits of human good and to the detailed
rules of conduct for promoting it, and not to the
general principle of love to mankind—that exception
is taken by people whose moral ideal is not that of
mere selfishness.   Such persons often admit the
enormous and beneficent moral revolution introduced
by that teaching, but it seems to them too much marred
by the limitations of a race and a period to be treated
as containing in any sense a full or final body of
ethical teaching suited for all races and all times.
To deal with these objections will be the best way, I
think, of removing misunderstandings, of bringing
out the real nature of Christian morality, and of laying a foundation for an answer to a further question
which I have had in view all through these Lectures—
the question in what sense the revelation of God in
Christ may be regarded as final or complete—in what
sense Christianity, looked at either on its purely ethical
or on its religious side, can be regarded as a universal,
or absolute, religion.

Of course there are ethical writers of the present
day who are out of sympathy with the very principle
of Love or universal Brotherhood, and not merely with
particular applications or misapplications or alleged
exaggerations of it.   There are, again, those who,

without (it may be) personally entertaining an anti-social ideal, take too naturalistic a view of the Universe to be able to find a place in their theory of it for the idea of moral obligation at all, whether in a religious or a purely ethical form. There are others (among whom the insane genius Nietzsche is the most conspicuous) who deliberately invert the Christian law, and defend a Morality based upon pure, unmitigated Egoism ; who hold that the superior person, the " Uebermensch," the " Super-man," has a right to assert his own individuality to the utmost possible extent, and to treat all other and inferior persons as mere means or instruments for his own enjoyment or " self-realization," who maintain in so many words that selfishness is noble, self - sacrifice mean and contemptible. I believe it can be shown that such an Ethic is as irrational and self-contradictory as it is opposed to the ordinary feelings of mankind.[1] Here,

[1] If anyone is inclined to think that Egoism, as an ethical doctrine, is capable of philosophical defence, I would recommend him to study E. von Hartmann's scathing criticism of Nietzsche's ideas in *Ethische Studien*, pp. 33–90, or G. A. Moore, *Studia Ethica*, p. 99 *sq*. The contradiction may be briefly pointed out. The Egoist says : " It is intrinsically reasonable for me (A) to promote my own good alone." But the meaning of good is something which is intrinsically valuable, something which ought therefore to be brought into existence so far as that is possible. It can only be reasonable for me to promote my own good alone, if it is the only good in the world. If that were so, another person (B) would also be bound to promote my good and that of no one else. But, if I tell B that it is reasonable for him also to be an Egoist and so to promote his own good and that of no one else, I imply that *his* good is the only good in the world. Here I contradict myself : I say that A's good is the only good in the world and ought to be promoted by everyone, including

however, I am not concerned with such fundamental objections, but with objections in point of detail—with objections which may be made by people who cordially accept the fact of moral obligation, and who may not even deny that the Christian law of love, rightly understood, is the fundamental law of Ethics, though it requires (they may think) a development and an interpretation different in some degree from that which was actually given it by our Lord Himself and by the early Christian Church. Before I attempt this task, however, I would emphasize the fact that the objections are for the most part to details, to applications, not to the fundamental principle. The applications which our Lord gives to His precepts are for the most part avowedly illustrations of the principle. We must expect that the illustrations should sometimes have a reference to the immediate circumstances of time and place, to the then condition of Jewish Society, to the environment and position of the teacher and the taught. It might be possible to go further than that, and to admit that some of His applications were mistaken or narrow or one-sided, even relatively to the circumstances of the time, and still to remain in a very real sense a follower of Christ and a believer in

B, and at the same time I say that B should think *his* own good as the only good in the world. Egoism therefore involves an internal contradiction—a conclusion which cannot be accepted by anyone who professes that his ethical system is rational. The irrationality of the national Egoism now defended by so many German writers may be exhibited in exactly the same way.

the Christian religion. I do not myself think that any such admissions are required, but the possibility should be faced with an open mind.

(1) The first objection to the Ethic of Christ which I shall consider is the general suggestion that it teaches exaggerated self-sacrifice, exaggerated un-selfishness—that it insists on love of neighbour and forbids the due and proper regard for self, that reasonable self-love of which so orthodox a Moralist as Bishop Butler has spoken with so much respect. Certainly such a consequence does not flow from the principle of loving one's neighbour *as* oneself, and Christ never taught that a man ought to love his neighbour better than himself. By the later Christian Church such a doctrine has more than once been formally condemned.[1] The very principle on which the rule of Altruism is founded would be inconsistent with such an exaggeration. The duty of loving one's neighbour springs from the truth—a truth which is the very heart and centre of Christ's teaching—that each individual human self or life or soul possesses an intrinsic value. That same principle requires there-fore that each man should treat himself as of no less value than his neighbour. Most of the exaggerations of self-sacrifice have sprung from forgetfulness of this principle. It cannot be reasonable that an individual

---

[1] In 1346 Nicholas de Ultricuria was condemned for maintaining even that a man ought to love better than himself a man who is better than himself. See Denifle and Chatelain, *Chartularium Universitatis Parisiensis*, T. II, No. 1124.

should sacrifice a larger amount of his own good for a smaller amount of another's ; or that he should lay down as a rule for universal observance a precept which, if universally obeyed, would prove fatal to the general interests of the whole community ; or that he should promote one man's interests at the expense of a much larger number of persons who are no less his brethren.

This seems to be forgotten by people like Count Tolstoi, who think it inconsistent with Christian principles under any circumstances to refuse relief to a beggar, or to punish a criminal. To give to beggars in the street when one knows that the effect of doing so habitually will be a doubtful boon to the recipient himself, and will certainly turn those who are now honest working-men into habitual mendicants ; to give in a way which will injure the self-respect of the receiver and encourage him in idleness and dependence ; to give away what ought to be spent upon the maintenance of a family and provision for the future ; even to give to an extent which, if generally followed, would lower the standard of life and of culture for the whole community—such giving cannot be a true application of the Christian principle of loving one's neighbour as oneself. How far, it may be asked, would our Lord Himself have recognized this interpretation of His words ? There is no reason to think that Jesus actually understood those laws of social Well-being which have only been discovered by the extended

experience, the accumulated observation, the social
and economic Science of later ages. In some ways
no doubt kinds of giving which are harmful when
carried out on a large scale in our highly complex
society may have been less harmful, or not harmful at
all, in a simpler society. To this day the poor give
to each other on a scale which shames the grudging
and scanty charity of the rich, and they do so very
often with the best results. There is no loss of self-
respect in taking money from a friend who knows the
reality of the need, when the receiver would be ashamed
to take it the moment he could do without it, when the
donor may the next day stand in the like need of
assistance himself. Even in their application to the
circumstances of His own day it is most improbable
that our Lord had actually thought out these questions as to the limitations of giving. But it would be
quite unreasonable to contend that, because He said,
" Give to him that asketh thee, and from him that
would borrow of thee turn not thou away,"[1] therefore
He would have refused to recognize that there might
be occasions on which it is right to refuse a dole.
Do we not all of us—the most enlightened and philosophic Moralist, the most stony-hearted charity
organizer, the most cold-blooded social scientist among
us—say to children " Do not lie, do not be hard on
other people, do not kill " ; although we fully recog-

---

[1] Matt. v. 42 ; Luke vi. 30 has : " of him that taketh away thy
goods, ask them not again " (ἀπαίτει).

nize on reflection that there are exceptional circumstances under which the interests of Society demand hardness or lying, and in which killing is no murder? All moral teaching has to be given in the form of general rules : we cannot at every turn be dealing with exceptions. Jesus Himself, by turning aside at times from the crowds who wanted Him to heal their sick, recognized the principle that one detailed moral rule may sometimes interfere with another ; that one good can sometimes only be attained by the sacrifice of some other and lesser good ; that we must think of the future as well as of the present, and do that which is best for our fellow-men on the whole. There were times when it was necessary for the eventual good of His disciples and of humanity generally that He should secure leisure for that meditation and communion with God from which He derived His power to succour them, or for teaching His disciples how to preach the Gospel of the Kingdom—more necessary than to relieve this or that sufferer or minister to the wants of this or that body or mind diseased.

Another way of putting the same thing is this. Our Lord fully recognized that the supreme moral law dealt with dispositions, intentions, the state of the heart. The true moral law, as it has been said, is internal.[1] The internal law has no exception. It is always right to love or to be charitably minded. But internal precepts must be illustrated and defined

[1] Sir Leslie Stephen, *Science of Ethics*, p. 155 *seq.*

by the acts which under ordinary or normal circumstances flow from them. The most obvious application of the rule " Be kind " is " Give, lend, refuse not."
But there are circumstances under which a truer
charity, more desire for our neighbour's good, will
show itself in the refusal to give or to lend than is
shown by the kindness which insists on giving even
when it will do more harm than good. I do not deny
that there may have been occasions when our Lord
might have said " Give " when a wider consideration
of social consequences would induce us to say " With-
hold " ; but I do not think there is any precept of IIis
which is inconsistent with the interpretation which
I have attempted to put upon them when they are
understood with the same allowance for possible exceptions or complementary principles which we should
make in interpreting any other moral teacher of any
age or country.

(2) The next objection which I shall notice is the
same in principle as the last, and ought, I think, to
be met in much the same way. It is said that our
Lord lays down principles of non-resistance, sub-
missiveness, meekness which are inconsistent with
manly self-respect ; and which, if generally observed,
would be fatal to the very existence of social order
and civil society. " Resist not him that is evil : but
whosoever smiteth thee on thy right cheek, turn to
him the other also. And if any man would go to law
with thee, and take away thy coat, let him have thy

cloke also "[1] and so on. In such injunctions Jesus was clearly not thinking of political problems at all. They lay entirely beyond His province. The people whom He was addressing had nothing to do with government or the administration of justice : they had no votes and did not sit on juries. This must not be distorted into the doctrine that Christianity has nothing to do with politics or social questions. The principles of Ethics, whatever principles they are that we adopt, must necessarily be applicable to all spheres of life. Those who have accepted Christ's principles of conduct must necessarily, when they find themselves in power, regard them as their rule of action in their official or civil capacity as well as in their business life and their private affairs. The principles must be applied to politics : but Christ did not so apply them Himself. He was speaking of the conduct of private individuals towards one another. The principle which He lays down is, I imagine, this—that the spirit of revenge is bad. The law of Brotherhood requires that we should love every human being, even the man who has done us an injury. His bad conduct cannot alter the fact that he is an end-in-himself, that his good is no less valuable than one's own ; even if he is actually bad, still he has capacities of goodness which give his life a value. The principle is the one which Plato—nearest of the ancients to Christ on this side of his thought, if not on all sides—so strenuously

[1] Matt. v. 39, 40. Cf. Luke vi. 29.

asserted, that we ought always to do good to every human being, and never evil, and that therefore punishment must be regarded as a medicine for moral maladies. We should never avenge an injury merely because we are angry, because it is *I* that have been injured, because *my* personal honour demands it. But there may be occasions when either the good of the offending person or the good of society requires some kind of resentment. The object should always be to do what is best for the person himself, so far as is compatible with the duty that we owe to other persons.

The most obvious way of showing another that, in spite of his injury, we care for his good, and of bringing him to repentance, is to forgive. But there may be cases in which some kind of resentment is best both for the individual himself and in the interests of society ; there are occasions when the interests of the individual ought to give way to the interests of society —that is to say, to the interests of a much greater number of persons who are also our brethren. But this is very much less often the case than most of us in our pride and our selfishness are apt to imagine. And when we do determine that some resentment is necessary, the amount and the form of it should be governed by the same principle of Christian love to the offender and to others. Sometimes literal forgiveness, in the sense of remission of penalty, will be best ; sometimes resentment ; at other times some combina-

L

tion of the two. Resentment may take a great variety
of forms : it may be a rebuke, a protest, the mere
showing that we are hurt, renunciation of friendship
or diminution of intimacy or a change of manner.
At other times the protection of society may make
self-defence a duty, and self-defence may sometimes
take the form of giving blow for blow, though in a
civilized and orderly society for obvious reasons no
one should take the law into his own hands (to use
the common phrase) except for some very good
reason, and on very exceptional occasions. At other
times the resentment that is called for will take the
form of legal prosecution. In no case, be it remembered, is the duty of forgiveness entirely abrogated by
the duty of resentment. In the words of Bishop
Butler, " Resentment is not inconsistent with goodwill : for we often see both together in very high
degrees; not only in parents towards their children,
but in cases of friendship and dependence, where there
is no natural relation. . . . We may therefore love our
enemy, and yet have resentment against him for his
injurious behaviour towards us. But when this
resentment destroys our natural Benevolence towards
him, it is excessive and becomes malice or revenge."
The injured person (to quote Butler once more)
" ought to be affected towards the injurious person in
the same way any good man, uninterested in the
case, would be, if they had the same just sense which
we have supposed the injured person to have of the

fault : after which there will yet remain real goodwill towards the offender."[1]

How far, it will be asked, would Christ Himself have
recognized this statement of the case ?   Are we not,
when we adopt such principles of action, really explaining away His teaching ?   I am quite sure of two things :
(*a*) that I am correctly stating the principles which
flow from that law of mutual love which Christ Himself laid down as the supreme moral law : and (*b*) that
if in any matter the spirit of Christ's teaching is seen
by us, in the light of wider knowledge and experience,
to be inconsistent with any application which He
actually gave or would have given in particular cases,
it is our duty to follow the spirit of that teaching and
not the letter, the principle and not the particular
application.   But I do not think that by interpreting
His rule of life as I have interpreted it we are contravening any command of His which He meant to
be literally observed in every possible case.   To what
extent Christ had actually reflected on the question
how far in some cases the requirements of social Well-
being made it necessary for men who wish to forgive
nevertheless to punish, for men who desire their
neighbour's ultimate good to inflict on them immediate
evil, how far He would have recognized the exceptions
for which I have been pleading in the application of

---

[1] Sermon ix. in *Fifteen Sermons*.   I have fully dealt with the
problems of Punishment and Forgiveness in my *Theory of Good and
Evil*, I, Pt. I, chap. ix.

His typical, startling, paradoxical illustrations of the principle which should govern the treatment of injuries by His followers, we simply do not know, and cannot know. But we have enough evidence to indicate that our Lord Himself did not intend His precepts to be taken with the deadly literalness which Western minds, bent either on a too literal imitation of the outward accidents of the Master's life on the one hand, or anxious to represent them as obsolete and impracticable on the other, have been disposed to take them. The most unsympathetic modern critic of Christ's utterances will not seriously contend that our Lord meant that men were to mutilate themselves in order to observe His precept about the offending member, or that He who bade us love all men really meant that His followers should hate—in the ordinary sense of the word " hate "—father and mother and child, or that forgiveness was to cease after 490 offences.[1] So to interpret Christ is to reduce His teaching to a mass of inconsistent, self-contradictory nonsense. He declared that to call a brother fool might be as bad as murder: yet He is recorded once at least to have used the word Himself,[2] and on other occasions used language of equal vehemence and severity. He forbade

[1] It is rather tempting to add that in accepting the High-Priest's adjurations (Matt. xxvi. 63, 64) Jesus gave evidence on oath before a court of Justice. But the High-Priest's " I adjure thee by the living God " is omitted in Mark xiv. 61 and Luke xxii. 67, and after all the " thou hast said " need not necessarily imply that the speaker accepted the adjuration.

[2] Matt. xxiii. 17. Cf. Luke xi. 40 ; Luke xxiv. 25.

men to resist evil : yet His driving out the oxen from the Temple, and overthrowing the tables of the money-changers were acts of physical force.[1] The language which He uses towards the Pharisees or in speaking of them is quite inconsistent with the idea that our Lord condemned all self-assertion, all vehemence of expression, all manifestations of hostility against the oppressor, the wrong-doer, the dishonourer of God.[2] If we are to regard as part of our Lord's real teaching the injunction to take complaints to the Church or Christian Assembly, to abide by their decision and to treat as a heathen man and a publican the unrepentant Christian offender against his brother, those words sanction the principle of organized social resentment. It is practically certain, indeed, on critical grounds[3] that we have here a development, an application of Christ's teaching—a quite legitimate application in the

[1] It is just conceivable that our Lord may even have thought seriously of using—not against an armed band, but against the attack of an assassin—the weapons which, according to Luke xxii. 38, He directed His disciples to procure. More probably the words were " a piece of ironical foreboding " (Burkitt, *The Gospel History and its Transmission*, p. 141) which a disciple took literally. The " it is enough " will then mean : " Drop that idea : my words were not meant seriously."

[2] Of course it is possible (with Mr. Montefiore) to condemn the language used by our Lord against the Pharisees. See below, p. 179.

[3] Matt. xviii. 17. The words are found in a section which has no parallel in the other Synoptists, and is exactly of the same type as not a few other sections peculiar to the first Gospel, passages referring to and intended to support the ecclesiastical institutions which had been developed by the time the Gospel was written. St. Luke (xvii. 3) has : " Take heed to yourselves ; if thy brother sin, rebuke him ; and if he repent forgive him " (R.V.). This is no doubt much nearer to what our Lord actually said.

circumstances of the early Christian community[1]—
but not an actual saying of the Master. Even the
words " *if he repent*, forgive him " are by themselves
a serious qualification of the principle that forgiveness
is to be unlimited. Even the command to forgive to
seven times in a day is confined to the cases in which
there is repentance.

(3) Another detailed criticism of the same order represents our Lord as hostile to the institution of property,
as teaching a kind of Communism or complete self-
renunciation in the matter of worldly goods. This
suggestion is founded chiefly upon the words to the rich
young man, " If thou wouldest be perfect, go, sell that
thou hast and give to the poor " (Matt. xix. 21). Now
here, in addition to the considerations we have already
dwelt on, we must remember this fact, which is very
essential for the understanding of Christ's teaching—
that when Christ called men to " follow " Him, He
did not mean merely that they should accept His
teaching and endeavour to practise it in their lives.
He was calling upon certain of His disciples to devote
themselves to His great missionary enterprise, to
join Him in going about the world to preach the coming
of the Kingdom. It is to such men that the severer
injunctions of the Gospel pages are addressed—to take
nothing for their journey, save a staff only, no bread,
no wallet, no money in their purse, but to go shod

[1] And yet perhaps " Jesus would hardly have spoken so harshly
of the ' tax-collector.' " Montefiore, *Syn. Gospels*, II, 681.

with sandals[1] and the like. The precepts form part not
of the Sermon on the Mount, but of what is sometimes
called the great ministerial commission.   Even the
words about hating father and mother may have been
intended for those who received this commission.[2] To
become a disciple of Christ in the strictest sense meant
no doubt to join Him in His missionary work. Many
of these injunctions have, of course, an application to
all who would be in our modern sense of the word
followers of Christ, believers in His Gospel, members
of His Church ; but in their immediate and primary
signification, they were addressed to His Missionaries,
not to all His hearers. In the conditions of the time
to make such a complete renunciation of worldly
goods, to take up something like the life of a mendicant
friar, was probably the most effective, perhaps the only,
way of carrying on the work which He felt called upon
to do, of communicating to mankind the good news
which He knew Himself divinely commissioned to impart. Here for once the anticipation of the immediate
Parousia may be allowed to have influenced the specific
advice given by Jesus to His hearers. And yet, after
all, he surely would be a bold man who would seriously
pretend that he knew a way of proclaiming the Kingdom
of Heaven, or the eternal truths which were for Jesus

---

[1] Mark vi. 8, 9 (Matt. x. 9, 10 ; Luke ix. 3.   There are considerable variations in detail).

[2] They are addressed " to the multitudes " (Luke xiv. 25–6), but
they refer to him who would be Christ's " disciple."   The Matthean
equivalent (in a weakened form) is in the Commission to the Twelve
(x. 37).

enshrined in that conception, that would have succeeded better than the way actually adopted by Him.
The advice was not given to all His hearers—still less
to all mankind—but to those whom He called or who
felt themselves called to this special work.[1] Jesus
never makes such complete renunciation necessary as
a condition of entrance into the Kingdom of Heaven.
He warmly commended the charity and honesty of
Zaccheus, who, under the influence of His preaching,
resolved to restore fourfold to the particular persons
whom he had wronged and to give half of his remaining
goods to the poor.[2] " To-day is salvation come to this

---

[1] This limitation may be thought inconsistent with the words:
" So therefore whosoever he be of you that renounceth not all that
he hath, cannot be my disciple " (Luke xiv. 33). The words need not
necessarily mean more than the words of the preceding verse (26):
" If any man cometh unto Me, and hateth not his own father and
mother, and wife, and children, and brethren, and sisters, yea, and
his own life also, he cannot be My disciple," which no one will
understand with absolute literalness—as an injunction to cruelty
or self-destruction. It may be understood as recommending complete " detachment " from worldly goods as from family ties.
Or more historically it may be taken as referring literally to disciples
in the full sense—those called to join the missionary band. The
saying immediately follows the parables of the man building a town
and the King going to war with another King. It occurs in Luke
only. Many of the strong sayings about wealth peculiar to Luke
are probably genuine, but these particular words (xiv. 33) may very
well be suspected of being Luke's amplification of the saying about
renouncing father and mother—his way of pointing the moral of
the preceding paragraphs. Loisy calls it " une addition rédaction-
elle." Cf. the same writer on Luke xiv. 26 : " Ce sacrifice est
imposé à qui veut ' suivre ' Jésus, et il n'est dit aucunement
que l'on puisse avoir, sans le ' suivre,' une part assurée dans le
royaume " (*Evan. Syn.*, I, 894).

[2] Luke xix. 9. The fourfold restitution was required by the
Mosaic Law in certain cases of theft, in others double restitution
(Exod. xxii. 1, 4).

house, forasmuch as he also is a son of Abraham."
We must not, of course, allow this consideration to
prevent our seeking to penetrate to the eternal
principle implied in the advice to the rich young man.
The meaning of what our Lord said was surely this :
" If you want to do the best thing in the world, sell
all that you have and give to the poor, and " (it is
no doubt implied) " come and join my missionary band,
and preach the coming of the Kingdom." He went
away sorrowful, we are told—not because an enlightened political economy had told him that this
renunciation would not be the best thing he could do,
not because he doubted whether it would, if generally
imitated, be conducive to the true good of humanity,
or because he felt a call to other work which could
better be done with his possessions than without them,
but simply because " he had great possessions." Was
our Lord wrong in saying that the reason why the
rich young man would not give up his possessions was
that he was too fond of them, that he had not love
enough to make the sacrifice ? Was He wrong in
saying that that is not the ideal of perfect love, or
that such an ideal of love and devotion should be striven
after ?[1]

[1] It is important to notice that the words " Thou shalt love thy
neighbour as thyself," which in Matthew are included in the commandments which the young man had kept from his youth, are
absent in Mark and Luke. If they are omitted, it is clear that he
was satisfied with bare compliance with the negative commands of
the Decalogue. Not only was his love imperfect: he had hardly
shown any positive love at all.

What, it may be asked, is the application of this principle to those who in modern times would accept the principle of Christ's teaching? Surely it is perfectly true that so long as a man is not willing, if and so far as he sees it to be for the good of his fellow-men, to renounce all worldly possessions in order to serve them, he is morally imperfect. It does not follow that in the existing state of human society the renunciation of all worldly possessions is the best way for serving our brethren which is open to all of us. There are ways in which those who have love enough, and who feel the call to do so, may serve their brethren most effectively by literally selling all their goods and giving to the poor, or more probably by renouncing most of the ordinary luxuries and comforts of well-to-do life and devoting life and income to the service of humanity in ways that are economically sound—that is to say, ways which really do benefit the recipients in the long run. It does not follow that this is the best thing for all, or even for all who have the willingness to do it. To love our neighbours enough to be willing to make this sacrifice for them is part of the Christian ideal for all : the duty for each is to make that use of his possessions which, he being what he is, circumstances being what they are, will enable him to do the best service for his fellow-men—the particular service to which he is called. Some even of those who have the love may not be called to the more exacting kind of self-renunciation : still more often those whose love is as yet very imperfect. The actual words, " If thou wilt be perfect," may be an addition of the first Evangelist, but it fairly represents our Lord's probable meaning, and points to the eternally true and important principle of Vocation. All are called to the loving service of their fellow-men : not all are called to serve in the same way. All modes of service imply self-denial and sacrifice, but not all imply equal self-sacrifice. At all periods of the world's history some men are called to sacrifices as great and as literal as that which was set before the rich young man, but not all men.[1] " Let each man do as he purposeth in his heart, not grudgingly or of necessity, for God loveth a cheerful giver " (2 Cor. ix. 7). That is a Pauline principle, which is as full of the spirit of Christ as it is of practical wisdom and good sense.

I may not linger on the wider social application of Christ's teaching about Property. To say that Jesus was a Socialist is, of course, as unhistorical as to say that He condemned Socialism or taught that " Religion has nothing to do with politics." The principle which underlies all His teaching about Property is simply this—that wealth should be treated as completely subordinate to the higher ends of human life, not only for the individual himself, but for the whole community. What is the best way under existing con-

[1] For further discussion of the problem, which at bottom involves the question of " Works of Supererogation," I may refer to my *Theory of Good and Evil*, Book II, chap. iv.

ditions of apportioning the enjoyment of the wealth
which is created by the common labour is the most
important problem which it is incumbent upon Christians of the present age to work out. They must work
it out in the spirit of the Master's teaching. But they
will not find in His express words any detailed
guidance for its solution. The one thing which we can
say with absolute confidence is that the present distribution of wealth, and the use made of the wealth
which they call their own by most rich men, would have
caused His sternest and most uncompromising condemnation. Many considerations may be urged in
favour of a social system which allows some inequality
in the distribution of wealth ; many considerations
of social utility may be urged in favour of individuals
allowing themselves more enjoyment and indulgence
than on a system of anything like equal distribution
would be possible for all; but we may be quite
certain that now as ever the spirit of Christ, no less
than the enlightened Reason of mankind, does call
for a much more rigid limitation of personal expenditure on the part even of people whom the world would
hardly call rich than conventional religious teaching
has usually insisted upon.

(4) The question of Property leads on to the question of Asceticism in general. It is often suggested
by the wilder kind of anti-Christian writers that Christ
taught a severe and morose Asceticism in which the
modern world does not and will not believe. Now

here I do not think the objector has even a plausible case. Our knowledge of Christ and His teaching is undoubtedly incomplete and fragmentary—that is a fact often forgotten both by ardent Christians and by sceptical critics. But, if there is one thing about Jesus which is made perfectly certain by all the records which we have about Him, it is this—that He did not encourage Asceticism in its stricter sense, either by His teaching or by His practice. The hardships which He endured and enjoined upon others were the hardships that were incidental to His mission and His work : their motive was simply love of His fellow-men. There is not the slightest trace of the idea that self-inflicted suffering is well-pleasing to God, or that it possesses any expiatory virtue for the doing away of sin, or that all innocent enjoyment is wrong. There is not even any encouragement of voluntary suffering, in the shape for instance of fasting, as a means of disciplining or strengthening character. The constant reproach hurled against our Lord and His disciples by the religious world of His day was that He was *not* ascetic. " Whereunto shall I liken this generation ? It is like unto children sitting in the market-places which call unto their fellows and say, We piped unto you, and ye did not dance ; we wailed and ye did not mourn. For John came neither eating nor drinking, and they say, He hath a devil. The Son of man came eating and drinking, and they say, Behold a gluttonous man, and a wine-bibber, a friend

of publicans and sinners."[1] "Why do the disciples
of John and of the Pharisees fast, but Thy disciples
fast not ? "[2] Our Lord accepted invitations to dinner
with rich tax-gatherers. Even those who are most
sceptical about the historical value of the fourth
Gospel may at least accept the story of the marriage
in Cana as showing that there was nothing in the
early traditions about His life which would make His
presence on such an occasion seem incongruous or
improbable. The argument from silence is not here the
precarious argument that it sometimes is. The legends
which grow up about a religious teacher, particularly
in the East, delight to represent him as exceeding
other men in Asceticism. Both the Jews[3] and the
early Christians believed in Asceticism, though in
both cases only to a moderate extent as compared with
the ideas of other oriental Religions or of the later
Christian Church. Had our Lord favoured Asceticism,
His utterances on this head are just those that would
most certainly have been reported. If therefore, when
critically examined, the records of His life and teaching
do not support the charge of Asceticism, we may be
quite sure that there were no such utterances to report.

It is true that legend has begun, even in the Canoni-
cal Gospels, or in the received text of them, to impart
an ascetic tinge to His teaching and practice, but

---

[1] Matt. xi. 17–19 (=Luke vii. 31–4).

[2] Mark ii. 18 (=Matt. ix. 14 ; Luke v. 33).

[3] The Pharisees encouraged the bi-weekly fast, but there was in
general among the Jews no tendency to favour celibacy.

criticism has here done a valuable service in enabling us to detect its operations. Mere criticism of the text shows that our Lord did not say, " This kind can come forth by nothing but by prayer and fasting " (Mark ix. 29) : in the R.V. you will find that the words " and fasting " have disappeared. In the case of the forty days' fast in the wilderness, we have to go behind the actual text, and apply the methods of historical criticism. It is easy to see how the story grew up. In the first Gospel, it is true, we read that " when He had fasted forty days and forty nights, He afterward hungered." But in the second Gospel we find what surely represents the earlier tradition : " He was in the wilderness forty days tempted of Satan."[1] In St. Luke's version also it is the temptation which lasts forty days, though that Evangelist goes on to say that " He did eat nothing in those days ; and when they were completed, He hungered." Is it not probable that the hunger implied by the first temptation suggested the idea that the forty days of retirement in the wilderness were also days of fasting ? And after all there is nothing (especially in Luke's version) to suggest that the abstinence from food was anything

---

[1] Matt. iv. 2 ; Mark i. 13 ; Luke iv. 1, 2. I do not think the probability of this view is lessened by the suggestion that Matthew and Luke used Q, and that Q is in general earlier than Mark. If Mark used Q, the absence of the words about fasting makes it doubtful whether they stood in his version of Q. Luke's version of Q does not suggest ' fasting ' as a piece of deliberate ascetism. If Mark did not here use Q, it will hardly be denied that in a particular case Mark may represent the more primitive tradition.

but the natural consequence of retirement to a food-less region.

When we have got rid of these allusions to fasting which reflect the Asceticism of a later age, there remain two genuine allusions to the practice. The first is the merely incidental allusion in the Matthean version of the Sermon on the Mount : " When ye fast, be not, as the hypocrites, of a sad countenance . . . but thou when thou fastest, anoint thy head and wash thy face ; that thou be not seen of men to fast, but of thy Father which is in secret ; and thy Father, which seeth in secret, shall recompense thee."[1] Here it is undoubtedly assumed that some of our Lord's hearers were in the habit of fasting, just as it is assumed that they would be taking gifts to the altar in the Temple. There is no emphasis on the practice, no express command to fast, but there is also no declared hostility. Not so in the teaching about the new wine and the old bottles.[2] It seems to me impossible to deny that our Lord had by this time come to realize that fasting—at least fasting in obedience to definite ecclesiastical injunctions at frequent intervals—was not congenial to the spirit of the new gospel of the Kingdom which He was pro-claiming.[3] It belonged to the old system of rites and

[1] Matt. vi. 16, 17. The saying has no parallel in Luke, who would certainly have had no bias against fasting. He might, how-ever, have omitted the saying because it was directed against a kind of hypocrisy which was not common among Gentiles.

[2] Matt. ix. 15–16 ; Mark ii. 19–22 ; Luke v. 33–39.

[3] It must be remembered that the Law of Moses prescribed but one fast in the year—the Great Day of Atonement.

ceremonies, not to the new religion of the heart and the life which He was preaching. There remains the difficulty of interpreting the words, " But the days will come when the Bridegroom shall be taken away from them, and then will they fast in those days." The easiest and most obvious way of understanding these words is to suppose them to mean " Fasting is a natural expression of sorrow, and is therefore unsuitable now." We must remember that with Orientals fasting was practised not merely as a religious observance, but as a sign of mourning : it was the usual accompaniment of rending the garments. You will recall the surprise of David's servants at his eating and drinking after his son's death. Our Lord's meaning may then be " Fasting will come as a natural expression of sorrow in due time, when the Bridegroom is taken away from them." It is even possible, on the assumption that the words were really uttered by Jesus, that He was not thinking of literal, intentional abstinence from food at all. You must remember the spirit of the objection. The Pharisees had taunted our Lord's disciples with the easy-going, unexacting character of the Religion which their Master preached. He may have met the spirit of the objection by saying : " Don't think the Religion I preach is an easy-going Religion. The call for self-sacrifice and suffering has not come yet, but it will come in due time. My disciples will have plenty to endure and plenty of calls to self-discipline and privation, when

M

I am taken away from them. Then it will be seen that the demands which their discipleship makes upon them, though they assume a different form, are not less exacting than the demands which John and the Pharisees made of their disciples."[1] But after all, I cannot but feel that the words, taken in any natural sense, are so difficult to reconcile with the previous saying about the new wine and the old bottles that M. Loisy is probably right in suggesting that here, too, we have an addition of the Evangelist, reflecting the growing asceticism of the later Church.

(5) I turn to another aspect of the ascetic ideal, its attitude towards Marriage. Can we attribute to our Lord any sympathy with the idea that virginity is superior to marriage ? I answer emphatically that we cannot. A high estimate of marriage is implied in this strict rule in regard to its permanence. How then are we to interpret the words " there be eunuchs which have made themselves eunuchs for the kingdom of heaven's sake. He that is able to receive it, let him receive it."[2] If the saying be genuine, the most natural way of understanding it is to suppose that our Lord meant that there is a peculiar blessedness in renouncing marriage in order the better to do the work of spreading the Kingdom of God among men. Even under normal conditions there are many kinds of spiritual or social work which are best undertaken by those

[1] Loisy remarks that our Lord did not usually speak of His " being taken away from them." These words suggest a later date.
[2] Matt. xix. 12.

who are willing to postpone indefinitely, or even totally to renounce, this great source of human happiness. That Jesus might have suggested to His disciples the blessedness of making, in view of the near approach of the Kingdom, such a sacrifice as He had made Himself is quite conceivable. But it is equally possible that this may be one of the numerous passages peculiar to Matthew which are due to the ideas of a later age, the days of an organized Christian Church, a more ecclesiastical spirit, a growing respect for celibacy. Under this category may confidently be placed the committal of the keys of the Kingdom of Heaven to St. Peter, the saying about the Church being founded upon him, the command to bring quarrels to the Church to be decided, and many others. The saying about the three kinds of eunuchs may well belong to the same class of ecclesiastical additions. A parallel but stronger instance of this kind of ascetic development may be found in the saying attributed to Jesus by the Gospel of the Egyptians, " I came to destroy the work of the female sex."[1]

(6) The question of Asceticism naturally leads on to the more general suggestion that Christ's ideal is one-sided and incomplete because it preaches the doctrine of self-denial, self-sacrifice, social activity, and says nothing about that other side of the moral

---

[1] Clem. Alex., Strom. III, c. ix. 63. The tone of both sayings has a certain resemblance to the collections of mystical " Logia " of our Lord which have recently been discovered, and few of these have the ring of genuineness.

ideal which is often summed up in the word self-development. The Gospel says nothing about the duty of self-culture, about the value of intellectual activity, or of intellectual knowledge. Two points ought, I think, to be unreservedly admitted about this matter :

(*a*) There is this other side to a true ideal of human life. Knowledge and the contemplation of Beauty, intellectual development and æsthetic development, Culture and the pleasures connected with it, are part of the true ideal of man. They are among the best and noblest things in human life : they form part of that good which the ideal man should promote for himself and for others. They are far higher and more valuable than mere pleasure, though not so valuable as goodness or willingness to do one's duty. Knowledge is good, but love is better. So much is a clear deliverance, as it seems to me, of the enlightened moral consciousness.

(*b*) It must be admitted that Christ did not explicitly insist on this side of the moral ideal. There is, indeed, nothing against it. Unlike many of the sterner moral teachers, the prophets of righteousness or enthusiasts of humanity, our Lord never depreciated intellect or culture or the love of beauty. There are, indeed, traces of the love of natural beauty in His teaching : " I say unto you that even Solomon in all his glory was not arrayed like one of these."[1] We

----

[1] Matt. vi. 29 = Luke xii. 27.

must remember, too, that our Lord was well acquainted with the only literature which was practically within His reach—the Old Testament and a few books belonging to the post-canonical literature of Judaism. Among the Jews alone in the ancient world, outside the countries affected by Buddhism, was there a system of popular education : and the teaching of Jesus implies a higher culture—even on the strictly intellectual side—than is sometimes admitted. There is no opposition to Culture in our Lord's teaching : but it is, of course, vain to look for any such sense of the high value of purely intellectual activity, of secular literature, of Art, of Science and Music as we find in the literature and philosophy of Greece and Rome.

And to say this involves the admission that the ethical teaching of Christ does require development, and that it can only be accepted as a final and permanent ideal for the modern world on the understanding that such a development is to be allowed. The mere scantiness of the record by itself involves the admission that many rules of conduct are necessary for the guidance of human life which are not explicitly contained in the teaching of Jesus—rules that were necessary even then, and others that have become necessary now. Some such rules are simply presupposed by the teaching of Jesus. There was no need to speak of them just because they were sufficiently recognized in the Old Testament and the current moral teaching of the time[1]; and others must be developed out of His teaching if it is to be made adequate to solving the actual problems of a modern Society. The very idea of a detailed code of morals suitable to all conditions of society is an obvious absurdity and impossibility. The details of morality must necessarily vary from age to age.

If Jesus had, indeed, put forward a set of rules which claimed to prescribe in detail the conduct suitable for all nations, all classes and all individuals in all future periods of the world's history, it would be a perfectly reasonable thing to say that the modern world could not accept such a code. The attempt to guide our conduct by such a code would put a stop to all social progress, and would be fatal to the moral life itself, which at its highest implies that men should be continually acting upon their own judgement, using their own moral and intellectual faculties, basing their lives upon their own sense of right and wrong. That our Lord never attempted to communicate to the world such a code of Ethics, we have already seen. What He did was to lay down a few great principles. These principles, I have contended, do appeal to the moral consciousness of the present as essentially true, and as the foundation-stones of all true Morality.

In detail the principles require infinite expansion,

---

[1] Still more obvious is the probability that what would be remembered would be the more revolutionary element in the Master's teaching.

application, development, in accordance with the growing experience of the race, and the altered needs and circumstances of successive ages. To effect this development is, according to the true idea of it, the work of the Church of Christ—that religious community which should be the highest organized expression of the enlightened Christian consciousness of the time.[1] The development began so early that the most minute criticism can hardly draw the line with precision between the authentic utterances of the Master and the development which they received in the consciousness of the Church. Belief in the continuous activity of the Holy Spirit in human hearts and human society is the necessary complement and corrective of the doctrine of a unique Revelation of God in a single historical Personality. Only on condition that that doctrine is firmly held and duly insisted upon can it be morally healthy—as I believe that, subject to that condition, it is morally healthy and expedient in the highest degree—to put the historical Christ in the centre of our ethical as well as of our religious life, and to make the imitation and the following of Christ into

[1] Father Tyrrell, after noticing the authority which may be claimed by any good man, goes on to say, " Such too in kind, though indefinitely greater in degree, is the authority of the Church, that is, of the Saints and of all good men gathered round and organised into one society under Christ, the Incarnation of Conscience. It is as the formulation of their collective experience that Catholic teaching commends itself to my reverence and assiduous meditation " (*Essays on Faith and Immortality*, p. 22). No words could better express the right relation between the three great authorities—Conscience, Christ, the Church.

the supreme concrete expression of our ethical ideal. The Christian Church has accepted and expressed that principle by making belief in the Holy Ghost and in a Holy Catholic Church into articles of its Creed side by side with belief in an historic Son of God.[1]

[1] " La Vie de Jésus et l'Histoire de la rédaction des Évangiles sont deux sujets qui se pénétrent de telle sorte qu'il faut laisser entre eux la limite indécise, au risque de paraître se contradire. En réalité cette contradiction est de peu de consequence. Jésus est le véritable Créateur de l'Évangile ; Jésus a tout fait, même ce qu'on lui a prêté : sa légende et lui-même sont inséparables : il fut tellement identifié avec son idée, que son idée devint lui-même, l'absorba, fit de son biographie ce qu'elle devait être " (Renan, *Les Evangiles*, p. 204). The passage is quoted with approval by Mr. Montefiore, *Syn. Gospels*, I, p. lix.

ADDITIONAL NOTE ON SOME DETAILED OBJECTIONS TO THE MORAL TEACHING OF CHRIST

It may be well at this point briefly to examine a few of the minor and more detailed objections which are made in various quarters to the ethical teaching, and in some cases the character, of our Lord :

(1) *The Unjust Steward* (Luke xvi. 1–8). The author of *The Diary of a Church-goer* writes (p. 211) : " Which of us has not been conscious of something like a gulp in accepting the parable of the Unjust Steward ? If the fraud of the Steward is not approved it is certainly not reprobated. We are left with an uneasy consciousness that we are invited to admire the clever trick of escaping suffering through the success of a dishonest manœuvre." It seems to me that this objection entirely misses the point of the parable. That point, as I take it, is just what is expressed by our Lord Himself in the words " The children of this world are in their generation wiser than the children of light " ; they show in the pursuit of their selfish and worldly ends a contrivance, a foresight, a common sense which the men of better intentions and higher aspirations too often fail to show in the pursuit of their higher ends. It is probable that the words were spoken by our Lord with more or less special reference to the use of wealth for purposes of Almsgiving. Wealth spent in this way will meet with its due reward in the Kingdom of Heaven. Certainly this is what was intended by the Evangelist, who adds to it a number of

sayings, perhaps originally independent, on the same subject: " Make to yourselves friends out of the mammon of unrighteousness " (Luke xvi. 9), etc. Wealth may be used in such a way as to secure something much better and more durable than wealth. Our Lord would hardly, perhaps, have thought of asking whether this reward—the " everlasting habitations "—was to consist in goodness or in happiness : had He asked it, it would (if we may judge from His general teaching) have said " both." If happiness is not a worthless thing, is there anything to object to in such teaching as this ? On the whole subject of our Lord's teaching about reward and punishment, see Appendix II.

(2) *The parable of the Householder* (Matthew xx. 1–15). The same writer continues : " In the parable of the House-holder and his Servants we are not exposed to so severe a strain, but we are still uncomfortable at the apparent inequity of the remuneration of the labourers. We do not allow, in judging the conduct of our fellows to-day, that the plea of contract is an answer to all complaints ; whilst the doctrine involved in the question ' Is it not lawful for me to do what I will with mine own ? ' is repudiated altogether as inconsistent with the obliga-tions of morality which bind us in the disposition of what is legally wholly under our control." The author goes on to say (p. 212) : " Enough of these captious criticisms. Let them be so called. I have no pleasure in them. Their strength lies in the claim of flawless perfection which provokes them, and against which a single fault is fatal. Considered by themselves, they are insignificant: they are lost in the beauty and the loveliness which break through the narrative of acts and words contained in the Gospels." How far I claim " flawless perfection " for the teaching of Christ will sufficiently have appeared from the preceding

lectures. Assuredly there is nothing in this parable to detract from it. Christ was not thinking of the question how labourers were to be paid or of any other economic problem. What he was denouncing was the claim that those who accepted the call to discipleship earlier in the day should have a reward greater than those who accepted it later.[1] (" What shall we have, therefore ? " they asked on another occasion.) He rebukes the commercial view of Morality which this spirit implied. " God," He tells them, " does no wrong by offering to those who repent at a later date the same full and free forgiveness which was offered to those who repented and became disciples earlier." " If you insist on discussing the question in the terms of ordinary commercial justice," He may be supposed to suggest, " this involves no wrong to the later comers." Would the writer really insist that God is bound to proportion reward in this life or the next exactly to the number of years of good service in the past, and not to the actual and present moral condition of the person ? Undoubtedly there are questions about the proper reward of labour which lay wholly beyond our Lord's mental horizon or beyond what He would have regarded it as His province to deal with—questions as to which it would be in vain to look for guidance in His teaching. But would the writer say that, even in the light of the coldest modern economics, an employer of labour, having paid to his employee the stipulated wage (assuming it to be whatever we understand by a just wage) was forbidden voluntarily, out of profits which he might justly have retained, to provide a club-house which should be open equally to his

[1] It may be that the Evangelist means to suggest that the Gentile was now spiritually on a level with the Jew. Our Lord, so far as there was any special application in His mind, would rather be thinking of the " publicans and sinners " as compared with the Pharisees and other respectable religious persons.

oldest and his newest employees ? If a body of modern
workmen were to make such conduct the motive for a
strike, I feel sure that the author of *The Diary of a Church-
goer* would be against them. Of course it might be argued
that these conventional notions about Justice and Benevolence, about money which I am bound to pay and money
with which I may do what I like, do not represent the
highest moral ideal ; but that objection can hardly be
urged by those who insist that the owner of the Vineyard
was bound to make pay exactly equal to work done. If we
are to argue the matter on grounds of economic justice,
the argument of the owner is a good one : if we say " these
ideas of economic justice do not represent the highest
Morality," then the objection has no relevance : the
argument was addressed to people who accepted these
ideas, and had never heard of Socialism. The lesson sought
to be conveyed is simply " Admittance to the privileges
implied by the Kingdom of Heaven is the free gift of God :
you must not be jealous because they are offered to others
who have done less for it, as you think, than you have
yourself." Would the writer seriously maintain that such
jealousy would be the note of a high morality, and that
a man who had gone to heaven after twenty years of a
good Christian life would be justified in complaining if he
found someone else there who had only been a Christian
for ten ? After all, the lesson meant to be taught by the
parable is only " God forgives the past freely when there
has been sincere repentance : the Pharisee must not
expect a higher place in the Kingdom than the converted
Publican." Well may Loisy remark : " Au fond la
parabole est la même que celle du Fils prodigue."[1] He

---

[1] *Evan. Syn.*, II, 229. Loisy regards Matt. xx. 16 (" So the last
shall be first and the first last "—the conclusion of the verse is
omitted by the best MSS.) as a saying not originally connected
with the parable (found also in Matt. xxii. 14).

adds that the teaching of this parable must be balanced by others which speak of higher and lower places in the Kingdom (e.g. the parable of the talents, Luke xix. 11–27 ; Matt. xxv. 14–30).   Mr. Montefiore, who is assuredly no official apologist, pronounces this parable " one of the greatest and most glorious of all."[1]   Much the same lesson is taught by the parable of the Servant, concluding with the words "Even so ye also, when ye shall have done all the things that are commanded you, say, We are unprofitable servants ; we have done that which it was our duty to do " (Luke xvii. 10)—which Mr. Montefiore pronounces to be " a highly noble, notable and important passage."

(3) *The cursing of the fig-tree* (Matt. xxi. 19 ; Mark xi. 12–14, 20).   The same writer treats the cursing of the fig-tree as an exhibition of " petulance " (p. 209).   There is a general disposition among critics to regard the whole story as a misunderstanding or materialization of the *parable* of the fig-tree.   The story of the miracle occurs in Matthew and Mark : and is omitted in Luke, who inserts the parable (xiii. 6, 7.   But cf. Matt. xxiv. 32 ; Mark xiii. 28).   Even apart from this, there would be little ground for accepting the saying by anyone who rejected the miracle, and surely a writer who so freely criticizes the morality of Christ is not likely to accept as historical a miracle of this character.   It will be observed that in Matthew the miracle is exaggerated.   In Mark it was on the return journey that the fig-tree was found to be withered : in Matthew it withers " immediately."

(4) *The cleansing of the Temple.*   Other writers have criticized the violent cleansing of the Temple.   Our Lord's conduct on this occasion cannot be understood without bearing in mind His conviction that He was the Messiah of

[1] *Syn. Gospels*, II, 700.

His nation. It is impossible here to discuss the exact sense in which the claim was made or the grounds which justified the claim :[1] it is enough for our present purpose to assume that He identified Himself in some sense with the Messiah of Jewish prophecy and expectation. As such He would naturally regard Himself as free to act in the way in which the Messiah was represented in prophecy as acting. The sight of the profanation would remind Him of the passage in Malachi (iii. 1–3) about the Lord suddenly coming to His Temple and purifying the sons of Levi. The thought would occur to Him : " Is not someone called upon to protest against these things ? And who more so than I, if I am indeed the Messiah ? " Nay, might not any Jew, conscious of a divine call to preach righteousness, conceive that he was justified in correcting what he regarded as a flagrant breach of the Mosaic Law ? Can we say that such a one was not justified in committing what possibly from the point of view of Roman (hardly perhaps of Jewish) Law may have been an illegality, as a means of protesting against what Jewish Priests and Rabbis must in their conscience have admitted to be inconsistent with the divine Law supposed to be contained in the Old Testament ? That the rebuke went home, is evident from the fact that the interference was, for the moment, quietly submitted to ; though it was, of course, the act which eventually provoked the arrest and crucifixion. As an illustration of the fact that " Criticism " can sometimes be as rash in its assertions as Orthodoxy, I may mention that I recently read an otherwise able Unitarian sermon in which it was assumed that the " scourge of small cords " was used on the owners as well as on the beasts. Of this, of course, there is no suggestion in the text, and it is observable that the scourge is only mentioned in the fourth

[1] I have said what seemed to me necessary in Lecture II.

Gospel. The Synoptists do not say exactly how the dealers were " cast out."[1]

If we do venture to conclude (which I for one should not do) that in the light of full knowledge of all the facts, the course adopted by Jesus was not the ideally best course, it will be because : (*a*) in the light of subsequent events and the inspiration vouchsafed to Christ's Church, we are able to see that Jesus was Messiah in a higher sense than the prophets conceived, and that not all the details of prophecy could properly be taken as precedents for His action, or (*b*) because we do not conceive of the inspiration of the Law and the prophets in the way in which they were commonly understood in His day,[2] and which to some extent—to some extent only, for He was far from giving a very literal interpretation to them—He shared ; or lastly (*c*) because we may have a stronger sense of the importance of social order in matters of this kind. There was nothing in the spirit or motive or principle of His action which does not appeal to the modern conscience as in accordance with the highest Morality. It does not follow, of course, that a modern man, full of the spirit of Christ and thoroughly accepting the principles of His action, should in an analogous case (so far as there can be an analogous case) act in precisely the same manner.

(5) *Alleged harshness : the words to the Syro-Phœnician woman* (Matt. xv. 26 ; Mark vii. 27). There are a few cases in which our Lord is alleged to have shown a harshness not in accordance with the spirit of His own teaching

---

[1] Matt. xxi. 12; Mark xi. 15 ; Luke xix. 45; John ii. 15.

[2] Perhaps we ought to add that this difference would carry with it some conclusions which were outside of our Lord's mental vision, as to the importance of civil order and the proper relation of the civil government to the ecclesiastical. But we must remember that the police of the Temple belonged to the Sanhedrin, and they were both a religious and a secular authority, basing their whole polity upon the Old Testament.

at its best. In particular there are the words addressed to the Syro-Phœnician woman : " It is not meet to take the children's bread, and cast it to the dogs." I do not think that here we can quite accept the conventional explanation that our Lord was only assuming the tone of one con- temptuously rejecting the woman's petition with a view to a trial of her faith. On the other hand, we need not see in them a piece of personal harshness, an actual defect of character. This incident may possibly represent a moment in the process of Jesus' emancipation from the ideas of His environment. He was, as it were, talking aloud to Him- self. The woman asks Jesus to heal her : He says : " Can it be really part of the Father's will that I should use the powers which He has given me, for the benefit not of Israel, the children of God, but of those whom Israel has always regarded as no more than mere outcasts ? " The woman's humble acceptance of the situation, her plea to be accepted as one who can hope for the leavings, as it were, of God's promises to Israel makes it easy for Him to decide the question in her favour. And thereby, perhaps, the mind of Jesus was led one step onwards in the road to that recognition of God's equal love of all men to which it is clear that He ultimately attained. Progress in moral insight there must certainly have been in Christ's case, as in that of all other human beings, if we accept the Evangel- ist's statement that " Jesus advanced in wisdom and stature."[1]

So far I have assumed the trustworthiness of the narrative. At the same time I may remark that it is open to some suspicion, not because it is connected with a narrative of miraculous cure, but because it presupposes a kind of miracle much more difficult to understand than most of our Lord's cures, which were by present, personal

[1] Luke ii. 52.

influence.   Alleged cures from a distance are open to peculiar suspicion.   Still, we are hardly entitled to treat the saying as altogether without historical foundation. Loisy remarks : " En soi, l'incident n'autorisait pas la prédication de l'Évangile aux païens.   Il est vrai seulement que la présence de Jésus en terre païenne, dans une maison qui est sans doute habitée par des païens, et où il reçoit l'hospitalité, témoigne, comme sa réponse touchant la pureté des mets, qu'il ne partage aucunement les scrupules pharisaïques sur les relations avec les étrangers " (*Évan. Syn.*, I, p. 971).

The words " I am not sent but unto the lost sheep of the house of Israel " are in Matthew only (xv. 24) and possibly represent the ideas of the Evangelist as to the personal mission of Christ (see Loisy, l.c., p. 973) : he was not of course opposed to the Gentile mission in his own days.   It is natural enough that St. Luke should have omitted the whole incident.

(6) *Give not that which is holy unto the dogs.*   " Give not that which is holy unto the dogs, neither cast your pearls before the swine, lest haply they trample them under their feet, and turn and rend you."

The passage occurs in Matthew only.[1]   He places it just after the command not to say " let me pull out the mote out of thine eye, and lo ! a beam is in thine own eye."   If Matthew has preserved the context, the words might well mean " Do not be too eager to offer good advice or rebuke, even when it is called for, unless you are sure that it will be well received.   Do not be censorious : be tactful in dealing with others."   But the passage has rather the appearance of an isolated saying.   To see in these words a prohibition to preach the Gospel of the Kingdom to Gentiles would be to attribute to our Lord an attitude unsupported by any-

[1] Matt. vii. 6.

N

thing else which He ever said or did. It is certain that not even the most Jewish of the Evangelists would have inserted it in his Gospel if he had understood it in this sense. It is not easy to find a meaning for the saying which is in harmony with the general teaching of our Lord on the assumption of its genuineness. It is far more probably an " ecclesiastical addition." In the Didache it is interpreted to mean " Do not admit the unbaptized to the Eucharist."[1] And something not quite so definite but in the same spirit may well have been the meaning which it bore for the Judæo-Christian consciousness. As Loisy suggests, it may have grown out of the saying to the Syro-Phœnician woman.

(7) *Depreciation of family ties.* I do not feel that the sayings about leaving father and mother to preach the coming of the Kingdom require any apology. The saying in which our Lord in a sense repudiates His earthly parentage ("Who is My mother and My brethren ? ")[2] was provoked by an attempt on their part to keep Him back from His mission on the ground that He was mad. There are occasions when family ties must give way to wider duties. No one would now blame such language in a tatesman calling upon his countrymen to take up arms at a supreme crisis in the history of his country. No Christian ought to object to similar language in an advocate of Missions calling upon men to become missionaries, provided he does not suggest that this particular call is one which comes to all men in all circumstances. Our Lord is not responsible for the monastic abuse of this principle.

---

[1] Didache, ix., 5.

[2] Mark iii. 33 =Matt. xii. 48. Matthew from mistaken reverence omits the words about being "beside Himself." Luke omits even the words "Who are My mother and My brethren ? " but retains the characteristic saying "My mother and My brethren are these which hear the word of God and do it " (Luke viii. 21).

Equally true is it that the spiritual union between the true servants of God is closer than the ties of blood. If so, " Whosoever shall do the will of God, the same is My brother and sister and mother" requires equally little apology.

(8) *Let the dead bury their own dead.* Another saying of the same class is " Let the (spiritually) dead bury their own dead " (Matt. viii. 22 ; Luke ix. 60). This also might well be justified by the circumstances, even if taken literally : but, considering the short interval which in the East commonly elapses between death and burial, it is extremely improbable that the father was actually lying dead at the time. " Suffer me first to go and bury my father " no doubt means " let me wait till the old man dies." I have met in some commentary with the remark of an Eastern traveller who was always sceptical of this explanation till similar language was actually used to him in Palestine of a still living parent ; but I cannot find the reference.

(9) *The denunciation of the Pharisees.* Mr. Montefiore, from the standpoint of liberal Judaism, condemns severely the attacks by Jesus on the Pharisees both as being un-justified in themselves and as inconsistent with His own teaching. To use the language of severe denunciation does not appear to me ethically unjustified or inconsistent with the spirit of the teaching which, in general, Mr. Montefiore approves : and what Jesus denounces in the teaching and conduct of the Pharisees certainly deserved such condemna-tion. It does not appear to me at all self-evident that Jesus, " if he had loved his enemies, would not have called them vipers, or enthusiastically predicted their arrival in hell " (*Syn. Gospels*, II, p. 524). The adverb, of course, is Mr. Montefiore's. That there was another side to the teaching perhaps of those very Pharisees whom Jesus denounced, and certainly of other Pharisees, Mr. Monte-fiore is quite entitled to point out, and Christians ought

freely to admit the fact. But it is hardly fair to speak of
such denunciations as merely calling " religious enemies
hard names " (*ib.*, II, p. 526). It was not the theological
doctrine of the Pharisees that Jesus denounced, but (1) the
immorality of their teaching and (2) their hypocrisy—the
contrast between their exacting teaching and their lives
of what seemed to Him easy, self-complacent religious
exclusiveness. In the very same page on which this
criticism occurs, Mr. Montefiore has some reflections—too
well deserved—on the intolerance shown by Christians
towards Jews which, though expressed in a more modern
dialect, mean much the same thing as the denunciations
of Jesus. That we have learned better to understand the
psychological causes of such aberrations as those of the
Pharisees may be admitted by any Christian who does not
assert that Jesus was omniscient. If some of the Pharisees
were not justly chargeable with all the bad motives which
Jesus attributed to them, or if there was more good in
them than He supposed, that is a question of fact. It may
be admitted that the historian's judgement about the
matter should not be based on these sayings alone.
But the important thing for us is whether He was right in
severely condemning certain elements in their teaching
and the state of mind from which He supposed it to spring.
I do not see in these denunciations any defect of ethical
principle. The denunciation of the Friars *as a class* by
men like Wycliffe and Luther seems to me a fairly parallel
case, and was equally justified, though, of course, there
were good Friars even in the worst periods of medieval
history. That there has been a further and fuller development of that principle of Universal Love which Jesus
taught should be fully admitted. The principle of religious
toleration was not actually taught by Jesus, though He
taught nothing contrary to it. It is a further development

of the principle which He did lay down, and yet, after all, this question is not much in point in this particular connexion, for there was no question of persecuting the Pharisees.

I am not competent to discuss the question whether Mr. Montefiore does not as much overrate the Pharisees as some Christian Theologians (liberal as well as orthodox) have unjustly depreciated them ; I will only say that he himself in his indignant protests against the onesidedness of Christian Theologians seems occasionally to forget the admissions that he elsewhere makes. That there was much in the teaching and conduct of the Pharisees which was justly rebuked by our Lord, could be proved out of Mr. Montefiore's own writings. Moreover, he is (if I may venture to say so) too apt to assume that all that is best in the rabbinic teaching of all ages must be supposed to have been equally characteristic of these particular Rabbis and Pharisees with whom our Lord had to deal. On the face of it, it is probable that the Pharisees in the day of their political ascendancy would show the characteristic vices of a dominant clergy more frequently than in the days of national humiliation and persecution. It would be grossly unjust to the French clergy of to-day to say of them what might justly be said of their predecessors in the time of Louis XIV. Nor can I discuss the question of reflex Christian influence on the later rabbinic teaching. It is improbable that the teaching of Christianity (however little illustrated by average Christian practice) should have produced no influence on their Jewish critics. It would be equally absurd to assume that the views about toleration or the relative unimportance of ritual now adopted by the best Roman Catholics owe nothing to Protestantism.

This will be a convenient place to examine another of Mr. Montefiore's reflections. " I thank thee, ἐξομολογοῦμαι [which may have its usual meaning of ' confess, acknowledge '], O Father, Lord of heaven and earth, that thou didst hide these things from the wise and understanding, and didst reveal them unto babes " (Matt. xi. 25 = Luke x. 21).

Mr. Montefiore asks : " Is he not only glad that God has revealed the truth about himself to the simple, but that he has *not* revealed it to the wise and the clever ?   Woe to the unbelieving Scribes, and yet thank God for their unbelief ! It is not pleasing to have to believe that Jesus said this."[1] For once Mr. Montefiore, in his resentment at Christ's language towards the Scribes, seems to me a little too prosaic and literal. If Jesus had been educated as a Jewish scribe or a western philosopher, and had carefully weighed His words before giving utterance to this sudden access of emotion, He would perhaps have said " I thank thee that thou hast revealed to the simple what those who pride themselves on their knowledge and their insight have failed, with all their education and their wisdom, to understand." If He did think of this " withholding " as a sort of penalty for the pride of learning, would such a point of view be wholly unjustified ? There is such a thing as the " pride of knowledge," though it seldom equals the pride of half-educated ignorance. I don't think Mr. Montefiore would have quarrelled much with this saying if he had found it in the Old Testament or the Talmud. That not all the Rabbis of our Lord's time or any other deserved such a censure, I have fully acknowledged.

Our Lord's denunciation of the cities which had rejected Him (Matt. xi. 21 ; Luke x. 13) may be dealt with in much the same way. The denunciation, according to St. Matthew, was called forth " because they repented not " : and this is implied in the words. There is nothing

[1] *Syn. Gospels*, II, 604.

personal about the resentment. The strongest saying, "Thou shalt be brought down to hell," clearly cannot be taken literally to mean that every man, woman and child in Capernaum would go to hell. In so far as they are applied to the whole city collectively, the words are clearly metaphorical—as much so as the previous words "which art exalted to heaven" or (R.V.) "shalt thou be exalted into heaven ? "

(10) *Undue Self-exaltation?* The much-disputed doctrinal passage "no man knoweth the Son but the Father," etc.[1] is followed by the words: "Come unto Me, all ye that labour and are heavy laden, and I will give you rest. Take My yoke upon you and learn of Me; for I am meek and lowly in heart" (Matt. xi. 28–29). These last words have been thought to imply undue self-approbation. Martineau, for instance, rejected them as inconsistent with the character of Jesus. Taken in their context—in connexion with the contrast (which immediately follows) between the light yoke of His teaching and the heavy burden laid on man by the Pharisees, I do not see that Jesus—quite independently of any claim to Divinity or even to Messiahship—should not have endeavoured to attract men by saying in Wellhausen's words "that He is not haughty, and does not, like the Scribes, despise the people, which knows nothing of the Law." But the passage is in Matthew only, and is of the kind which *might* well be an ecclesiastical addition. Beautiful as the words are, spiritually true as they have

[1] It would be out of place to discuss the genuineness of this passage here. The differences exhibited by Matthew and Luke and by different MSS. and versions are considerable. Harnack (*Sayings of Jesus*, p. 295) accepts them in their simplest and least elaborated form. It is probable that they represent some genuine saying, but it is difficult to be confident that even Harnack's reading is absolutely primitive.

abundantly been shown to be, they are not unlikely in their present form to represent the experience of the early Church, though it is quite conceivable that some genuine saying of Jesus about the lightness of His yoke may underlie them. The words are largely inspired by a passage from Jeremiah and the praise of Wisdom in Ecclesiasticus.[1] Loisy doubts their historicity in the mouth of Jesus, and remarks that for the Evangelist they mean, " le joug de Jésus est la loi chrétienne, si douce et légère relativement à la Loi mosaïque interprétée par les pharisiens " (*Évan. Syn.*, I, 913–14).

(11) *Alleged admission of moral imperfection.* " Why callest thou Me good ? none is good save one " (Mark x. 18). These words are appealed to as a proof of our Lord's consciousness of moral shortcoming. That they represent the true version of the saying (which the true text of Matt. xix. 17 waters down—" Why askest thou Me concerning the good ? ") no one who takes criticism seriously can doubt ; nor can I regard them as merely spoken *ad hominem*, from the point of view of the questioner, ignorant of the divine nature of Him who spake. They constitute, it seems to me, a real disclaimer of such absolute goodness as He ascribed to the Father. Yet I do not think that they amount to the admission of actual sin. The only evidence for the belief in the absolute sinlessness of Jesus that can be produced is negative evidence—the marked absence of that sense of sin which is so prominent a feature of the religious consciousness in the men who have otherwise most closely approximated to the goodness of Christ. (I assume that our view of the fourth Gospel will not permit of our appealing to John viii. 46.) He appears not to have felt oppressed by any consciousness of sin or sinfulness which would constitute an obstacle to complete

[1] Jer. vi. 16 ; Ecclus. li. 23 *sq.*

communion with God. Still, it is so difficult to form a clear conception of what we mean by absolute sinlessness, and so impossible, considering the extreme imperfection of our record, to *prove* such sinlessness, that it seems to me best to avoid attempts at definition. The picture handed down by the Gospels presents to us the character of one in whom we can see no consciousness or evidence of sinfulness. That is as far as we need go. Throughout this book I have assumed that it is because it is confirmed by the moral consciousness of the modern world that we accept the moral teaching and character of Jesus as the highest expression of absolute and permanent moral truth that we possess. It is chiefly the essential principles of Christian Morality that are of importance to us, and I have admitted the need of development in the light of later knowledge, thought, and experience. Still, I do not allow that any particular precept is inconsistent with these general principles, viewed in the light of existing social conditions and of what was then known of social laws, or that on any occasion whatever our Lord (so far as we know) acted in a way, or exhibited a character and temper, which can be pronounced inconsistent with them.

I have said nothing in this connexion about the saying in the fourth Gospel : " Which of you convicteth Me of sin ? " (John viii. 46), or other passages which involve similar self-assertion. The self-assertion of the Johannine Christ does strike us just occasionally as a little harsh, and inconsistent with the moral ideal which we should recognize as becoming in a thoroughly human consciousness, and with the character actually exhibited by the Synoptic narratives. It is not that the things which the Johannine Christ says about Himself may not be regarded as having truth in them ; but it is difficult to understand how Jesus could have thought and said such things about Himself, and retained the limitations without which a human consciousness ceases to be human. To my mind it is one of the positive religious gains of Criticism that we can read the statements of the Johannine Christ as expressing a disciple's sense of the value of Christ and His revelation of the Father, and not as assertions actually made about himself by an historical person engaged in controversy with his opponents. So considered, many of these statements may be regarded as eternal truths of the highest religious value. There is real truth in the statement that Christ was the light of the world, and that no man can come to the Father—in the fullest and completest degree—except through the avenue of approach instituted by this historical revelation. But it is difficult to think of a perfectly good human being actually making such a declaration about Himself ; and in the light of the Synoptic Gospels it is extremely improbable that He did so. There are no doubt many pieces of strong, though legitimate, self-assertion in the Synoptists, but they are of a different kind—of a kind intelligible enough in the light of Jesus' belief in His own Messianic calling. There are, too, in the Synoptists severe things said of the Pharisaic opponents, but they are different in character from the tremendous denunciations of the Johannine Christ. It is a relief to be able to regard these last, not for purely subjective reasons, but on the strongest critical grounds, as the work of a disciple who had in general marvellously entered into the spirit of his Master's teaching, but who was consciously developing rather than reporting that teaching, and who looked at it in the light of a theological theory, which was itself part of the development. I prefer to think of sayings like "All who came before me were thieves and robbers " as a disciple's impassioned tribute to his Master rather than as the Master's words about Himself.

(12) *The Parable of the Marriage Feast: Humility for the sake of Reward* (Luke xiv. 7–11). " When thou art bidden, go and sit down in the lowest place, that when he that hath bidden thee cometh, he may say unto thee, Friend, go up higher : then shalt thou have glory in the presence of all that sit at meat with thee." This has been objected to on the ground that it makes the desire for honour the motive for humility, and Jo. Weiss has suggested that it is a certain section of the Christian community that is here speaking rather than Jesus. I imagine that to win the favour of God would have seemed to Jesus too pure a motive to be identified with ordinary ambition or love of honour. And no one could well demur to His thinking so, if only the conception of God is kept high and pure enough. There cannot be too much desire to be approved by One whose judgements are absolutely just. It is the form which the desire to obey the Categorical Imperative necessarily assumes to the Theist, though, no doubt, the desire to win favour with God may easily degenerate into an ambition which is none the less selfish because the reward is posthumous. Others have taken it merely as a piece of practical advice. It is not bad or degrading advice to say, " It is better to leave it to others to give you a high place than to take it yourself." But this does not seem to me much in the spirit of Jesus, though there is no reason why the greatest of ethical teachers should not sometimes have given homely, practical advice in matters of the minor morals. It is quite possible that the Evangelist or tradition may have given some genuine saying of Jesus a turn which made it a warning against undue ambition for ecclesiastical office.

(13) *The discouragement of Prudence.* It has often been suggested that the teaching of Christ omits that whole side of Morality which may be summed up in the word Prudence.

The command not to be anxious for the morrow (Matt. vi. 34) may be taken as a sufficient illustration of the teaching which is objected to. Such an injunction, it may be said, would, if generally acted upon, be in the highest degree injurious to the interests of Society. It would tend to destroy the commercial prosperity of a modern industrial community, and would produce a population of Neapolitan beggars. What are we to say to this suggestion ? In the first place, I would submit that the objection probably owes a good deal of its plausibility to the mistranslation " Take no thought " instead of " Be not anxious." In the second place, it must be remembered that the neglect of material interests which was prescribed by Christ was only comparative. It was in comparison with the Kingdom of Heaven that the question of meat and drink was un-important. And, thirdly, we must remember that in a community which did systematically put the Kingdom of God first, no socially injurious consequences could result from the preference. In a community in which everyone did systematically care for the things of others and not for his own things, there could be no neglect of the general welfare in material any more than in higher ways. If all its members did systematically seek first the Kingdom of God and His righteousness, the other things certainly would be added to such a community. Unselfishness would be as powerful a stimulus to industry and invention as selfishness. That is a proposition which can be established from the point of view of the most severe economic Science. When anything like a socialistic or communistic community has been realized, it has often been attended by the highest economic prosperity. Whatever difficulties may have arisen, whatever objections there may be to such com-munities from other points of view, want of sufficient food and raiment has rarely been among them. The practical difficulty lies in extending such systems from a community of carefully selected enthusiasts to communities in which men of all characters have to be included. When the teaching of Jesus comes to be taken as the working rule of life for communities of average men, it undoubtedly needs to be interpreted by much complementary teaching. It can be easily shown that to earn one's own living and not become burdensome to others is a duty which results directly from the fundamental Christian principle of love to one's neighbour ; but undoubtedly it is a deduction or corollary which required to be pointed out and insisted upon. St. Paul discovered that necessity, and supplied the complementary teaching required.

Mr. Montefiore has some fine remarks on this text : " 'Not to be anxious' means to have a free heart, to be courageous and active, to accept our life every day fresh from God's hand and to trust in Him. But such composure of mind is not only not a hindrance, but is even an inexhaustible source of strength for a successful struggle for existence. And how shall we attain such freedom from anxiety ? Jesus says to us, ' Fill your soul with a great purpose, endeavour after the kingdom of God, battle for the victory of good in the world, strive after personal perfection, and then what has hitherto oppressed you will appear to you petty and insignificant ' " (*Syn. Gospels*, II, 545).

(14) *The alleged impossibility of Universal Love.* It is surprising to find intelligent persons finding a difficulty in Christ's requirement of Universal Love on the ground that it is impossible to love all men equally. It is not Christ alone but almost all the higher Moralists who have used the term " love " to indicate two things : (1) a state of the desires, emotions, and will directed towards the good of one's fellows, and (2) the spontaneous feeling of special

attachment to particular persons—affection such as our Lord is recorded to have expressed for the rich young man, for Lazarus and his sisters, for the " disciple whom Jesus loved."[1] This fact—I suspect a universal fact—of language has obviously a foundation in the facts of moral Psychology. The ideal relation between human beings is one in which the will of each is as steadily directed towards the good of every other human being as it is towards his own good or that of persons towards whom he feels the strongest emotional attraction ; and in proportion as this attitude is realized, an emotion is felt which is to some extent the same, though to some extent different, from the feeling entertained towards friends. The feeling entertained towards the personal friend is the feeling of good-will based upon personal liking or attraction. Language can only express the ideal feeling towards one's fellows as such by generalizing the terms naturally used to indicate personal affection (ἀγαπή, φιλία, amor, dilectio, caritas). A reasonable Ethic will approve of this generalization without denying that the feeling becomes in some ways different by being extended towards a large circle of persons, known and unknown. When Aristotle said that one ought to be a greater friend to truth than to beloved individuals, nobody takes him to mean that one must feel towards truth exactly as one does towards one's nearest friends or relations. There is a kind of thoughtlessness which is possible in theological (or anti-theological) discussion which cultivated men are never guilty of in any other connexion.

Sometimes the same kind of objection is made to the place which the love of God occupies in the Christian ideal. The objector asks, for instance : " Did any man ever love

---

[1] Mark x. 21 ; John xi. 5, xx. 2. Cf. Aristotle's use of φιλία for a universal human duty and for a special social relation. *Eth. Nic.*, iv., 1126 b. ; viii., 1155 a., 1161 b., etc.

God as he has loved some human beings ? Did he ever derive from the love of God a greater inspiration for all good things and thoughts than from the love of some one or other child of earth ? " (Garrod, *The Religion of All Good Men*, Ed. I, p. 169). On this objection I would remark (1) that the author seems naïvely to suppose that an ideal is shown to be false because it is not fully realized by most of us : on this side the objection would best be met by some well-known quotations from Plato. (2) He has largely answered himself when he goes on to say, " Did he never feel that in the love of some single human being he was loving God ? " If the love of God not only does not exclude, but expresses itself in the love of particular persons, why does he object to the Christian language ? If the writer does not mean that the moral ideal is *adequately* satisfied by the love of a single human being to the exclusion of all others, it is clear that the love of all Good will express itself in the love, not merely of a single human being, but of all human beings.

The love which ought to be felt towards all men as such is the desire of the true good for particular human beings, and such love is the same in principle as the love of God, in whom whatever is good in human beings is realized in a transcendent degree, and whose Will is (as Christians believe) directed towards the good of those beings. The emotion which naturally accompanies such a direction of the will normally shows itself in the love of particular individuals, or quite as often in devotion to particular societies of individuals. Love of country, of Church, of the ideal represented by Christ has often, in point of fact, been quite as intense as that felt for a wife or a friend. The highest degree of devotion to the general good does not exclude the existence of feelings towards particular persons which it would be a psychological impossibility to feel towards all. Nor does it follow that on all occasions the best man will behave towards all as he does towards his best friend. The love of Humanity shows itself largely, though not entirely, in performing services for particular individuals. The extent to which, and the ways in which the good man will promote the good of any particular individual will depend upon the nature of his relation towards them. There are obvious reasons why a man should in practice promote the good of his own family more actively and persistently *in certain ways* than the good of strangers. Somewhat similar considerations will prescribe that *in certain other ways* we should promote the good of those to whom we are attracted by natural and spontaneous affection rather than that of strangers. The existence of such natural affection is one of the things—but only one—which determines for which of all possible human beings we should specially perform good offices. What I imagine the Christian and rational precept of love towards mankind as such to prescribe is that the ultimate laws of human conduct should be determined by the principle that every man should be treated as an end-in-himself according to his intrinsic value. This ultimate law will prescribe that our conduct even towards those for whom we have most natural affection should be duly controlled by, and subordinated to, the requirements of general social well-being. The selection of the persons towards whom should be performed the kind of services which cannot be performed towards all should be determined likewise by the supreme rule of promoting universal well-being. This supreme rule will prescribe, for instance, that a man is free to a large extent to choose his companions according to his own tastes, and that he may spend much of his leisure in their company. It would, however, clearly not be a rule fit for law universal that he should leave to his personal friend the money which by the social custom of his community and the implied understanding at his marriage should go to his wife and her children, even if he chanced to feel more affection for the friend than for the wife.   And the same principle will require that neither personal friend nor wife and children should interfere with the discharge of his professional duties or his willingness to fight for his country in the hour of need.   But I feel I am here straying into broad questions of Moral Philosophy which it would take too long to discuss here.

It may be suggested that, while it is possible for a man to *act* upon such principles, it is not possible for him to control his feelings and emotions and affections to the same extent.   I should reply briefly (i) that the man whose will is steadily directed towards such a rule of conduct does fulfil the command of universal love : the love towards all men which the Christian rule and rational Morality demand is primarily a direction of the will.   The fact that a man is willing to prefer the interests of Humanity to those of his wife and family (where such a preference is really demanded), actually proves that he does desire their good more than that of wife and children.   Will is a name for the dominant desire which has passed into action.   (ii) In so far as the emotional accompaniments of such a desire can be distinguished from the desire itself, they will tend to grow into conformity with the rule upon which the man habitually wills to act.   (iii) In so far as the emotion that we feel towards particular persons is of a kind that we cannot feel towards strangers or towards collective humanity, there is no inconsistency between the strongest devotion to Humanity and the tenderest affections towards individuals.

After all, the best answer to Mr. Garrod is to point to the

o

actual character and conduct of the best Christians in all ages. The Christians who have left home and family and friends to become missionaries, or who have refused to seek safety in time of danger for fear of leaving their wives widows and their children fatherless, or who have done things which involved the risk of pecuniary ruin to their families rather than be dishonest, have felt the ties of kinship and personal affection as keenly as other men : yet the fact that they acted as they did is a proof that they did love God or Christ or Humanity more than all these. The candour and sincerity of Mr. Garrod's enquiry deserve respect, but he is not the only writer who has criticized Christianity without showing much knowledge of what the best actual Christians have shown themselves to be like either in history or in his own day. When personal experience fails, a little study of Christian biography may be recommended as an essential qualification for writing upon the comparative merits of the Christian, the Hellenic, and the " Gothic " ideals of life.

LECTURE V

THE PRINCIPLE OF DEVELOPMENT

IN my last lecture I endeavoured to make it plain
that the ethical teaching of Jesus could be regarded
as the supreme guide for conduct in modern life on
two conditions only—firstly, that that teaching is
understood as laying down general principles and
not detailed regulations of eternal obligation: secondly,
that the necessity for development is admitted in the
amplest possible manner. The first condition is one
which may be said to have been fully recognized by
Jesus Himself, since He never attempts to do more than
lay down principles: any applications which He gives
to them are avowedly mere illustrations or applications of those principles to the conduct of particular
individuals under particular circumstances, which can
only be applied to other individuals and other circumstances by disengaging the general principle from
the particular application. And this implicitly carries
with it the other principle, the principle of Develop
ment ; for, if one can discover no detailed rules in the
teaching of Christ, it is obvious that we must make
them for ourselves. How far we can discover any ex-

press recognition of that necessity for development in the teaching of the Master Himself will depend largely upon the view that we take of the fourth Gospel. The doctrine of the Holy Ghost contained in that Gospel obviously implies this principle. It was to be the object of the Spirit's indwelling to take of Christ's and show it unto His disciples. The Spirit was to say to them many things which at present they could not bear, and therefore His going away from them was the very condition of their moral and spiritual advancement. I do not myself think that this teaching about the Paraclete in the Church can have had more than a rudimentary germ in the teaching of Jesus Himself. There was a germ of it in that recognition of the existence of Conscience on which I have already dwelt, and in the many sayings which speak of a Holy Spirit working in the hearts of men. The fourth Evangelist's doctrine of the Paraclete, and of the Church as the Society in which the Spirit dwells and works, is just an illustration of that very development of which I am speaking. It involves the principle both in the region of Theology and in that of Ethics. In the present lecture I must confine myself to the ethical side of this development.

It is well that we should set before our minds quite clearly and definitely what is meant by this principle of ethical Development. We have already dealt with the kind of ethical evolution which went on in the Jewish mind before the time of Christ, and which cul-

minates in His teaching. In that teaching, as I have
tried to show you, we do discover a supreme and
final principle which we do not expect to be transcended—the rule of universal love, which (expressed
in cold philosophical terms) implies that human duty
consists in the promotion of the true good for all mankind, the good of one being considered as of equal
intrinsic value with the like good of every other. Why
is this principle insufficient for the guidance of life
without any further expansion? For two reasons :
in the first place we want to know the means by which
human good is to be promoted : and in the second
place we must know what in detail constitutes this
" good " which we are to promote for all mankind.
It is obvious from the nature of the case that there can
be no finality in either of these directions. The discovery of any fresh means of promoting human good
not only adds new rules of life to the ethical code ;
it actually cancels old rules. Not only has the course
of social and intellectual development opened up a
thousand duties of which no one living in the time
of Jesus could well have dreamed, of which the
wisest of men, Jewish, pagan or Christian, never had
dreamed, but many acts which to the world of that
day seemed right have become wrong in the light of
fuller knowledge of detailed fact and of natural or
social law. Indiscriminate almsgiving became wrong
when it was discovered that it does more harm than
good—generally to the actual recipient, always to

others. It has become wrong to spend time in organizing solemn processions as a means of averting plague now that we know that plague is produced by neglect of sanitary precautions, and that energy devoted to sanitary reform is a more effective way of averting it than the organization of processions. It has become wrong for religious men to turn aside from politics now that we realize how much improved social arrangements may do not merely for human happiness but for the improvement of human character and for the elevation of human life on its most spiritual side. This principle, when once pointed out, is too obvious to need further illustration; and yet it involves the absolute abandonment of the attempt to derive detailed guidance in matters of conduct from any final and closed system of moral rules, whether it be the teaching of Christ or of the New Testament or of the most elaborate authoritative Casuistry. The more elaborate and detailed the rules become, the greater ere long becomes their inapplicability to a world in which circumstances are constantly changing and knowledge advancing. Simple as the principle is, I do not think it has ever yet been sufficiently grasped by the mass of religious people or by their religious guides. It is still too often assumed that we cannot make the promotion of Socialism a Christian duty unless we can show that Christ Himself was a Socialist, or that we can refute Socialism by showing that He was not. There is still too much disposition among Christian people to settle ethical controversies by the appeal to isolated texts or to ancient ecclesiastical rules.[1]

It is the other kind of development which creates the most difficulty—the development in our conception of what this ideal consists in, this " good " which we recognize it as a duty to promote for all mankind. It is here that it may most plausibly be contended that the principle of development has actually been carried by almost all modern Christians to a point which really makes it impossible to treat the moral teaching of Jesus as any longer expressing an ideal which enlightened modern minds can recognize as their own. It has become fashionable to express the contrast between the ethical teaching of Jesus and the ideal which most modern men profess by saying that the ethics of Jesus were " world-renouncing " and that ours are " world-affirming."[2] I should like to face that question as honestly as I can—to ask firstly how far this contrast holds between the teaching of Jesus and the ethical ideal which most cultivated modern Christians actually profess ; and secondly, whether, in so far as this is the case, it prevents our

---

[1] I am afraid that some of the publications even of so enlightened a body as the Christian Social Union have not been altogether free from the tendency to erect a social system upon the basis of texts from the Old and New Testaments.

[2] See, for instance, Professor Troeltsch's brilliant work *Protestantism and Progress* (trans. by W. Montgomery). The weak point of that otherwise valuable enquiry seems to me to lie in the acceptance of this distinction, without much analysis, as adequate and absolute.

sincerely giving to that teaching the supremacy which Christians have always claimed, and still claim, for it.

To a great extent I have already dealt with these questions in asking how far the eschatological ideas of Jesus really prevent our accepting His fundamental ethical principles. In fact, I do not think I need do much more than remind you of the conclusions at which we have already arrived. If these conclusions are true, we shall answer our present problem by saying two things : (1) That there is room for much development in our conception of what the ideal good consists in without giving up the fundamental principle that the supreme precept in Morality is that which enjoins the promotion of this good for all mankind : and (2) that the extent to which it can justly be said that the ideal of Jesus was world-renouncing has been greatly exaggerated. Undoubtedly the ideal of Jesus was world-renouncing, if that means the renunciation of selfishness, of selfish ambitions, of sensuality, of pride ; if it means that in the ideal life the highest place was to be given to a goodness of which love is the supreme element, and in which the spiritual is regarded as of much more importance than the carnal. Nobody who does not acknowledge the truth of His teaching on such fundamental points as this—nobody (to put it more definitely) whose ideal does not include the condemnation of adultery and fornication and sensuality in thought, of drunkenness and every excessive indulgence of appetite—is likely even to claim that his ethical ideal is a legitimate development of Christ's. But neither His ideal nor His practice were world-renouncing in the sense of despising and condemning all ordinary human pleasure—still less in the extremer sense of positively courting pain. He, as we have already seen, neither practised nor enjoined fasting. He spent much of His time and energy in curing diseases of mind and body. He made little of bodily pleasures and satisfactions in comparison with higher things. But He never condemned them, or urged that they should be given up except as a means to something higher—that something being, for His immediate disciples, the preaching of the Kingdom of Heaven and, for all, the effort to become fit for entrance into that Kingdom. And that really implies that in principle His ideal was not world-renouncing. There is absolutely no idea or suggestion in His teaching of self-renunciation for its own sake—of the ideal which would extinguish all pleasure, all desire, all individuality. If in the exercise of our moral consciousness we judge many things in life to be good of which He knew little and thought little, it is a quite legitimate extension and development of His teaching to include these things in our conception of the good which the rule of Universal Love bids us promote for others.

Indeed, it may, I think, be shown that the ascetic view of life is logically inconsistent with the teaching which makes the heart of Morality consist in love—love as Jesus understood it. He certainly recognized it as a duty to promote bodily health, and a certain measure of enjoyment for others.   His injunctions to charity are constantly directed towards the satisfaction of bodily wants, and no sober criticism can well deny that He claimed to heal some kinds of bodily disease by spiritual influence.   If these things are good for others, they must be good for myself also —in due subordination to the claims of others : up to that point therefore it cannot be wrong for me to enjoy them myself.   Nor is there any reason why, whether for ourselves or for others, we should stop at precisely that minimum of enjoyment which is represented by a sufficiency of food and clothing.   We cannot set up a rule of unlimited giving or self-sacrifice for the sake of others without raising the question : " To what shall the energies of a community be devoted when once food and clothing have been secured to everyone ? "   If it is suggested that the rest of their energies ought to be devoted to the promotion of righteousness, it must be remembered that there is a limit to the extent to which time can effectively be spent in the promotion of righteousness.   Too much zeal for edification ceases to edify.   Let us suppose that we have secured a community in which nobody takes more than his share of the lower goods, and in which, so far, nobody is wanting in love.   Is all the rest of the time and energy of the community to be spent in religious contemplation or spiritual exercises ?   If not, to what is their time to be devoted if not either to some increase of lower pleasures or enjoyments above what is absolutely necessary for life and health, or to such higher enjoyments as Science, Art, Literature, and the like ? Are we not then to include these things in our conception of the ideal life ?

It might, indeed, be contended that from the actual nature of things it is impossible that everyone should enjoy more than a very moderate amount of such higher goods as Art, Knowledge, Culture, and that no one ought to get more of these things than is possible for everyone. But, as a matter of fact, it is quite impossible that all should enjoy even a moderate amount of culture unless some men enjoy a much higher amount. The scientific discoveries which all may know of, and the scientific inventions which all may use, have resulted from the labours of men who have devoted the bulk of their time and energy to Science. The books which all may read have been written by men who have devoted their lives to reading more, and thinking more, than those who read them. The little insight into the nature of the Universe and the little enjoyment of beauty which are possible to those who spend most of their days in manual labour, come from the work of those who have spent most of their time in intellectual or artistic pursuits. In this way it may be shown that there is an inner contradiction in the position of those who, without denying that some enjoyment of the best things is part of the ideal life, would set very severe limits to that enjoy-

ment, and practically look askance upon any serious
devotion to artistic or scientific or literary pursuits
by anyone professing to accept the Christian ideal of
mutual service. The severer the Asceticism, the more
logical it becomes. Only when Asceticism becomes
severe, it becomes hopelessly irreconcilable with the
teaching and practice of Him whose example Christians profess to respect. If the Science which has
resulted in so much saving of pain to humanity is a
bad thing, why was it right for Jesus to go about
curing disease ? If a ball is in itself wrong (I am putting
aside for the present the question how much time and
money ought to be spent upon such enjoyments),
why not the simple village wedding feast ? If abstinence and the depression which it causes are really
better than the health and cheerfulness which springs
from moderate eating and drinking, why did not
Jesus teach His disciples to fast as the disciples of
John and of the Pharisees fasted ?

After all, there is no arguing about these ultimate
judgements of value. Physical Science it is difficult to
condemn for anyone who shares the Christian ideal of
Brotherhood, on account of its practical applications :
but if anybody likes to say that the world would be
a better world if there were in it no drama, no novels,
no poetry except hymns, no music except hymn-tunes,
no Art except what is directly conducive to edification,
no learning beyond the biblical exegesis of the Sunday
School, no Philosophy which seriously faces ultimate

questions, he cannot be positively refuted. If this be the result of appeal to the moral consciousness, there is no more to be said. I can only say to my own mind this is certainly not the case ; my own moral consciousness unhesitatingly affirms that these things are good ; and so does that of most modern men. The austere religionists who even now are inclined to depreciate all employments which do not minister to the relief of strict bodily necessities on the one hand or to immediate edification on the other, generally admit so much of the modern view of life that they can be convicted of intellectual inconsistency, or at least of arbitrary limitations, if they refuse to go further. They look with suspicion on the man of Science ; yet they will travel in railway trains, and use telephones, and regard it as a thoroughly religious task to secure the best medical treatment for the sick. They cannot quite get over the suspicion that there is something profane and presumably godless about the occupation of a Philosopher, or a researcher, or an Artist ; yet they will hang photographs of the Artist's picture on their walls, and, when the ideas of the Philosopher or the discoveries of the researcher have filtered down into school text-books, they will be heartily zealous that children should read them. They condemn the stage, but they will read Shakespeare at home—and so forth. The most hopelessly inconsistent of all are the religious people who do not condemn a very consider-able indulgence in the lower good things of life, but reserve all their asceticism for the higher intellectual pursuits. Have we not known of rich bankers or wine-merchants who spend their lives in ministering to the luxuries of other rich persons and much of their profits in luxury for themselves, but who would regard almost as a lost soul a son who wanted to become a philosopher or a scholar or a painter ? I have myself heard a clergy-man speak about a brilliant school contemporary of his who had remained all his life an Oxford don as one would speak of a respectable man who had taken to drink or otherwise gone to the bad. Had he gone to the Bar and made a fortune, that would have been all right : had he taken Orders and worked in the slums, that would have been still better. Had he emerged from the slums to become a Bishop, that would have been best of all. But the work of a "mere scholar," why, that was to make the worst of both worlds !

Once again then, if we accept this modern view of Morality, which after all by this time most Christian people do accept, does it not imply that we are desert-ing the teaching of Christ ? Most emphatically I maintain that we are not—under two conditions, two conditions which practically come to very much the same thing : (1) In the first place, we must recognize that these things, which we consider to be elements in the true good for ourselves, are elements in the true good for others also ; and that therefore it becomes a Christian duty to promote them for others as well as for ourselves—for the many as well as the few—for other people, other classes, other races than our own. Selfish, dilettante, anti-social Æstheticism is, indeed, hopelessly at variance with the fundamental principle of Christ's teaching. A specialized devotion of one's life to Art or Science, to Literature or to learning, can only be justified from the Christian point of view when in some way or other the results of such a life-work are shared by the community in general or some part of it. For the Christian the intellectual or artistic life must become a Ministry. (2) Secondly, even for ourselves moral goodness must be put higher than intellectual excellence of whatever kind. The view of life which regards Art as a sort of optional alternative or substitute for Religion and Morality—a view of which there are traces in the language of many Philosophers and other writers besides those who would seriously maintain such a thesis—cannot by any ingenuity whatever be represented as a legitimate development of Christ's Morality. The Morality which I have sketched—that is to say, the Morality practically accepted by most cultivated Christians of the present day—is not inconsistent with the fundamental principles of Christ's teaching ; but it involves, and it should be most fully recognized that it involves, a considerable development of what actually was taught by Christ Himself.

Christ's teaching was world-renouncing, if by that is meant that He put universal human interests before self and the spiritual above the carnal : and in that sense Christian Morality must always be world-renouncing. Christ's teaching was world-affirming in so far as He held that there are many good things in life which should not be renounced, but, on the contrary, should be promoted for others as well as for ourselves. In that sense there was for Him no incompatibility between world-renunciation and world-affirmation. Nor need there be for us, though we may recognize the value of many things which are not explicitly recognized in His actual ideal : and so long as we limit our own enjoyment of these good things by the claims of others to their due share in them.

No doubt when we turn from Christ's own teaching to the Morality of the Christian Church in the past, there is more truth in the contrast—more ground for the complaint that Christian Morality has been world-renouncing, in a sense in which ours is not and cannot be. And yet, after all, this is by no means the whole truth. Up to a certain point the actual development of the Christian ideal has been towards an increasing recognition of the value of many things in life from which Christ's own immediate followers turned aside. Those very complaints of the " acute secularizing " of the Church in the post-apostolic age with which Harnack has made us familiar, testify to the fact that the development was not all in the direction of increasing renunciation of things in the world which were harmless or even desirable. Unless Harnack is really prepared to say that all these things are wrong (which it is impossible to suppose), it may be doubted whether he is justified in speaking of such "secularizing" as though it necessarily involved a decline from the true Christian ideal, and whether he ought not to regard it rather as an evidence of that work of the Spirit in the Christian Society which the fourth Gospel had foretold. Even St. Paul himself, though his ideal was more affected than that of his Master by the thought of the coming Parousia, found that an excessive preoccupation with that thought, an excessive devotion to talking, speculating, meditating about spiritual things, militated against true spirituality. He therefore laid down in a very emphatic way the paramount duty of earning one's own living, —and something more that we may have to give to those who are in need.[1] All the industrial virtues to which Christianity has sometimes been supposed to be indifferent are enjoined by implication in St. Paul's precepts to the idle busybodies of Thessalonica. This so-called secularizing of the Christian ideal may better be described as a perfectly legitimate and indispensable development of it.

The history of the first four Christian centuries is to a large extent a record of the gradual absorption into Christian life of what was best in pagan Literature, Art, Philosophy, even Ethics and Theology. From political life Christians were necessarily excluded, though they had politics of their own within the Church

---

[1] 2 Thess. iii. 6–14 ; Rom. xii. 11 ; Eph. iv. 28. Cf. 1 Tim. v. 13.

P

which afforded a sphere for great statesmen and administrators and for much social activity of a highly democratic kind. When the Christianization of the Empire threw open political office to Christians, the work of Government came to be recognized as a possible sphere of Christian service; and much of what we may call the political morality of the ancient world was embodied in the current conceptions of Christian duty. Though the old sharp distinction between the Church (now very largely identified with the clergy and the monks) and the world to a large extent survived, the mere fact that the writings of Cicero were highly popular with the Fathers, and the Ethics and Politics of Aristotle with the Schoolmen, shows how much of the ancient ideal of life was absorbed into the current teaching of the Church. Hundreds of pages of St. Thomas Aquinas' *Summa Theologica* are little more than a reduction to scholastic form of the Ethics of Aristotle. The highest Ethics of the ancient world were, to use Professor Gardner's happy expression, " baptized into Christ " ; and that means that the ideal practically accepted by the Christian world absorbed considerable elements of the best pagan thought. Protestantism has still more fully and unreservedly recognized all kinds of public office and all lay callings as possible spheres for the exercise of the highest Christian virtues. The very Theology of the Church represents a fusion of ancient Philosophy with the Theology of

Judaism and the teaching of Jesus and His Apostles. After a long struggle, pagan literature was accepted as part of the training of Christian youth; and the pretence that Grammar and Rhetoric were cultivated only as conducive to the understanding of Holy Scripture was laid aside. In the later Middle Ages it is not too much to say that the promotion of Culture was recognized as one of the duties of the clergy—even of the Friars, although there was still a disposition to justify secular knowledge either (as in the case of Law and Medicine) on account of its practical utility to the commonwealth, or (in the case of liberal studies) to regard them as in some way preparatory and conducive to the all-important study of Theology. The Renaissance led to a still further relaxation of the ancient Christian austerity and a still further recognition of Culture—even in the Catholicism of the Counter-reformation, still more so in Protestantism.

But, of course, there was another side to this matter. Side by side with this broadening and expansion in the Christian conception of life—this absorption into it of the best elements in the pagan world which it had killed—there was a continuous narrowing of it ; an increase of Asceticism, anti-intellectualism, other-worldliness. The tendency began to assert itself very early. Even the Apostolic Church never quite acquiesced in Christ's refusal to enjoin fasting ; the post-apostolic Church began to tamper with the text of the New Testament to conceal the fact, although

even in the Pastoral Epistles it is recognized that
" bodily exercise [i.e. Asceticism] profiteth little."[1] The
severer Asceticism was at first a characteristic rather
of heresy than of the Church. But even within the
Church there was an increasing tendency both toward
Asceticism in its ordinary sense and towards the
devotion of life to religious observances and religious
contemplation. And this gradually hardened into
Monasticism. It is important to note that the
tendency to exalt contemplation, asceticism, and
celibacy was a tendency of the times by no means
peculiar to Christianity. Neo-platonism had more
to do with it than the teaching of Jesus or of His
Apostles. It is not improbable that definite Monasticism
was an imitation of paganism. And the introduction
of Monasticism implies that the collision between the
two kinds of development which we have seen going
on in the Christian Church has now become so marked
that the Church has split up into two sections.
There is now an increased toleration of " worldly "
pursuits, amusements, culture for the many ; while
the renunciation of these things which is demanded
of the few—of those who aim at a perfect fulfilment of
the Christian ideal—has become more extreme. Moreover, the doctrine of original sin and the whole system
of thought which is associated with it—the idea that
the world is wholly under the dominion of the wicked
one—though its influence has, I think, been exag-

---

[1] 1 Tim. iv. 8.   Some translate "for a little time."

gerated, undoubtedly deepened the cleavage between those ideals of life which we commonly associate with the ancient Greeks and the ideal which was set before Christians. Thus there was a tendency all through the patristic and medieval periods to an ideal of life which was gloomy, austere, intensely other-worldly. Even in the austerest Religionists of these periods there are, indeed, to be found many sayings and ideas which are quite inconsistent with the view that the world lay under a curse, that all its good things were created by God simply to give men the opportunity of earning merit by renouncing them. St. Augustine admits that there is some good in all that exists. The patristic writings—those of St. Chrysostom, for instance—show an appreciation of the beauty of Nature of a kind which we are accustomed to think of as peculiarly modern, and which we certainly should find it hard to parallel in the classical writers of Antiquity. The doctrine of original sin in its Augustinian form was not universally held, nor the view of the Universe which was associated with it.

Ascetic as they are in their attitude towards all bodily pleasures, there is no anti-intellectualism in the great Alexandrians, Clement and Origen ; and in the Greek Church generally there was much less of it than in the West. On the whole even the Latins do not condemn intellectual activities, though their attitude towards the pagan classics was hesitating and

uncertain. Art, too, was never condemned (except in
so far as it involved Idolatry), though it was largely
consecrated to the service of Religion. Immense
qualifications must be introduced before the epithet
" world-renouncing " can be accepted as a true
account even of the patristic and medieval ideals.
On the whole, however, it must be admitted that the
ideal of other-worldliness—the ideal which made it
the chief object of the present life to escape the pains
of Hell and to win the joys of Heaven largely by the
renunciation of all joy in the present—does represent
the predominant tone both of the later patristic and
of the medieval Church.

And it is true also (as has recently been contended
by Professor Troeltsch) that Protestantism—as judged
by its formal expressions, by its official professions,
and by the vein of sentiment prevalent in some of its
religious circles—has not wholly thrown off this other-
worldliness. By abolishing purgatory, by the emphasis which it laid on the Augustinian doctrines of
election and arbitrary decrees, by withdrawing to
a great extent the encouragement which medieval
Christianity practically conceded to Art under cover
of an often merely nominal enlistment of it in the
service of Religion, it has even in some ways emphasized the austerity of the ecclesiastical ideal, and
diminished the joy of human existence. On the other
hand, in other ways it has enormously mitigated the
antagonism between ecclesiastical Christianity and

the best elements of the old Hellenic ideal in more, and more direct, ways, I think, than Troeltsch is disposed to admit. Protestantism has never favoured the more extreme kinds of Asceticism. Its doctrine of salvation by faith *only*, anti-moral as its tendency has often been, did at least put a stop to all devices for winning Heaven or escaping Hell by self-torture or mere ecclesiastical observance. It abolished the hard-and-fast distinction between the religious and the secular life, and discouraged all monastic withdrawal from the world. It peremptorily refused to recognize any moral superiority in the celibate life. It has always acknowledged, fully and ungrudgingly, the possibility of leading the most religious life in the most secular callings. If the clergy of Protestantism have sometimes claimed a control over life which, if conceded, would have been injurious to liberty and intellectual progress, they have claimed it rather as exponents and interpreters of a divine law, than as having any *jus divinum* to rule men's consciences : and consequently Protestant pastors have seldom been able effectively to exercise this control except where they have really represented the moral consciousness of the community for the time being.

It is possible, of course, to suggest (as has been done by Professor Troeltsch) that the contribution of Protestantism to intellectual progress and emancipation has been due rather to its accidental association with the Renaissance than to its own official prin-

ciples. But the Renaissance had so large a share in
producing Protestantism that it becomes a very
speculative enquiry to ask how much was due to
Protestantism, and how much to the Renaissance.
Protestantism without the Renaissance is a mere
abstraction. Protestantism without the Renaissance
would certainly not be the Protestantism that we
know. Doubtless there was from the first an inherent
inconsistency between some of the ideas which Protestantism took over from medieval Catholicism and other
ideas which it owed to the New Learning, or to that
New Testament which the New Learning had given
back to the Church. And the change which has taken
place in the ethical development of Protestantism
since the days of the Reformers and of the Puritan
Revolution in England may be said to be due to a
gradual triumph of the Renaissance-element in Protestantism over its medieval element. But, whether we
put it down to a direct or to an indirect effect of
Protestantism, there can be no doubt that the ideal
which most modern Christians in their hearts accept
does involve a very considerable departure from the
ideals either of the Middle Ages or of early Protestantism. There is then a certain, but only a certain,
measure of truth in the now somewhat hackneyed
assertion that Christianity in the past has been " world-
renouncing," while, in the form in which most modern
Christians accept it, it has become " world-affirming."

Of course, it may be contended that, in so far as this

is so, modern Christianity is wrong. There are people who will be prepared to contend that the world-renouncing medieval ideal was right, that it alone is faithful to the spirit of the Master's teaching, and that, if it differed in any way from that teaching, it was the legitimate development of it. This view is sufficiently often asserted—sometimes in real earnest, more often, I think, in a spirit of sentimental admiration for a past which the critics know cannot be revived and have no intention of imitating even at a discreet distance—to make it worth while for us seriously to ask ourselves whether we are really prepared to accept this world-renouncing interpretation of Christianity. Few, I suppose, will quarrel with my taking the "Imitatio Christi" as a representative of the old medieval ideal on its monastic and world-renouncing side. It is by no means an extreme representation of that ideal. It emanates from that religious movement of the later Middle Age in Germany and the Low Countries which was largely a movement towards a more spiritual Christianity, and which culminated in the Reformation. There is in it little advocacy of austerities. It is full of moral maxims which go straight home to the most modern conscience—maxims about the control of temper, charity towards individuals, abstinence from severe judgements of others, patience, humility, self-examination, penitence. But most of us do not really think that the highest kind of life is to renounce all liberty or responsibility for one's own acts, to be under complete obedience to another human being, to be alone and in a cell for as many hours a day as possible, and to occupy nearly the whole day in religious services, prayer, or meditation. The main theme of the " Imitatio " is the disparagement of all worldly affairs, of business as well as pleasure, of all secular joys, of all secular learning and literature—even of sacred learning beyond what is absolutely required for instructing the individual soul how to get to heaven. There is singularly little about works of charity or philanthropy even in their most conventional forms, or about being useful to other people even in the most directly spiritual ways. We do, indeed, know that Thomas à Kempis sometimes preached and taught ; and the mere fact that he wrote his reflections down for the benefit of others shows that he was by no means an idle or useless or spiritually selfish person. But even this measure of altruistic work seems almost a deviation from the ideal which he sets before his readers. Most modern Christians outside the Roman Catholic Church and many of those within it would regard the ideal of Thomas à Kempis, taken seriously and literally, as at the best a very one-sided ideal. Even those who would defend it as an ideal life for some persons would wholly refuse to follow him in condemning or at least disparaging, as he would actually have done, the life of the politician, of the lawyer, the merchant, the craftsman, the scholar, the artist. If we do reject it, we have to admit that the ideal of modern Christianity is not the same as that of the Middle Ages. The "Imitatio" does, indeed, represent only one of the numerous ideals which express themselves in the life of the patristic and the medieval Church. It is far more world-renouncing, for instance, than the vigorous and highly intellectual ideal of St. Thomas Aquinas. But it does represent a type of life which it has been the general tendency of the Christianity of the past to put highest. There is, as I have so often said, no arguing about ultimate ideals. I can only say that most of our contemporaries—most of the very best men in instructed Christian circles—do fully recognize the value in different degrees of many things which Thomas à Kempis treats as contemptible vanities. And I believe that the modern world is right. A development has taken place, and a development in which I for one am prepared to recognize the work of God's Spirit. In so far as the austere religionists are still disposed to the disparagement of Art and Science and Literature and Learning, I believe them to be wrong, and I recognize the necessity for a still further development of the Christian ideal in this direction.

But in this development are we moving further and further away from the Christianity of Christ ? Most emphatically I believe we are not. The ideal of Thomas à Kempis was very unlike the ideal of Jesus— much more so than the ideal of the best modern Christianity. The view of God's character which Christ taught was quite unlike that of those who made all life an anxious striving to escape from Hell. The idea of God's Fatherhood is scarcely to be detected in the meditations of Thomas à Kempis. The God of Jesus promised forgiveness of sins on the one condition of sincere repentance : a life of solitary meditation— to say nothing of self-torture—was not required as the price of forgiveness. The Christ of whom we hear so much in the " Imitatio " has not very much in common with the Christ of the Gospels. The historical Christ did not live in a cell, but did go about doing good. That solitary, world-renouncing absorption in one's own soul which commended itself to Thomas à Kempis would have seemed to Him mere selfishness, and not at all the way to enter the Kingdom.

It will no doubt be thought by some that the element of Christ's teaching which we have left standing, if we fully accept this principle of Development, is a very small one. It comes, it may be said, to little more than this—that Morality consists in the unselfish pursuit of the good for all men, and in the recognition of the supreme value of moral goodness as the highest and most important element of that good. And that, it may be urged, is a very small element in a moral system—one which might be equally accepted by those who in practice would adopt very different maxims of conduct and recognize very different ideals of life. I should reply, Yes, if you compare the sheer bulk of these precepts with the mass of detailed rules which are required in practice for the guidance of our complicated modern life, their bulk is, indeed, small ; but ethically speaking it is the one thing needful. And no one has ever taught this supremely important truth with the same clearness, consistency, and force as Jesus, or illustrated it so forcibly by the whole of the life and character. And, therefore, in spite of all the enormous development which has taken place in the past, and which doubtless will take place in the future in our conception of the good in detail, and in the rules which we recognize as necessary to the promotion of it, those who accept this principle of universal love as the supreme and all-important ethical command—with all the corollaries and implications of it taught by none so penetratingly as by Him—are true disciples of Christ. And, in so far as the modern Church is getting rid of so many elements of the ecclesiastical ideal which were inconsistent with this supreme principle, we may claim that it is only going back to Christ—to the very heart of Christ's own teaching. From one point of view the difference between the moral standard (say) of the Middle Age and that of the best modern Christianity is undoubtedly a development which owes much to other sources than the actual teaching of Christ and His Apostles—the teaching of ancient Greece and Rome, of the Renaissance, of modern teachers and modern movements which have not been avowedly and at all points Christian ; but from another point of view it has been a real return to the Christianity of Christ. In its broader philanthropy, in its tolerance, in the rejection of immoral devices for getting rid of punishment without getting rid of sin, in the more systematic effort not merely to cure existing evils, but to prevent their recurrence, in the attempt to remould all social life in accordance with the ideal of human brotherhood—in the Christianity which recognizes these things as part of the Christian ideal, however little as yet they form part of average Christian practice, we may recognize that there has really been a return to the spirit of the Master's teaching even when these things involve much development of the letter.   There is more of the spirit of Christ in the modern ideal than there was in the teaching of St. Augustine or of Thomas à Kempis.

And here I should like to guard against two possible misunderstandings of what I have said.   In the first place do not suppose for one moment that I am attempting to represent that *all* the current modern ideals are in harmony with a legitimate development of Christ's own ideal.   It is, indeed, an absurdity to talk as though there was only one ideal of Morality in existence at any one time or place.   It is absurd to do this in regard to the patristic age or the medieval period, although at that time all the competing ideals professed at least to be Christian.   It is a still greater absurdity at the present day to speak as though there were one single ideal of life which we can call essentially *the* modern view whether within the limits of professed

Christianity or outside it. And some of our modern ideals I do not attempt to represent as Christian at all. More and more in fact the real battleground between the Church and its foes will turn, I believe, on this question of the moral ideal : more and more the theological differences themselves will be such as directly flow from the ethical differences. Of those who seriously accept the Christian ideal of self-sacrifice for the common good and whose conception of that good is not mere indulgence of the flesh, we can say that, inasmuch as they are not against us they are for us—even though they may not always follow with us on theological matters. Nietzsche's ideal of pure selfishness ; the ideals of Mr. H. G. Wells in the matter of sexual relations ; the exaltation of æsthetic culture above humanity and charity to which there is at least a strong tendency in many quarters ; the defence of unlimited, cruel, relentless competition which sometimes (quite illogically I venture to think) attempts to ground itself on the Darwinian survival of the fittest—these and many other current moralities or immoralities can never be " baptized into Christ." [1] There is a sense in which we may justly say that the modern Christian ideal " accepts " or " affirms " the world, but not the world just as it stands with all its commonplace, conventional moralities and its still

[1] I might add now the international Immoralism of Treitschke and Bernhardi, more or less sanctioned by not a few German Theologians, Roman Catholic, Liberal, and Orthodox Protestant.

lower practice. There is still and always will be a " world " which the Christian has got to renounce, as remorselessly as ever.

Secondly, it must not be supposed that in what I have said as to the return of the modern Church to the ideal of Christ Himself, I am attempting to defend the version of the Christian ideal which is often accepted even in professedly religious communities and circles as one which is really in accordance with the ideas of Christ. The most that I have ventured to claim for the ideal which modern Christians acknowledge is that we have made a beginning towards a return to the true spirit of Jesus. If there is one thing which can be claimed as a definite discovery of modern Christianity, as a really new idea in Christian Ethics, it is this—that we have got not merely to remedy social evils when they have once arisen, but to take measures against their arising. The great defect of the Christian ideal as it has commonly been understood in all past times, whether we think of the Apostolic Church, of the patristic Church, of medieval Christendom, or of modern Protestantism, is this—that Christian Charity has contented itself far too much with curing sin, with relieving suffering, with removing injustices, with mitigating poverty, instead of trying so systematically to organize human society that suffering and injustice shall, as far as possible, not arise, and that undeserved poverty shall altogether cease. We have only just begun to recognize this as the true aim of

Christian morality : how much remains to be altered in our ordinary manner of living, in our ordinary standards of comfort and expenditure, in our ordinary manner of doing business, in the manners and view of life which are practically received and acted upon by most religious people, I must forbear to estimate. I will only insist that the change that seems to be called for is very great and far-reaching. There may be many different opinions as to the way in which human society ought to be reorganized so as to realize the closest possible approximation to Christ's ideal of a society in which all men treat each other as brothers. That such a reorganization is required, and that Christians are bound to strive for it, is a matter about which there ought to be no doubt or difference of opinion among Christians. We have not the excuses which Christians of past ages could plead for neglecting this side of Christian Ethics. We do not believe that in consequence of the first man's sin the world has been given over to the dominion of the devil. We do not believe that human nature has been so deeply corrupted that no trace of the divine image is left in it ; we do not believe that the world is just on the point of coming to an end, so that there is no use in trying to make things better for those who come after us ; we do not believe that in moderation the pleasure and enjoyment in which rich people indulge—still less their education and their intellectual activities—are so hopelessly vile and contemptible that it would be

Q

positively wrong to try and extend them in some measure to the poor. And therefore, whatever the spirit of Christ may have prescribed to those who did entertain these beliefs, that same spirit prescribes a very different course to ourselves. And, whatever view we may hold as to the proper means of social regeneration, one thing is certain. It is simply impossible that the poor can ever be made even a little richer without the rich being made, whether by legislation or by their own voluntary action, a good deal poorer. And therefore it must not be supposed that the modern interpretation of Christ's ideal will ever cease to include the element of self-sacrifice. Self-inflicted pain, pain for its own sake, is no part of Christ's ideal : self-sacrifice for the sake of others—as a means to social good—represents the very central idea of all Morality ; and it is just because it does assert the supreme value and necessity of this self-sacrifice for the good of all in a way that no other historical religion has done, that Christ's ideal maintains its identity through all the inevitable and legitimate developments in detail which it has undergone ; that it is still the ideal which the modern world wants, and which all that is best in the modern world consciously or unconsciously acknowledges.

ADDITIONAL NOTE ON CHRISTIAN ETHICS IN THE APOSTOLIC WRITINGS

In a more extended course the natural sequel of Lecture V would be a lecture, or several lectures, on the Ethics of the New Testament outside the actual teaching of Christ, but to attempt such a task with any thoroughness would carry me beyond the limits prescribed by the scheme of these lectures ; and if all the New Testament writings were to be included, it would be difficult to avoid extending the enquiry some way into the early history of the Church, for the latest New Testament writings are possibly later than some uncanonical writings. In lieu of any such systematic treatment, I will endeavour to exhibit in very brief outline the chief lines of development which Christian Ethics underwent in the hands of the most important New Testament writers.

(1) St. Paul was probably the first fully to grasp the Universalism implied in the teaching of our Lord Himself, and formally to proclaim that the Jewish ceremonial law was not binding on Gentiles ; though the way for his work was largely prepared for him by St. Stephen (Acts vii.), and the men of Cyprus and Cyrene who for the first time preached Christianity to Gentiles at Antioch (Acts viii. 4 ; xi. 20). St. Paul seems personally to have observed the Law, but to have done so rather as a matter of expediency and national custom than as a matter of strict moral obligation. He refused to observe the letter of the law, or at least the rabbinical amplification of it, in so far as

227

that forbade social and religious intercourse with Gentiles. This principle is fully accepted by all the other New Testament writings, where they explicitly touch upon the subject. This Universalism is especially prominent in the Johannine writings, which (whoever was their author) are assuredly not independent of Pauline influence.

(2) The distinction thus effected between the moral and the ceremonial law made it possible for the Apostles to assert the essential principles of our Lord's teaching—the inclusion of all Morality in the duty of brotherly love—in an absolutely explicit way. " Owe no man anything, save to love one another : for he that loveth his neighbour hath fulfilled the law. For this, Thou shalt not commit adultery, Thou shalt not kill, Thou shalt not steal, Thou shalt not covet, and if there be any other command- ment, it is summed up in this word, namely, Thou shalt love thy neighbour as thyself " (Rom. xiii. 8, 9 ; cf. also Gal. v. 14). In the same spirit love is recognized as superior in intrinsic value to all other personal qualities, even to spiritual gifts of the highest value, even to Faith and to Hope : " but the greatest of these is Charity " (1 Cor. xiii. 13). Completely consonant with this is the teaching of the Johannine writings. " This is the message which ye heard from the beginning, that we should love one another " (1 John iii. 11). " He that loveth not knoweth not God ; for God is love " (1 John iv. 8). The whole of the first Epistle is a magnificent embodiment of the inmost essence of Christ's own teaching.[1] The Epistle of St. James has been supposed to have a Jewish tone about it, but nowhere is the supremacy and all-inclusive- ness of the command " Thou shalt love thy neighbour as

---

[1] The same may be said of many portions of the fourth Gospel, even where the sayings cannot be treated as actual records of the Master's teaching.

thyself" more fully recognized (James ii.). Cf. 1 Peter i. 22, iii. 8, iv. 8 ; Heb. xiii. 1.

(3) Those special virtues and duties which, though they may in a sense be regarded as all embraced in Love (since they all contribute to the true good of Humanity), are not obviously coincident with mere kindness, are enforced with more detail than in the teaching of our Lord. The necessity for such enforcement naturally arose with the growth of organized Christian communities, especially of Gentile communities in which ordinary Jewish moral ideas could not be taken for granted. In particular it became necessary to insist emphatically on abstinence from various sins of the flesh, from drunkenness and revelling, and from " filthy talking" (Rom. xiii. 13; 1 Cor. v., vi. 9–20; Eph. iv. 19, 29 ; v. 3–12 ; 1 Thess. iv. 3–8 ; 1 Peter ii. 11, 12 ; iv. 1–7). There is for the most part nothing in this teaching which goes beyond ordinary Jewish ideals, except that our Lord's teaching about the permanence of marriage is pre· supposed wherever the subject is touched upon. The doctrine of love is further developed and applied to the details of personal conduct with far greater minuteness than is the case in the teaching of Christ, who could pre-suppose the ordinary Jewish Morality, and who aimed chiefly at arousing conscience and insisting upon a few great principles, especially those not generally recognized. Thus we get in St. Paul long lists of virtues or qualities which may be said to be closely akin to love, and of the vices which are opposed to it. See Rom. i. 28–31 ; xii. 9–19 ; Gal. v. 16–26 ; Col. iii. 5–14.

Among the virtues specially insisted upon are Veracity and Humility. Both of these are based upon the principle of Love. " Wherefore, putting away falsehood, speak ye truth each one with his neighbour ; for we are members one of another " (Eph. iv. 25 ; cf. Col. iii. 9). " In love of the brethren be tenderly affectioned one to another, in honour preferring one another " (Rom. xii. 10 ; cf. Phil. ii. 3, 4 ; 1 Peter v. 5 ; James iv. 6). In various other directions the duty of love is translated into distinct precepts. In all the Apostolic writings there is a strong insistence upon the duty of Almsgiving, which was made particularly necessary by the circumstances of the early Christian Church at Jerusalem and by the prevalence of petty persecution : the organization of Charity was one main function of the Christian communities and their leaders (Rom. xii. 8; 1 Cor. ix., xvi.; 2 Cor. viii., ix., xi. 8, 9). The expectation of the Parousia and the reliance upon extensive Charity from the Church made it necessary to insist with peculiar emphasis on the duty of all to work for the support of themselves and their families (Eph. iv. 28 ; 1 Thess. iv. 11 ; 2 Thess. iii. 10–12).

(4) The circumstances of the early Church raised various questions of Casuistry, which demanded explicit solution for the guidance both of individual Christians and of the Christian Communities and their rulers. Of these the most important were the question of meats offered to idols (Rom. xiv. 14 ; 1 Cor. viii., x.) ; intermarriage with the heathen (1 Cor. vii. 12–17 ; 2 Cor. vi. 14–18) ; the marital relations of Christians (1 Cor. vii. 3–5) ; divorce (1 Cor. vii. 39). It will be generally admitted that the decisions of St. Paul were on the whole entirely in accordance with the dictates of Christian common sense. As to divorce (1 Cor. vii. 39) St. Paul seems to forbid remarriage on the part of the wife, apparently even if divorced by her husband: he does not deal with the parallel case of the husband, nor explicitly with the question of divorce in the case of adultery. In one matter he defines a point which his Master had naturally not defined ; he allows a husband or wife converted from heathenism, whose partner

refuses to continue the co-habitation, freedom to depart, and apparently to marry again. And this is the principle upon which the Christian Church has always acted, so far as the dissolution of the heathen marriage is recognized by the civil law of the country (1 Cor. vii. 15).

(5) The organization of the Christian Churches called for the enforcement upon Christians of a number of new duties — duties of attendance at public worship and perseverance in Christian devotion, public and private (Col. iii. 16) ; proper behaviour at the love-feasts and other religious gatherings (1 Cor. xi., xii., xiv.) ; good government on the part of rulers, obedience to ecclesiastical authority on the part of those ruled (1 Cor. xvi. 15–18 ; 1 Thess. v. 12) ; the promotion of internal harmony and the avoidance of quarrelling or litigation among fellow-Christians and of party spirit (Rom. xii. 17–19 ; 1 Cor. i. 10–12 ; vi. 1–8 ; 2 Cor. xii. 19–21 ; Phil. ii. 1–3 ; Col. iii. 12, 13) ; zealous performance of various functions in connexion with the spiritual as well as the charitable work of the community (Rom. xii. ; 1 Cor. xii., xiv.) ; a combination of severity with mercy in the exercise of discipline by rulers and communities (1 Cor. v. ; 2 Cor. vii., xiii. ; 2 Thess. iii. 6) ; hospitality to fellow-Christians (Rom. xii. 13) ; the duty of supporting those who devote themselves to Apostolic work, though St. Paul personally declined to avail himself of such support (1 Cor. ix.). The exact degree of value—temporary or permanent—which we ought to recognize in all these regulations would involve a treatise upon the Church, its functions, and its organization. Suffice it to say that anyone who recognizes the absolute necessity of ecclesiastical organization for the carrying out of Christ's work and the diffusion of His principles throughout the world must admit the necessity of some

such rules ; and few will be disposed to deny that on the whole the precepts of St. Paul and the other Apostolic writers on this head do represent a thoroughly legitimate application to the circumstances of the early Christian communities of the fundamental ideas of our Lord's own ethical teaching. The obligation to obey such rules is based upon the principle of mutual Love, which carries with it the duty of co-operating with others, of subordinating individual interests and inclinations, and even to some extent private judgement in matters of unessential detail, for the good of the Christian community and the extension of its work among " those that are without." The chief point on which exception might be taken to St. Paul's actual rulings is his treatment of the position of women in the Church Association (1 Cor. xiv. 34–36). This is a point on which the Christian world is still divided ; but few will dispute the wisdom for St. Paul and the Church of his day in deferring to the general sentiment of their time.

(6) Another department of duty which called for more explicit treatment than was required in our Lord's own teaching was that of obedience to the State. This is enforced by St. Paul and by the author of 1 Peter in a way which was no doubt demanded by the circumstances of the time, however unfortunate the precedent they have supplied for doctrines of " divine right " and absolute non-resistance in later ages (Rom. xiii. 1–7). The principle that the State, according to the true idea of it—even a non-Christian State—is a minister of God for good to its subjects, may be regarded as a new ethical principle of enduring value (cf. 1 Peter ii. 13–17).

(7) Patient endurance of suffering is one of the duties which the circumstances of the first Christians obviously called upon their teachers to enforce. It is frequently

insisted on in all the Epistles, and is the main subject of the first Epistle ascribed to St. Peter. Since effective resistance to the State was for the first Christians wholly out of the question, and would have been absolutely fatal to the progress of the Christian faith, it cannot be said that there is undue insistence upon the idea of passive submission. The prominence of such exhortations in the Epistles has no doubt sometimes suggested a too passive interpretation of the Christian ideal; but this tendency has been chiefly theoretical except when the abuse of these passages suited the purpose of a political or ecclesiastical party.

(8) Another kind of development is to be found in the application of general principles of Christian conduct to the various special relations of life. St. Paul in particular insists on the mutual obligations of husband and wife (Eph. v. 22–33 ; Col. iii. 18, 19 ; 1 Peter iii. 1–7), of parents and children (Eph. vi. 1–4 ; Col. iii. 20, 21) ; of master and slave (1 Cor. vii. 21–24 ; Eph. vi. 5–9 ; Col. iii. 22–25 ; 1 Peter ii. 18–20). The details of these duties are conceived of in accordance with the best ideas of the time alike among Jews and Gentiles ; but a new spirit is infused into them by the prominence which Christian teaching gave to Love and mutual goodwill in all the relations of life. This is especially prominent in the case of the mutual obligations of slave and slave-master. There is of course no opposition to the institution of slavery in itself. It required a thousand or eighteen hundred years more of development before anything of the kind became possible. But the principles laid down by St. Paul contain in themselves, if duly carried out, the condemnation of the whole institution. Doubtless St. Paul never contemplated that they would have that effect ; but, if he had done so, the course which he took would still have been regarded by wise men as the only

one immediately practicable—to lay down moral principles and leave the political applications to the future. The only point of immediate application on which a modern Christian would be likely to differ from him would be in his advice to the slave to remain a slave if he had the opportunity of being free ; but it is not certain that his " Use it rather " (μᾶλλον χρῆσαι, I Cor. vii. 21) does not mean " Avail yourselves of the opportunity."

So far we may, I think, recognize the ethical teaching of the Epistles as a legitimate development of our Lord's actual teaching, and as supplying a type and pattern for the kind of development which must always be going on if the Christian spirit is to be applied to the needs of widely different ages and countries, and if what is true and noble in other ethical ideals and systems is to be accepted and brought into its proper relation with those fundamental Christian ideas. But it would be too much to say that the spirit of the Apostolic and Sub-apostolic age was altogether after the mind of Christ, or represents in every respect a model for our own imitation. It may be well briefly to notice the points on which some reservation is necessary :

(1) There is something in the spirit of the Apocalypse which may be thought Jewish rather than Christian. The book is probably based upon an old Jewish Apocalypse, or rather many Apocalypses, edited by a Christian hand or hands; but the editing—whoever was responsible for it —is hardly sufficient to warrant its use as an authority for Christian conduct. It exhibits a certain ferocity towards heathen persecutors, but it does not contain much in the way of ethical precept. We know too little of the errors denounced in the Epistles to the Churches to be able to judge how far they were merely theological mistakes or how far they involved a moral laxity which

justified strong denunciation. To a considerable extent it is probable that this last was the case.

(2) The expectation of the Parousia narrowed the Christian outlook upon life. For the most part the ethical deficiencies which it brought with it were negative. Men expecting a catastrophic judgement of the world in a few years' time were not likely to attach their true value to Art, Knowledge, schemes of widely expanded and gradual social improvement (such a limitation, by the way, is almost equally characteristic of the best philosophic Ethics of the time). It involved almost inevitably (though not perhaps logically) some tendency to other-worldliness—though the extent of this may very easily be exaggerated. The temptations which it brought with it to idleness, undue religious excitement, neglect of family obligations and the like were fully appreciated and corrected by the Apostolic leaders themselves (see especially 1 Thess. iv. 11 ; 2 Thess. iii. 6–15).

(3) There are few traces of excessive Asceticism in the Apostolic or Post-apostolic ideals. Extreme asceticism, and a disposition to rely upon it, was a characteristic of the heresies with which they were engaged in combating. Dogmatic prohibitions or scruples about particular kinds of food or drink are severely condemned. Still, we cannot quite positively say that even St. Paul actually adopted our Lord's attitude towards fasting (see above, p. 160 *sq.*). If we may rely upon Acts (x. 30 ; xiii. 3 ; xiv. 23), the practice of fasting was kept up in the earliest Church. But the allusion to fasting in 1 Corinthians vii. 5 is due to a transcriber (rejected in R.V.) ; and it is doubtful whether in 2 Corinthians vi. 5, xi. 27, St. Paul is referring to ecclesiastical fasting or (as seems more probable) to privations endured in the course of Apostolic journeys. 1 Cor. ix. 27 is too vague to be appealed to in this con-

nexion ; all Christians recognize the duty of self-control in the matter of bodily appetites.

(4) St. Paul's idealization of the married relation, which he used to typify the relation between Christ and His Church, began that spiritualization of the marriage ideal which has been one of the most undoubted achievements of later Christianity. But in practice he does not seem himself to have advanced very much beyond the average Jewish view of marriage. He looks upon it too much as a mere preservative against worse evils (1 Cor. vii.). All through his treatment of the subject, especially in his condemnation of second marriages, there is a distinct inclination to the ascetic disparagement of Marriage, though his strong common sense and experience of the evils arising from the undue exaltation of celibacy prevented his carrying the tendency far. His attitude was largely no doubt due to the expectation of an immediate Parousia. The emphatic contradiction of St. Paul's advice in 1 Timothy v. 14 (" that the younger widows marry ") may no doubt be attributed to a waning confidence in the nearness of this event, and to experience of the evils which the exaltation of virginity and widowhood had brought with it.

(5) The most serious deduction from what has been said as to the generally Christian temper of the Apostolic Morality is to be found in the attitude which the development of the visible Church (considering the intellectual limitations of its leaders) almost necessarily involved towards heresy, schism, and every form of rebellion against ecclesiastical authority. The Christian Conscience can hardly approve " the Lord reward him according to his works " (2 Tim. iv. 14, there is much MS. authority for " shall reward "). But it is in the Johannine writings that the tendency towards the

identification of all persons, all forms of life, and all forms of belief outside the legitimate Church with the " world "—a world regarded as actively hostile to Christ and all good—is carried furthest. The existence of quite unjustified and savage persecution from outside and the strong disposition of the early heresies to associate themselves with moral laxity may go far to excuse this temper as regards heretics within (or claiming to be within) the Christian fold ; while the moral condition of the pagan world (especially as regards sexual morality) fully justified the conception of a broad ethical contrast between the two worlds. Christians were justified in regarding with horror and hostility the dominant temper of ordinary pagan life, though doubtless there was more good in the best circles of the pagan world than some of them could recognize. But it is hardly possible to deny that the germs are to be found in the New Testament itself of that tendency to attribute high merit to orthodoxy of belief and of that intolerance towards unbelievers or unorthodox believers which constitute such an appalling set-off to the enormous benefits which the Christian Church has conferred upon the world. So far even the best and greatest of Apostles and Apostolic men fell below the spiritual level of their Master. Even in the attitude adopted towards actual sin, the doctrine of the Epistle to the Hebrews (vi. 6) that no repentance for wilful post-baptismal sin was possible must be regarded as a falling off from our Lord's own teaching on the forgivingness of God. Happily that attitude was soon corrected by the charity and the common sense of the Church.

I have rarely used the Pastoral Epistles for illustration ; though much in them may well come from the pen of

St. Paul, it is probable that, in their present form, they represent the ideas of a generation later than the Apostolic age : but there is in them, in the way of positive precept, little which is not quite in the spirit of St. Paul. They consist for the most part in the application of the general principles of Christian Morality to a more developed—but still fairly simple—ecclesiastical organization.

For an elaborate examination of the moral ideal and especially the internal moral condition of the early Christian communities I may refer to the excellent work of Prof. von Dobschütz, *Christian Life in the Primitive Church* (Trans. by Rev. G. Bremner). Though the Professor belongs to a school rather disposed to deny the necessity or value of " development," the book affords striking testimony to the historical fact of such development at least within the ethical region, and constitutes on the whole a vindication of the form which it assumed.

LECTURE VI

CHRISTIAN ETHICS AND OTHER SYSTEMS

I HAVE endeavoured in previous lectures to establish three points : (1) That in its fundamental principles the ideal of life presented to us by Christ Himself still commends itself to our moral consciousness ; (2) that these principles require development, and (3) that the development which is demanded by the Christian consciousness of to-day is one which can be recognized as a true and legitimate outgrowth of the Master's own teaching. At this point the question may be raised, " Granted that this ethical ideal is true, is it at all peculiar to Jesus ? Can we not find in other ethical systems the same fundamental principles, and are not those principles equally capable of such a development as is being actually given to them in the Christian Church of to-day ? Is there any reason why at the present day we should regard ourselves as in any paramount or exclusive sense disciples of Jesus ? " These are the questions which I propose to discuss in the present lecture.

I should like to begin by saying that from a practical point of view—for the purposes of the individual religious life—it is not a matter of *primary* importance to determine how far the ethical teaching of Jesus was original when it was first given to the world, or how far other teachers may or may not have taught the same principles since His time. If those principles are true, if the development that has been, or at all events may now be, given to them within the limits of the Christian Church is a legitimate development, they will be none the less true because the same truths may have been taught by other teachers also. That remark holds also of the distinctively religious or theological side of Christianity. The fact that the same truths had been revealed to others through other teachers would not alter the truth of the revelation in Christ. To admit that might no doubt involve some change in our ideas about the Person of Jesus Himself ; but so long as we are looking upon Him simply as an ethical Teacher, the fact that other teachers have taught the same things, will not supply us with any reason for ceasing to regard ourselves as disciples of Christ.

We ought therefore to examine the originality and distinctiveness of Christ's teaching with a perfectly open mind. How far then, to take the central point of His teaching, has the doctrine of universal Brotherhood been taught by others besides Christ and independently of Him ? First, I will say something as to the teaching of Moralists outside the great historical Religions. I have already endeavoured to show how far Aristotle fell below the teaching of Jesus—how far in many respects he fell below the moral standard of the later Judaism—the standard which is presupposed by the teaching of Jesus Himself. But it would be quite unfair to look upon Aristotle as representing the highest ethical thought of the ancient world. Some writers—notably the revered Thomas Hill Green— have at times encouraged the notion that such was the case. They have written as though the Morality we now profess was substantially the Morality of Aristotle a little widened and expanded by Christianity, as though no important ethical development had intervened between Aristotle and Christianity. As a matter of fact, Aristotle represents not the highest ethical standard of the ancient world, but in some respects one of the lowest among highly civilized Moralities. His is the least modern, the least universalistic, the least humane—the most intensely aristocratic, particularistic, and intellectualistic—of ancient Moralities. It is the Morality of the little slave-holding aristocratic class in the autonomous City-state. In the very next generation, when the destruction of the ancient Polis system by Aristotle's friend and master Alexander the Great had begun to do its work, we find a higher and more cosmopolitan Morality. You find little or nothing about the brotherhood of man in Aristotle. You begin to find it in the writings of Aristotle's own pupils—in Theophrastus, for instance. There had been a little more of it in Plato, and there was much more of it in the later Platonists. But it is

R

above all in the writers of the Stoic school that we
encounter the closest parallels to the teaching of Jesus
and of primitive Christianity. Is there anything in the
teaching of Jesus—I am confining myself now to His
ethical teaching—which you do not find in the Stoics ?
I think it may fairly be said that the fundamental
principles of the Sermon on the Mount are to be found
in the great Stoic writers. The essential principle that
we ought to treat every human being as an end in
himself as philosophers say—that we ought to love our
neighbour as ourselves or to treat him as a brother
as Christian Morality more simply expresses it—is
fully taught by such writers as Zeno, Seneca, Epictetus,
and Marcus Aurelius. The supreme value of moral
goodness—as the most important element in human
good—is as fully and completely expressed by them
as it has been by any Christian writer. The superiority
of spiritual good to carnal is duly emphasized, nor
can it be said that there is any over-estimation of
intellectual activity—rather perhaps too little appreciation of any knowledge or culture which has no
direct bearing upon individual character or social
welfare.

Here are a few of the passages in Seneca which
afford the closest approximation to the Sermon on
the Mount. " We will enjoin him to hold out his
hand to the shipwrecked, to point out the way to
the wanderer, to divide his bread with the hungry,"[1]

[1] Ep. Mor., XCV. Seneca is singing the praises of Friendship.

" You must live for another if you would live for yourself,"[1] " I will so live as if I knew that I was born for others."[2] There is no fundamental distinction between the slave and the freeman. " They are slaves," you urge, "nay, they are men. . . . They are slaves, nay, they are humble friends. They are slaves, nay, they are fellow-slaves, if you reflect that fortune has the same power over both. . . . Let some of them dine with you, because they are worthy—others that they may become worthy. . . . He is a slave, you say, yet perchance he is free in spirit."[3] " I will be agreeable to friends, gentle and yielding to enemies."[4] " We will not cease to serve the common good, to help individuals, to give aid even to enemies."[5] " If you imitate the gods, confer benefits even on the unthankful : for the Sun arises even on the wicked, and the seas are open to pirates."[6] " One ought so to give that another may receive. It is not giving or receiving to transfer to the right hand or to the left."[7] " Expect from others what you have done to another."[8] " Let us so give as we would wish to receive."[9] The intrinsic value of goodness, the importance of pure intention, the inwardness of true virtue, are taught in language which, both on its strictly ethical and on its religious side, is closely parallel to sayings

---

[1] Ep. Mor., XLVIII.
[2] De vit. beat., 20.
[3] Ep. Mor., XLVII.
[4] De vit. beat., 20.
[5] De Otio, 28.
[6] De Benef., iv. 26.
[7] *Ib.*, v. 8.
[8] Ep. Mor., XCIV (in a quotation).
[9] De Benef., ii. 1.

of Jesus. " So live with men, as if God saw you ; so speak with God, as if men heard you."[1] " Cast out whatsoever things rend thy heart ; nay, if they could not be extracted otherwise, then thou shouldest have plucked out thy heart itself with them."[2] " Apply thyself rather to true riches. . . . It is shameful to depend for a happy life on gold and silver."[3] There are a number of other parallels (collected in the well-known Essay of Bishop Lightfoot),[4] both to the teaching of our Lord and of St. Paul so close that, if it were not quite impossible in the case of our Lord and highly improbable in the case of St. Paul, an incautious critic would be certain to pronounce that there must have been borrowing on one side or the other.

Much the same spirit pervades the writings of M. Aurelius and Epictetus. " Love the human race. Follow God," says M. Aurelius.[5] " It is the characteristic of man to love even those who do wrong."[6] " Whatever action of thine has no bearing, either directly or indirectly, upon the social end, tears thy life asunder and destroys its unity and involves sedition "[7] ($\sigma\tau\alpha\sigma\iota\acute{\omega}\delta\eta\varsigma$). " Anger is not manly ; but meekness and gentleness, as they are more human, so they are more masculine."[8] M. Aurelius is particularly full of exhortations to forgiveness and gentleness towards

---

[1] Ep. Mor., X.   [2] *Ib.*, LI.   [3] *Ib.*, CX.
[4] Appended to his edition of the Epistle to the Philippians.
[5] Meditations, VII, 31.   [6] *Ib.*, VII, 22.
[7] *Ib.*, IX, 23.   [8] *Ib.*, XI, 18. Cf. the whole chapter.

those who injure or revile one : and he was a man who had opportunities of dealing with detractors as Nero and Domitian dealt with them.

Exhortation to universal Benevolence is a little less prominent in Epictetus, but he is full of the thought that man is a citizen of the world,[1] and the religious aspect of Morality is more marked in him than in the other two writers. His conception of God is a distinctly ethical conception, if he more often speaks of His essential rationality than of His love.[2]

As far as they go, such maxims as I have quoted must be pronounced wholly in accordance with the spirit of Christ. But, as I have so often found it necessary to observe, the real concrete meaning of an ethical formula can only be discovered from its context—the context in which it stands in the whole teaching and ideal of the teacher. It would be possible to collect from the great Stoic writers a considerable list of maxims quite inconsistent with the Christian

---

[1] " Thou art a citizen of the world and a part of it, not one of its subjects but of its rulers. . . . The whole is more important than the part, and the city than the individual citizen " (Arrian, *Discourses of Epictetus*, ii. 10).

[2] God is " Intellect, Knowledge, Right Reason " (l.c., ii. 8). Man is " a spark of God ; thou hast a piece of Him in thee " (*ib.*). " Philosophers say that we ought first of all to learn that God exists and takes thought for the Universe, and that we cannot escape His notice not only in what we do but even in the secret thoughts of our hearts." " He who would please the Gods must endeavour to become like them so far as he can. If the Divinity is faithful, he too must be faithful : if free, he too must be free ; if beneficent (εὐεργετικόν), he too must be beneficent ; if generous, he too must be generous. And so in everything else he must act and speak as befits an imitator of God " (*ib.*, ii. 14).

principles which they elsewhere profess. At one time, for instance, Seneca urges forgiveness ; at other times he practically adopts the maxim, " Thou shalt love thy friend, and hate thine enemy." He has not fully understood the principle which Plato might have taught him, that, when punishment should be inflicted, it is really a kindness. It is only consistent with this cruder and lower side of Stoic morality that, though personal insults are often to be ignored, forgiveness of moral wrong-doing is actually condemned.[1] As to their teaching on the sexual side of Morality, I will only say that there is some difficulty in understanding what it was, and that it seems to have fallen far short of the Christian standard.[2]

Moreover, if we penetrate to the fundamental principles of the Stoic school, we shall find in them three elements which were really inconsistent with their own teaching about universal Benevolence. (a) In the first place the very exaggeration of their doctrine that moral goodness was the sole good of Humanity, the

[1] De Clem., ii. 5–7. So to be indulgent to the sinner would imply that the man had not sinned voluntarily (μὴ παρ' αὐτὸν ἡμαρτηκέναι). Stobæus, Floril., 46. 50. The paradoxical doctrine that there are no degrees of virtue, and that all sins are equal, is in accordance with this line of thought. The parable of the talents and the saying about many stripes and few stripes correspond much better to the moral instincts of unsophisticated Humanity.

[2] The idea of living according to Nature seems sometimes to have been understood in a coarse and immoral sense. It is suggested that in an ideal state there would be a community of wives, and the duty of recognizing the accepted restrictions is based solely on the authority of the State. See Zeller's *Stoics, Epicureans and Sceptics*, E.T., 1870, p. 290 sq., and the passages there quoted.

only thing necessary to happiness, militated against Benevolence. If pleasure is no good for myself, it is no good for others, and I need not trouble myself about other people's pleasures : if pain is no evil, why should I seek to mitigate it ? The Stoic idea of Apathy required the suppression of the altruistic as much as of the egoistic passions. And this conclusion was explicitly drawn by the Stoics themselves. They often (though happily not with complete consistency) despised and condemned pity, and their exhortations to forgiveness were too often tinged with contempt. " There is no reason why thou shouldest be angry; pardon them, they are all mad."[1]   (*b*) Secondly, this condemnation of pity was only a part of a general condemnation of feeling. They deliberately attempted to suppress and exterminate all emotion. They held, no doubt, that the wise man will often do in obedience to Reason the things which less wise men do from emotion. He will relieve suffering, but he feels no pity for the sufferer. He will punish the wrong-doer, but righteous indignation must be suppressed no less than the spirit of personal revenge. The Stoics were right, no doubt, in thinking that mere affection for individuals not guided or controlled by a Reason which attempts to be impartial or universal is not Virtue at its highest. But it was scarcely possible that thinkers who condemned the emotion which is and practically always must be the chief inspiring source of Benevo-

[1] De Beneficiis, v. 17.

lence, should give its right place in Ethics to Love.
Nobody ever served men more heartily and con-
scientiously than M. Aurelius. Perhaps he loved them
too : but in his attitude towards the vast majority
there was a touch of contempt. It is impossible to discover in him that recognition of undeveloped possibilities of goodness in the publican and the sinner
which was so conspicuous a feature in the character of
Jesus. Virtue was only possible to the wise man. And
wise men, it was admitted, must always be few even
among the intellectual. Wisdom, and therefore the
highest virtue, was not possible for the uneducated or
the stupid. And this is closely connected with a third
radical defect in Stoic Morality. (*c*) The starting-point
of the Stoic Morality was the desire to find peace or
unruffled tranquillity for the individual soul. The
fundamental tenet of the school was that nothing was
really good or evil which was not dependent solely on
the will. Virtue was recommended because it was
the only good which depended entirely upon the man
himself. Thus the Stoic was too much disposed to
commend Virtue not because it was good, but because
it was *his* good. Such an ideal produced a self-sufficiency and self-absorption which did not conduce to—
perhaps were hardly compatible with—the highest
unselfishness. And it certainly tended towards that
excessive sense of personal dignity which we commonly call pride. Hence the encouragement to suicide,
even in cases where a man's opportunities of social

service were by no means at an end. It was in order
to be independent of the accidents of human life, to
be sure of attaining the true good for himself, that the
Stoic school originally recommended men to think of
nothing but Virtue.

I do not, indeed, hold, as has been strangely suggested in some quarters, that whereas all the other
virtues could be discovered by the natural capacity of
the moral consciousness, a special and strictly supernatural revelation was required to teach the value of
Humility.   There is something singularly grotesque
in the notion of a man being humble because, though
he could not see any essential beauty or excellence in
it, he had received a supernatural communication of
the fact that he ought to be humble. Rather should
we say that Humility at bottom (in the form in which
it really is a virtue) is only a particular form or manifestation of the love which cares for others, for their
rights and their virtues and their achievements, as
much as for self. The want of humility in the Stoic
ideal is just one of the little indications that, in spite
of all the formal correctness of its maxims, the beauty
of unselfishness was not yet fully appreciated. There
was an ambiguity about their fundamental principle
of living agreeably to nature. In so far as this meant
living in accordance with the true nature of man, it
was a sound and Christian maxim.[1] But its original
meaning was perhaps simply to live in accordance

[1] Cf. Butler, Sermon I.

with the actual nature of the physical Universe ; and
it never altogether lost this side of its significance. So
understood, it amounted to little more than a prudential counsel to avoid setting one's heart upon
things which fortune might take away. There was,
indeed, the root of all true Morality in the idea
that moral conduct was to act on universal principles,
and this implied that a man should regard himself as
a citizen of the world and promote its good. But the
school never quite succeeded in escaping from what
seems to have been the original thought of its founder
— that virtue was the right means to that unruffled tranquillity of the whole life which the Epi-
curians less wisely sought in pleasure. The Stoic
Apathy ($\dot{a}\pi a\theta\epsilon\acute{\iota}a$) was not so very far in principle
from the untroubled calm ($\dot{a}\tau a\rho a\xi\acute{\iota}a$) of the Epicurean,
though much nobler in practice. The later develop-
ment of the school was on the whole away from this
original Egoism. The altruistic, universalistic side of
Stoicism steadily gained upon the individualistic, and
reached its final achievement in the teaching and the
life of M. Aurelius Antoninus.[1]

[1] The opinions of Zeno himself, as distinct from those of his
followers, are not known with much certainty, but on the whole the
account of the growth of Stoicism in Zeller and the authorities
which he cites support this view of its development. The origin of
Stoicism was a pessimistic turning away from politics and social
life in its old narrow, civic form. The individual, unable to find
true happiness in active political life, was thrown back upon himself. It was only gradually that the growth of the Roman Empire,
and the widening of ethical ideals which accompanied it, suggested
that the service of Humanity supplied a nobler sphere for practical
activity than the ancient Polis.

And yet, apart from all dogmatic considerations, few people feel that M. Aurelius is the equal of Jesus. The defects of Stoic Morality on which I have already dwelt are discernible even in him—in his teaching and in his character. It was not altogether through mere accident or mere misunderstanding that the best of pagans became the persecutor of the community in which his own ideal of life was more nearly realized than it was among any other section of his subjects. Under no possible circumstances can we imagine Jesus becoming the persecutor of a group of men who, whatever their tenets, worshipped that common Father of whom M. Aurelius vaguely spoke, and made it their chief aim to love one another. When Christians took to persecution, they had largely ceased to be followers of Jesus, and one great source of the corruption lay in an infusion of that very imperial spirit of ancient Rome which, with all his cosmopolitanism, revealed itself in M. Aurelius' persecution of the Christians.

And then I would once again call your attention to the principle that, when we are treating of an ethical system not as formal Philosophy but as practical teaching intended to appeal to the emotions and inspire the will, the form is as important as the substance. You can find, as we have seen, beautiful expressions of the duty of love and mercy and forgiveness—some of them so closely parallel to passages of the New Testament as to produce a fallacious appearance of imitation. And yet, taken as a whole, they do not appeal to us as the Sermon on the Mount and the parables of the good Samaritan and the Prodigal Son. They do not make so deep an appeal to the educated— still less to the uneducated. Stoicism was no Gospel for the mass of men. And therefore it was no mere historical accident that, in so far as the Stoic Religion and the Stoic Morality were identical with the Christian, it was not through the Stoic school, but through the Christian Church, that they came to be the accepted Morality of the modern Western world.

Even if we could get over the shortcomings and inconsistencies of Stoicism, if we could identify its theological and ethical teaching with that of Christianity to a greater extent than we can reasonably do, there would still remain this fundamental difference between M. Aurelius and Christ. Christ founded a Religion and a Church : the Stoics founded neither. This is a point of immense importance when we are considering the personal greatness and the historical position of Christ : it is simply decisive when we are discussing the reasons for transferring to M. Aurelius or some other Stoic hero anything like the allegiance that Christians actually own to Christ. There is, indeed, much truth in Mark Pattison's view that, during the three centuries or so before Constantine, Philosophy had been working out a creed which on its ethical side, and to a great extent even on the theological side, was identical with the creed at which the Christian

Church had arrived by quite another route—through the adoption of the Jewish ideal, universalized and completed by Christ and developed by His disciples.[1] But the fact remains that it was Christianity and not the Stoic or any other Philosophy which converted the world to Monotheism and the Ethics of universal Brotherhood. And, further, when Christianity came into contact with Græco-Roman culture, the two parallel currents of spiritual development began to fuse. The teaching of the Christian Fathers absorbed much of what was best in the teaching of Philosophy— especially of this Stoic Philosophy with which we are immediately dealing. There is no need whatever to minimize the close resemblance between the Stoic ideal at its best and the teaching of Christ and of those who drank most deeply of His spirit. The early Apologists were right in appealing to the correspondence between the best teaching of Philosophy and that of the Christian Religion as so much evidence in favour of Christianity, when taken in connexion with the enormously greater success of Christianity in moulding men's lives into conformity with that teaching. To anyone who seriously proposed to revive the Stoicism or the Eclecticism of the later Roman world as a working rule of modern life I should say, " You need not trouble to do that. The Christian Church has already absorbed what Stoicism had to teach. The

[1] See his *Sermons*, which are almost all devoted to the working out of this idea.

best way of practising all that is best in Stoicism—all in it that any modern Conscience is really likely to accept—is to be a Christian."

I do not, of course, deny that at some periods the actual working ideal of Christendom fell in some respects far below Stoicism, or that there were unchristlike elements in it which a renewed study of Stoicism might help us to get rid of. All that is said of " Christianity " here must be taken to mean " Christianity in so far as it has remained faithful to the spirit of its Founder."

I have dwelt thus elaborately on the differences between Stoicism and Christianity because, if one wishes to establish the supremacy of the Christian Ethic, it is fair to compare it with the highest non-Christian ethical system that one knows. Outside Christianity I know of no higher Morality than that of the Stoics. But to those who feel the need for a Religion and a Church or religious community, Stoicism could not possibly be an alternative to Christianity, even if the parallelism between their teaching were closer than it is. In the rest of this lecture I shall speak only of systems or ideals which have embodied themselves in still living historical Religions.

There are at the present day many people who would heartily admit the difference between an ethical philosophy and a religion, and who would freely recognize that Religion is possible on a large scale only in and through some actual historical religion, but who seem to think that it makes little or no difference which, at least among the higher religions, a man belongs to. They will, it may be, consider themselves Christians because they happen to be born in a Christian country, but they do not think the difference between Christianity and other religions—they often forget to mention precisely which religions—sufficient to justify them in supporting a mission whose object it is to invite members of other religions to become Christians. Such persons talk about a " religious experience " which they assume to be the same in all the higher religions. The Theology of the various religions is for them merely the outward historical embodiment of this religious experience, and is an unessential and separable element of such religions. As a matter of history and psychological fact, I believe this position to be profoundly mistaken. I do not mean, of course, that there are no common elements in the higher historical religions, or that there is any great religion in which there is not a measure of truth. The best missionaries of the present day fully and gladly recognize that the Spirit of God has spoken to men through many religions besides the Jewish and the Christian. But two things I regard as certain— (1) That every religion, whatever else it is, always includes a theory of the Universe, and incompatible theories of the Universe cannot all be true. It is as absurd to talk about all the religions being equally true as to talk about all philosophies, or all systems of

Astronomy, being equally true ; (2) that the character
of the religious experience which is possible to any
individual is largely determined by the theory of the
Universe at which he has already and independently
arrived. To get the religious experience characteristic
of a religion, you must believe in its theory of the
Universe. The experience of communion with or love
of a personal God is only possible if one believes in
a God who is capable of loving and being loved. The
experience which Hindoo mystics attempt to describe,
the experience of union with an All which is essentially
non-personal and non-moral (whatever may be its
value), is only possible to one who already believes in
such a non-personal and non-moral Absolute, and
who can share the genuine Hindoo contempt for
Morality as a purely human and transitory affair.
And the two experiences, so far as can be judged
from the expressions of them in language and literature, are profoundly different and incompatible. I
must not enlarge further upon the difference between
the great historical religions on their theological side.
My subject confines me to the ethical differences. And
here, by way of focussing the problem with which we
are concerned, I will allude to a letter which appeared
during one of those correspondences on religious subjects in the newspapers in which the most prominent
part is usually taken on both sides by the now large
class of half-educated persons who believe themselves
to know all about everything. The gentleman in

question informed the world that after a comprehensive survey of all the religions of mankind he had made a great discovery. He had come to the conclusion that there were two elements in every religion —a theological element which varied but was unimportant, and an ethical element which was important but was always the same. Is this really the fact ? Could anyone who has arrived at the conclusion that the ethical teaching of Christianity, as we have understood it, is true reasonably transfer his allegiance to any other Religion on the assumption that its Ethics were the same, even supposing he were right in imagining that the theological differences were unimportant ?

Now in the first place we may, I think, put aside for practical purposes all the lower religions. Roughly and broadly speaking, the higher religions are distinguished from the lower just by the fact that they are, in the full sense of the term, ethical religions. That does not mean that the lower religions have in them no ethical element. There has always been a very close connexion between Religion and Morality : but the nature of this connexion is variable. The primitive religions were primarily systems of rites and ceremonies by which it was thought possible to procure the favour of the gods : and the favour of the gods was not supposed to depend wholly or mainly upon the moral conduct of their worshippers.[1] Some

[1] It may be said that there was always this much that was ethical even in the lowest religions—that they always prescribed the doing of what was beneficial to the tribe ; and attempts have

S

gods, no doubt, did punish some kinds of moral offence :
but the gods were not all of them thought of as ideally
moral beings—some of them were thought of as
grossly immoral and as delighting in certain kinds of
immorality.   Unless a religion at least professes to
identify the will of the supernatural being or beings
whom it worships with the morally good, we need not
seriously discuss its claims to be considered on ethical
grounds an optional alternative to Christianity.   And
this consideration at once limits the religions which it
is necessary to consider to a much smaller number than
might be supposed from the airy talk which we often
hear about the substantial identity of all religions.
Is there then among the few higher religions of the
world any one which teaches substantially the same
Ethics as Christianity ?

I need not say much more than has already been
said about Judaism.   Judaism, as we have seen,
before the coming of Christ never quite rose to the
Christian ideal of universal Brotherhood.   Undoubtedly
there are enlightened Jews of the present day who
heartily accept that supreme ethical truth ; but they
have certainly not arrived at it without direct or

---

been made to draw a sharp line between Religion and Magic on
this basis, practices which were supposed to benefit the individual only being treated as belonging to Magic, and not to Religion.
For some purposes this may be a convenient distinction, but the
distinction cannot be made very sharply.   Even the early Jewish
prophet was much concerned with the recovery of lost property,
and yet it would be absurd to treat Samuel as only a magician and
as having nothing to do with the religion of Israel.

indirect help from Christianity, and they can only consistently teach it by repudiating (as of course is done by Jewish teachers who have accepted the critical position as to the Old Testament) much of the official teaching of their religion.[1] I am not now speaking of possible reforms of the Jewish or other historical religions, but of the religions in their historical, traditional, and official forms. Taking Judaism in that sense, the Ethics of Judaism must be pronounced (to say the least of it) very defective by anyone who has accepted the Christian doctrine that men of all races are equal in the sight of God and equally neighbours to one another, and who denies that the performance of rites and ceremonies such as those prescribed by the Jewish Law can be matters of ethical obligation.

Of Mohammedanism it may still more unequivocally be said that it is founded upon a doctrine of inequality. It is, indeed, universalistic inasmuch as it recognizes no distinctions of race, and has abolished such distinctions in practice more completely than is unfortunately the case with large numbers of professing Christians. But it does not recognize the duty of brotherhood towards men of all creeds. The Koran requires idolaters to be slain, and the Mussulman to be treated as intrinsically the superior of Jew or of

[1] No doubt this was already done to some extent in the teaching of the Hellenistic Judaism of the Dispersion, and possibly in the teaching of some of the Rabbis, as regards the duty of Gentiles; but I do not know that any Jewish teacher actually put the righteous " worshippers of God " spiritually on a level with the observers of the Law.

Christian. That doctrine of Intolerance which was only introduced into Christianity by the malign influence of St. Augustine, is included in the original and fundamental title deeds of Mohammedanism. That religion recognizes a limited polygamy and an unlimited concubinage. It proclaims the essential and enormous inferiority of women. It avowedly bases morality upon the arbitrary will of God. And the plenary inspiration which the Koran claims for itself creates a serious and probably insurmountable obstacle to any development of the Religion which shall practically emancipate it from these limitations. It is inconceivable that any man who really believes in the essential principles of Christian morality should regard it as a matter of indifference to a people or to an individual whether they accept the morality of the New Testament or that of the Koran. Expressions of sentimental sympathy with Mohammedanism generally come from people who do not seriously profess to accept the most characteristic elements of Christian Morality. Anti-religious writers have, for instance, sometimes represented Mohammedanism as the least objectionable of all religions precisely on account of its indulgence to human frailty in the matter of sexual relations :[1] while those who look at

---

[1] See, for instance, Lanessan, *La Morale des Religions*. As a specimen of the gross ignorance exhibited by this ostensibly scientific work, I may mention that the author treats St. Paul as the author of the Epistle to the Hebrews without a word of apology (p. 381).

Religion chiefly from a political point of view often regard Mohammedan missions with more favour than Christian just because they avowedly treat Mohammedanism as an inferior religion suitable for inferior races, and one useful to their rulers on account of the support which it affords to arbitrary and anti-democratic systems of government.

Far more might be said in favour of an attempt to represent the ancient Zoroastrianism—now represented by Parseeism—as a religion which a Christian might accept. Its original Dualism is believed to have passed into a practical Monotheism at an early date : and at all events modern educated Parsees are Monotheists. And their Monotheism is of an essentially ethical caste. But in the Ethics of the Zend-Avesta ceremonial transgressions are regarded as far more grievous than moral.[1] The greater part of the Vendi-

---

[1] " Thereupon came Angra Mainya, who is all death, and he counter-created by his witchcraft a sin for which there is no atonement, the burying of the dead." Zend-Avesta, Vendîdâd, Fargand, i, 13. Trans. by Darmesteter (Sacred Books of the East, Vol. IV).

" O Maker of the material world, thou Holy One ! If a man shall bury in the earth either the corpse of a dog or the corpse of a man, and if he shall not disinter it within half a year, what is the penalty that he shall pay ? Ahura Mazda answered : ' Five hundred stripes with the Aspahê-astra, five hundred stripes with the Sraoshô-karana ' " (l.c., F., iii, 36). But he may inflict a wound which is healed in three days for fifteen stripes (l.c., iv, 26), or if he hurts a man " sorely," the penalty is thirty (l.c., 30). If he smite him " so that he gives up the ghost," the penalty is only ninety stripes (l.c., 40). On the other hand, the law of Mazda (i.e. acceptance of it) " takes away from him who confesses it the bonds of his sin ; it takes away (the sin of) breach of trust ; it takes away (the sin of) murdering one of the faithful," etc. (l.c., iii, 41). But this is apparently only in the case of one who has not previously professed

dâd—the most ancient portion of the Zend-Avesta—
is taken up with the mode of avoiding ceremonial
pollutions and warding off the influence of evil spirits,
many of its rites being of a rather disgusting character.
Like the Koran, it recognizes a fundamental distinction between a man's duty towards fellow-believers
and his duty towards others.[1] Its ethical precepts
never rise above the level of the Pentateuch : it
never, I should say, comes up to the level of Deuter-
onomy.   Doubtless many modern Parsees neglect
many of its almost intolerable restrictions ; they may
read into its exhortations to goodness and purity
an Ethic which is largely identical with that of Christianity.   But it is impossible to represent that Par-

the law of Mazda, and who " confesses it and resolves never to
commit again such forbidden deeds " (iii, 40).

" He who has riches is far above him who has none " (l.c., iv,
47).   And " he who fills himself with meat is filled with the good
spirit much more than he who does not do so " (l.c., iv, 48).

" If a man shall throw on the ground the whole body of a dead
dog, or of a dead man, and if grease or marrow flow from it on to the
ground, what penalty shall he pay ? Ahura Mazda answered : ' A
thousand stripes with the Aspahê-astra, a thousand stripes with the
Sraoshô-karana ' " (l.c., vi, 24, 25).

The moral teaching of the Zend-Avesta contains many fine
sayings about Benevolence, Humility, and Chastity ; but it nowhere
lays down the principle of Universal Benevolence as the law of life.
Its teaching is not without elevation but it is vague : and the form
in which it is conveyed can nowhere be compared whether in literary
beauty or in practical impressiveness with the noblest passages of
the Old Testament—to say nothing of the New.

[1] " If a worshipper of Mazda wants to practise the art of healing,
on whom shall he prove his skill ? On worshippers of Mazda or on
worshippers of the Daêvas ? Ahura Mazda answered : ' On
worshippers of the Daêvas shall he first prove himself,' " etc. (l.c., F.,
vii, 36, 37).

seeism, taken in its traditional and official form, teaches an Ethic which would make Christian Missions a superfluity—even if the matter is to be decided on ethical grounds alone.

Turning to the indigenous religions of India, it will not be necessary to say much of orthodox Hindooism. Its system of caste is absolutely opposed to the fundamental principle of Christian Ethics. A religion which forbids an out-caste to come within so many paces of a Brahmin, which denies that the Brahmin has any duties to the Sudra, and which, to speak generally, interprets the neighbour to whom duties are owed as the member of one's own caste or (for some purposes) of a caste superior to one's own, cannot be said to teach the Christian doctrine of Brotherhood. When Indian civil servants defend such a system, as they sometimes do, they only show how little they have really grasped the principle of human brotherhood which (if Christians) they profess with their lips; and which if they do not make any such professions, they would theoretically perhaps admit to be the teaching of enlightened Philosophy.[1] All that is enlightened and progressive in Hindoo thought is already revolting against the system, however much social tradition may still secure the observance in practice of caste rules. It is not really of Hindooism as it is, but only of

---

[1] Of course if all that they urge is that the destruction of the system would be bad, unless its place was taken by a higher religion, they would have much to say for themselves.

some actual or possible reformation of it, that the defender of what we call Equi-religionism can reasonably be supposed to be thinking when he suggests that, though Christianity may be a suitable religion for Europeans, there is no reason for the Oriental to abandon his ancient faith.

Among the attempts at a reform of Hindooism, the most ancient and the most important is, of course, the religion known as Buddhism. There we do, indeed, encounter a religion which is, in a sense, on the same level as Christianity. It is absolutely universalistic. It has repudiated caste and all exclusive priestly pretensions. It is highly ethical, and its Ethics are of an elevated and exacting order. It rests on a philosophy which is at all events highly metaphysical and highly intellectual. In its earlier and purer forms it commits its adherents to no belief that is obviously impossible to highly educated Westerners. Rites and ceremonies are completely subordinated to a purely ethical end. Even in its lowest and most degraded form it has hardly sunk lower than Christianity at its worst. It is sufficiently free from stereotyped and authoritative standards of doctrine to admit much liberty of thought, and much development both of doctrine and of practice. In some of its sects there actually has been much development ; and it is capable of more development in a direction which increases the resemblance of both its Ethics and its Theology to Christianity. It is not too much to say that here we have the one ancient historical religion of the East that could conceivably be regarded by the civilized European as a possible alternative to Christianity for himself. It is the one religion which a few educated and intelligent Europeans have formally joined,[1] and which powerfully attracts the sympathy of many who have not done so. But are its Theology and its Ethics the same as those of Christianity? Most assuredly not. Of its Theology it is enough to say that in its original and most philosophical form it is strictly atheistic : in popular forms of it its atheistic Founder has been deified.[2] And this is certainly not the same Theology as that of Christianity. But once more I must confine myself to the ethical side of the Religion. Now here, so long as we think only of practical precepts which Buddhism sets before the average man, there is a very close resemblance between its teaching and that of Christianity at its best. It does teach universal Benevolence, Humanity not merely towards men but towards animals, Chastity, Humility ; and it cannot fairly be said that it teaches anything inconsistent with these virtues as regards the duties of the ordinary man living in the world. The Christian may very well see in these teachings an outpouring of the Spirit of God second only to that which he recognizes in the highest Judaism and the Chris-

[1] The Englishmen who have become Mohammedans may fairly be regarded as " cranks."

[2] Of course not to the exclusion of other " Buddhas," or incarnations of Deity.

tianity in which it culminated. But, when we turn
from the precepts for outward conduct to its inner-
most ethical temper, and in particular when we turn
from the ideal which it sets before the average man to
the ideal of perfection which it holds up to its monks
and its saints, then, amid much which attracts us,
we cannot but recognize that there is also much which
is absolutely contradictory to the Christianity of
Jesus. The charity preached by Jesus was a disinterested desire for the good of others : the Asceticism
which He approved (if it is to be called Asceticism) was
self-denial for the sake of others—for the sake of bringing others into the Kingdom and procuring for them
health of body or health of soul. To the Buddhist, we
are told, self-denial is prescribed for its own sake : the
others whom he benefits are treated not as ends-in-
themselves, but as a means to his own good. The
supreme ideal is not Love, but Self - renunciation.
And the rationale of that self-renunciation is that all
personal existence, and all the desire which springs
from personal existence, are bad.[1] The object of life

[1] Cf. the following passages from Buddhist Scriptures :

" By passing quite beyond the mere consciousness of the infinity
of reason, he, thinking ' nothing at all exists,' reaches (mentally)
and remains in the state of mind to which nothing at all is specially
present—this is the sixth stage of deliverance."

" By passing quite beyond all idea of nothingness he reaches
(mentally) and remains in the state of mind to which neither ideas
nor the absence of ideas are specially present—this is the seventh
stage of deliverance."

" By passing quite beyond the state of ' neither ideas nor the
absence of ideas ' he reaches (mentally) and remains in the state
of mind in which both sensations and ideas have ceased to be—

is to escape from life—to escape from desire, to escape from personality, perhaps (according to some interpretations of Nirvana) to escape from consciousness itself. Nobody, it must be remembered, can be a true Buddhist but the monk or the nun : the life of the layman is a mere concession to human weakness. Salvation can never be attained by a layman till his soul has been reincarnated in a monk. And the ideal of the monks—though in practice, like their Western equivalents, they have not been so socially useless as might be supposed from their ideal—is in the main renunciation of all ordinary human duties and human enjoyments, a life of solitary meditation and absorption in the Absolute. And even in laymen the most necessary duties of good citizenship are at best tolerated. It is strictly inconsistent with Buddhist principles to use force even in the most necessary administration of Justice. War is practised, but the Buddhist admits that, in however just and necessary a cause, it is not strictly lawful.[1] The Jew or the Christian will justify war as a necessary means to securing the best things of life and the just distribution

this is the eighth stage of deliverance " (Book of the Great Decease, iii, 39–41, *Sacred Books of the East*, Vol. XI).

" Hinder not yourselves, Ânanda, by honouring the remains of the Tathâgata. Be zealous, I beseech you, Ânanda, in your own behalf ! Devote yourselves to your own good ! Be earnest, be zealous, be intent on your own good ! " (l.c., chap. v, 24).

" You have done well, Ânanda ! Be earnest in effort, and you too shall soon be free from the great evils—from sensuality, from individuality, from delusion, and from ignorance " (l.c., chap. v, 35).

[1] Cf. Fielding Hall, *The Soul of a People* (chap. vi).

of such things : to the genuine Buddhist nothing in
life can be worth fighting for, or even struggling or
laboriously working for.   Can anything be more
wholly opposed to the ideals whether of the best
modern Christians who labour for the improvement
of human life or of the average Western man who,
whatever his professed religious or non-religious
belief, is profoundly convinced that business, politics,
culture, and ordinary social life are worthy spheres of
human activity ?   It is possible, of course, to suggest
that the Buddhist ideal is true and the Christian false :
it is simply trifling with the subject to maintain that
they are the same.[1]

It may, no doubt, be suggested that Christianity
has in the past at times approximated to the Buddhist
ideal.   No doubt it has.   Asceticism has sometimes
been far more extravagant among Christians than
among the followers of Gautama, who had a very
limited belief in the spiritual value of positive as
distinct from the negative kind of Asceticism.   The
ideal of Christian Monasticism, especially in its earlier
form, is open to precisely the same objections as the
ideal of Buddhism.   Those Christians who are called
in the narrow and more technical sense of the term
mystics have often approximated to the Buddhist
type of religious thought and feeling, though some of

---

[1] It is true that the selfishness of the Buddhist ideal is practically (if illogically) redeemed by its insistence upon the duty of
inducing others to make similar self-renunciation : the monk must
make other monks.   But this only emphasizes the anti-social
character of the ideal.

them have at the same time practised laborious works of Charity which to the strict Buddhist would seem but so many fallings off from the true ideal. And even in the ecstasies of the Christian mystic, the " love " of which their utterances are so full has never quite forgotten that it is a desire for the good of other persons, and has seldom become merely a name for the destruction of all desire in order to attain that true good of self which is the extinction of self. As to certain modern and quite unmonastic mystics who profess much sympathy with quasi-Buddhist modes of thought and expression, I will only say that their ideal appears to be consistent with an attitude towards the pleasures, enjoyments, and ambitions of this life which does not perceptibly differ from that of non-mystical Christians, and which would seem to the really Buddhist monk as inconsistent with the life of the true philosopher as it is with that of the true religionist. But in so far as the Western man is ever sincere in his professions of sympathy with the thoroughgoing Buddhist ideal, I freely admit that I do not see why he should ask a Buddhist to become a Christian. I will go further, and say that the difficulty is to justify his remaining a Christian and not becoming a professed Buddhist. The attitude that is really intolerable is first to complain of Christianity on the ground that it is too " world-renouncing," and then to patronize a religion which is on any view vastly more world-renouncing, world-contemning,

progress-hating, other-worldly than Christianity has
ever been at any period of its history—certainly
more so than it is now.   In one respect the most
ascetic and world-renouncing form of Christianity has
always been poles apart from Buddhism.   World-
renouncing Christianity—except in mystics who have
fairly passed outside the bounds of Christian orthodoxy
—has always aspired after a better life hereafter : to
the Buddhist hope of a future life is one of the deadly
sins.[1]

It is true that just as Christianity has sometimes
been tinged with Buddhist ideas, so it is possible to find
in some phases of Buddhism a much closer approximation to the best Christian ideas.   Among the practical
Japanese, for instance, the speculative, world-renouncing, anti-social side of Buddhism has never had any
profound influence.   One of its sects has become much
more theistic than the religion of Gautama.[2]   The
language used about salvation by belief in Amida
closely resembles the Christian language about salvation through Christ.[3]   Its Eschatology, through
association with the Shinto ancestor-worship, has
become more like the Christian hope of personal

[1] " The virtues which . . . are untarnished by the desire of
future life "—Mahâ-Parinibbâna-Sutta, ii. 9 (*Sacred Books of the
East*, Vol. XI.).

[2] The Jodo Shin Shu.   See two very interesting articles by
Dr. Estlin Carpenter on " Religion in the Far East " in *The Quest*
(Vol. I, Nos. 3 and 4, 1910).

[3] See *The Praises of Amida, Seven Buddhist Sermons*, translated
from the Japanese of Tada Kanai.   By Arthur Lloyd.   Tokyo,
published by the Kyōbunkwan : Yokohama, Kelly and Walsh, 1907.

Immortality. And the Ethics of the sect have undergone corresponding developments. The ascetic world-renunciation tends to disappear, and to be transformed into a high standard of social duty such as would be recognized by the modern Christian as the true interpretation of Christian Love. This development has been, up to a certain point, quite independent of Christianity : but in recent times the Buddhist ideal has shown a strong tendency to assimilate avowedly and consciously the ideal of Christ. Buddhist priests sometimes boast that they are teaching Christian Morality.

In the same way, in India and elsewhere, attempts are being made to regenerate the old historical Religions in a way which is obviously due, sometimes to an unavowed, sometimes to an avowed, influence of the Christian ideal. The best known of such attempts are the movements or rather religious communities known as the Arya Somaj and the Brahmo Somaj. In the Brahmo Somaj the influence of Christianity is particularly conspicuous. Its Theism, its hope of Immortality, and its Ethics are often quite of the Christian type. The language in which Keshub Chunder Sen, the founder of its most liberal branch,[1]

---

[1] The original sect was founded by Rajah Rammshun Roy in 1844. There is another branch of the Brahmo Somaj founded by Debendranāth Tagore in 1844; Keshub Chunder Sen in 1866 founded the " Brahmo Somaj of India," which became so famous that its connexion with the older movement which, though influenced by Christian thought, professes closer affinity with a regenerated Hindooism, was often ignored.

speaks of Christ is very much what would be used by many Unitarian Christians. Somewhat similar tendencies may be detected within the old Persian religion now known as Parseeism. As to Judaism it is difficult to say when it did not begin to be influenced by Christianity. And certainly there are many modern Jews whose Ethic is practically at all points Christian. Some modern Jewish Reformers advocate the reading of the New Testament, and regard Jesus as at least one of the prophets—if not as the prophet by whom at last the eternally true element of Judaism has been fully brought out and separated from the element in Judaism which was particularistic, unethical, transitory.[1] If they still advocate a modified observance of the ceremonial law, it is only as a particular form of universalistic Theism, suitable to the needs of a particular race with a special history but by no means of any strictly ethical or universal obligation.

It is only, as it seems to me, as regards these modern attempts to reform ancient religions under the avowed or unavowed influence of Christianity[2] that the question can seriously arise whether they can be regarded as alternative forms of Religion which could

[1] See, for instance, the *Liberal Judaism* and other writings of Mr. Claude Montefiore.

[2] The argument will not be much affected if it is contended that the approximation to Christianity has been independent of even indirect Christian influence—very difficult as such a contention appears to me to be.

possibly appear so far satisfactory to one who shares the Christian ideal that he would feel himself precluded from asking their adherents to leave their old religions and to join the Christian Church. As regards members of such bodies, we ought, I think, seriously to face the question what ought to be the attitude of the Christian to them. Ought we to abandon direct proselytizing propaganda in countries where such religious communities exist, and to direct our missionaries' energies rather towards helping and assisting such efforts at reform from within? In answer to this question I would say three things :

(1) We ought to recognize that this Christianizing of other bodies is distinctly one of the ways in which the Kingdoms of the world are already becoming, and are likely in the future still more to become, the Kingdom of our God and of His Christ. In so far as these reforms mean the practical acceptance of that conception of God and that ideal of life which Jesus taught, Christians must rejoice, and thank God that such a work is going on. Already the best Missionaries recognize that the indirect results of missionary effort are as important—perhaps more important—than the direct results as regards the more civilized races and the more educated classes in them. These results by themselves constitute a sufficient and splendid justification of those missionary efforts in the past towards which some of our enlightened Equi-religionists adopt such a supercilious and depreciatory attitude. We

T

must not let the mere non-use of the word Christianity blind us to the presence of the spiritual reality when it is actually there. The attitude of Christians towards such religious movements ought to be in the highest degree friendly and sympathetic. It does not follow that we can remain wholly satisfied with their position ; or that, even if we could, avowedly Christian missions ought to cease. Even if the Brahmo Somaj were a completely satisfactory equivalent of Christianity, the forces of all the Christians and all the reformed Hindooisms between them would assuredly be no more than adequate to the task of fighting against the idolatries and superstitions and the caste-moralities of unreformed Hindooism. We may freely admit that direct proselytizing effort had better be concentrated rather upon those who are in the most spiritual need of it than upon those who have adopted some quasi-Christian form of belief under another name. And yet it is probable that the more complete Christianization of such movements will be best carried on by the continuance of independent missionary effort directed towards the making of avowed members of the Christian Church. The people of India are quite capable of appreciating the idea that the same God can be worshipped under many forms : they are not likely to be much impressed by a Religion which does not believe in itself sufficiently to proselytize.

(2) I think it should very distinctly be realized that the truth and value of the Christian Ethic does not

depend upon the fact of its having been taught by Jesus Himself—still less upon its having been taught by Jesus exclusively. If it could be shown that the sayings which we have been in the habit of regarding as most characteristic of the historical Jesus were in reality none of His, if it could be shown that there never was an historical Jesus or that we know nothing to speak of about His teaching, the truth and the value of the teaching attributed to our Lord in the Gospels would not be one whit diminished. Still less could it be affected by the fact that others have taught the same ideal. And what is true of the ethical teaching is true equally of the religious teaching of Jesus—if we put aside those few genuine sayings which speak of His own divine Sonship or Messiahship. If that is so, it is a possibility that a religious community which did not formally adopt the name of Christian might come to teach the Ethics and the Theism of the Christian Church. Whether any actual religious community has reached this position is a question of fact upon which I will not venture to pronounce any positive opinion.

(3) There remains the question, " If an individual or a community has reached this position, what would be still lacking to them ? " That is a large question, to answer which fully would involve almost a treatise on dogmatic Theology. But, so far as the answer can be given in a single word, I believe the answer to be this. If it could be shown that the Jesus of the Gospels was un-

historical, what we should lose would be *the personality of Jesus.* The Christian ideal might be recognized where the words of Jesus are not known or reverenced, or the words might be accepted where the historic Jesus was not believed in : but they would not come home and appeal to us as powerfully as they do when we think of them as the expression of an actual Person who once lived in this world of ours, who once enjoyed and still enjoys that loving and intimate communion with the heavenly Father of which the Gospel pages tell us. The influence of an ethical ideal embodied in a Person is greater—I do not think it easy to say how much greater—than the influence of an ideal considered as a body of ideas or of precepts. And for this influence of the personality of Jesus to reach its highest efficacy, it must be recognized as supreme and paramount. Assuredly, if we believe the words of the Gospel, there are many who have in various degrees lived out Christ's ideal, though they have not taken His name upon their lips. " Inasmuch as ye have done it unto one of these My brethren, even these least, ye have done it unto Me." But, speaking broadly, it is easier to follow Christ when we know whom we are following. The influence of Jesus will not be supremely felt in a community which puts Him side by side with the Buddha or the Bâb or Keshub Chunder Sen. The embodiment of the moral ideal in a Person, the concentration of moral effort upon the following of that Person, the recognition of a unique spiritual authority and supremacy in that Person, the belief in the possibility of approach to God through Him—these have always been characteristic notes of the Christian Religion : and to these it has always, I believe, owed its highest spiritual effectiveness. A Christianity without Christ—or a Christianity in which Christ is not emphatically put above other masters—will always be a maimed and not very effective Christianity.

While therefore we may recognize to the full that there may be many genuine followers of Jesus in the Brahmo Somaj or in some reformed Jewish Society, I believe that Jesus will always be better followed in a society which actually recognizes His unique position. If a community actually came consciously to realize this unique position of Jesus, it would, I should imagine, sooner or later wish to acknowledge the fact by adopting the name of Christian, by identifying itself with the body of Christ's followers throughout the world, and by claiming as its own, deliberately and consciously, the whole spiritual treasure which has come down to them from the Christianity of the past. It would not follow, of course, that it would renounce all spiritual affinity with the spiritual past of its own race. Christianity has already appropriated much spiritual truth which is not of Christian origin. What it has done in the past, it will probably do in the future. The Christianity of the East may hereafter appropriate to itself, and be palpably coloured by, all that is best in the teaching of Confucianism, of

Hindooism or of Buddhism. But these teachings are not very likely to be " baptized into Christ " as fully as truth demands where the central position of Jesus in the religious history of the world is not formally recognized. Even from the point of view of Psychology— that science to which our Equi-religionists are so fond of appealing—we may treat it as an established fact that a certain exclusiveness and concentration of devotion is essential to the religion producing its fullest effect upon heart and life. No teacher ever did much who only believed in his religion as one of many equally permissible forms of approach to God. This consideration would not justify our professing to find in Christianity a uniqueness or a superiority to other religions which is inconsistent with the facts of history. But it does make it important that we should not suffer ourselves to drift into these fashionable modes of exaggerated toleration unless we feel absolutely compelled to do so by loyalty to truth. As far as I understand them, the facts of religious history support the unique position which Christianity claims for its Founder.

I have so far avoided the use of definite dogmatic language or reference to the dogmatic formulæ of Catholic Christianity. I have so far said nothing which might not be accepted by those Unitarians who do actually give Jesus a supreme and central position in their envisagement of the Universe—such Unitarians, I mean, as Channing or Martineau or Dr. Drummond. But if we do agree to put Jesus in this supreme place—to regard Him as the supreme Example, the supreme Prophet, the supreme Revealer of God— if we come to regard the Religion which He founded not merely as one of many parallel Religions, but as the final or absolute Religion, the culminating product of all religious evolution, then the question will arise in what language this conviction may be most suitably expressed ; or, better, what view of the relation of Christ to God supplies the best interpretation of the facts revealed by history and religious experience. On this very difficult enquiry it is no part of my present task to enter. I will only say a very few words as to the relation in which it stands to the question I have been actually discussing.

We have most of us come, I imagine, to recognize the historical fact that traditional Christian doctrine is the result of the Church's reflection about its Founder. It expresses the sense which Christ's followers have entertained of His unique spiritual importance. It has expressed that sense in terms which were taken from the metaphysical dialect of the ancient Græco-Roman world, and which implied the ideas of that metaphysic. That metaphysical dialect is not ours : some of the metaphysical conceptions which it implies are not ours. We do not naturally think in terms of Ousia and Hypostasis, Logos and Perichoresis, Generation and Procession. And therefore I do not believe that Christianity is eternally committed to the formulæ of the past : we may not say that a religious body has ceased to be Christian which has abandoned some of these terms and adopted others. But there is always an enormous presumption, within the religious sphere, in favour of keeping up our spiritual continuity with our own past. If we are agreed that it is ethically and religiously healthy to give Christ a supreme and a unique position in our religious and ethical life—to think of Him as occupying a unique position in relation both to God and to Humanity—the traditional Catholic language has a strong presumption in its favour. Whether we can put Christ into this position depends in the main upon the importance which we attach to His moral and religious teaching, and to the estimate which we form of His character considered as an expression of His ideal. The strictly religious side of His teaching is excluded from our present subject. In these lectures I have endeavoured to give reasons for thinking that we *can* attribute a supreme position and unique value to the moral teaching of Jesus Christ and to the character which is disclosed in His teaching, His life, and His death. I believe that an examination of the strictly religious or theological side of Christ's teaching would yield the same result—that we should find His teaching about God, and about man's relation to Him, the highest teaching that the world has known. And it is a teaching which is not altogether separable from a certain view about His own nature and relation to God. For it is just in His supreme consciousness of a filial relation to God, of intimate union with God, in which we see exhibited the true attitude of Humanity in general to God. And the two lines of enquiry—the ethical and the religious—are closely connected. For if we start with the conviction that God exists and that He may best be thought of in the light of the highest moral ideal known to Humanity, then it follows that, wherever we discover this highest moral ideal, there we must recognize the highest revelation of God which the human mind can apprehend. We have seen that Jesus was the first to teach in its full purity that moral ideal which, so far as it can be condensed into a single principle, expresses itself in the words that Love is the fulfilling of the Law. He was the first to teach also—with full clearness and purity—the idea that God must be thought of in the light of this ideal, as the common Father of Humanity whose nature is best expressed by the word Love.[1]

---

[1] In *The Teaching of Christ*, by the Rev. E. G. Selwyn, an attempt is made to deny that Jesus " revealed God as ' Father ' " (p. 56). The grounds for this somewhat surprising statement seem to be that " the teaching about the Father, where it is direct and not parabolic, is given to those who have already responded to His preaching. . . . The Sermon on the Mount, we are told, was uttered after ' His disciples came unto Him.' " Surely if this last statement be accepted, it would not alter the fact that Christ did teach it ; but, if there is a certain result of criticism, it is that the introductions to our Lord's discourses and the joinings of His sayings are frequently literary devices of the compilers and cannot be implicitly relied upon as history. Nobody now supposes that the Sermon on the Mount as a whole was delivered on any one occasion. Further, he

And His life and the character which it reveals impress us as having been in completest harmony with that ideal. This is briefly the line of thought which leads us up to the conclusion that it is in the teaching, the mind, the Personality of Christ that the highest

contends that (1) the idea of God's Fatherhood was already known to the Jews, and (2) that Jesus did not teach that " God's Fatherhood was a truth independent of the believer's relation to Himself." Surely these two reasons are mutually exclusive, unless Mr. Selwyn is actually prepared to say that the prophetic belief in the Fatherhood of God was unfounded, and the second assertion chiefly rests upon the fourth Gospel. If he appeals to that Gospel, will he say that, even to its author, " God is love " means merely " God loves all members of the Christian Church " ?

Mr. Selwyn further asserts that " He no more teaches the Brotherhood of Man than the Fatherhood of God " (p. 109) on the ground that the early Christian writers only apply the word " brother " or " brethren " to fellow-Christians, and not to the Gentiles. Even if this were true, it would not show that our Lord did not teach the wider truth Himself. No doubt Jesus was always speaking to Jews, and did not often explicitly consider the case of Gentiles. But does Mr. Selwyn seriously mean to say that our Lord—e.g. in the parable of the Good Samaritan—meant that the term " neighbour " was to be understood only of the brother Jew or the fellow-Christian ? If not, the idea of the Brotherhood of all men is clearly latent in that parable as in all the teaching which implies the doctrine of universal love. The question whether the *word* " brother " is used is comparatively unimportant.

With regard to the later Christian Church it is true that " brother " meant primarily " fellow-Christian," but it would be a libel on the early Church and opposed to all the historical evidence to say that it did not teach the duty of loving pagans. What is the difference between loving a man as oneself and treating him as a " brother " ? No doubt the ideal of love is not *fully* reached till it is mutual, but that fact does not destroy the duty of trying to realize it. It is a pity that a writer otherwise not illiberal or uncritical should have allowed the desire to prove that the " liberal Protestant " has always been wrong to get the better of him, and should so frequently insist on reading back into the teaching of Jesus not merely the germs but the developed ideas of later " Catholicism." In the writings of liberal Protestants he complains of " the sudden and secret irruption of the subjective element into discussions which purport to be objective and scientific " (p. 56). I do not deny that and completest Revelation of God has been made. And this is the fundamental truth which Greek religious Philosophy expressed by saying that the Son or Logos, the Reason or Word of God, was incarnate in Him. " The Word took flesh and dwelt among us, and we beheld His glory, the glory as of the only-begotten of the Father." If I were to develope the arguments which justify the application to Jesus of theological language such as is used by the Christian Creeds, I should lay the chief stress upon this—that now after the lapse of nearly two thousand years the teaching of Jesus about God and about the moral ideal still appeals to us as containing the vital essence of all Religion and of all Morality ; that it presents itself to us as the true basis of all further development whether in the sphere of Theology or of Morality, and that it is in the Church which Jesus founded that such a development has taken place and is taking place in the fullest and richest measure. I do not believe that Jesus is the only man in whom the Word or Reason or Wisdom of God has dwelt. That God has been revealed in some measure by other great prophets and teachers, that He dwells to some extent in the Conscience of all men, was fully and cordially recognized

the complaint has sometimes been justified, but Mr. Selwyn seems to me to have merely exchanged one subjective bias for another. The fact that he has done so is to my mind the chief defect in an otherwise excellent book. Fortunately the belief that God is the common Father of men, and that Christ taught the Brotherhood of man is not often explicitly repudiated either by Catholics or Protestants.

by the philosophical Greek Fathers. But the unique
appeal which Christ still makes to our Conscience
both by His teaching and by His life and death of self-
sacrifice, taken together with the supreme place which
the religion founded by Him has occupied, and still
occupies, in the spiritual history of the world, justifies
us in saying that with Him the Logos was united in
a supreme manner, that in Him God is most fully
revealed to men, or, in the language of St. Paul,
that in Him dwelleth all the fullness of the Godhead
bodily. And the greatest advantage of putting Christ
in this position is that it enormously strengthens the
influence of Jesus and the ideal which He represents,
over the moral and religious life. And therefore I
believe that it is in religious communities which retain
the ancient Catholic tradition, or at least recognize in
some explicit way the fundamental idea which has
expressed itself in that tradition, that the influence of
Christ's ideal is likely to attain its maximum intensity.

There are followers of Christ who have not taken
His name upon their lips. There are others who do
assume that name but who scruple to speak of Him as
God incarnate. That should not prevent our recognizing these last as fellow-Christians and co-operating
with them in all manner of Christian activities; but
equally it should not prevent us from affirming that for
ourselves the following of Christ is made easier by thinking of Him not only as the supreme Teacher and the
supreme Example, but as the Being in whom that

union of God and Man after which all ethical Religion aspires, is most fully accomplished, and through whom the individual soul can attain in the fullest measure that degree of complete likeness to God which its spiritual capacity admits.

APPENDIX I. ON THE LOVE OF GOD

THE question may be raised, " In what relation does the love of God stand to the love of man? " There is no explicit attempt to reconcile or reduce to unity the two commandments in the teaching of Jesus Himself. But if the conception of God taught by Him is that of a loving and righteous Father who wills the true good of all His creatures, it is a fair deduction that the love of God will show itself in the love of man. Will it show itself in nothing else? The answer to that question will depend upon the view we take of the attitude of Jesus to the ceremonial law, a subject which has already been briefly discussed. If the view I have taken on that subject be correct, we may say that, in so far as Jesus recognized the non-permanence and non-essentiality of the Mosaic Law, He must be taken by implication to have recognized that in their actual content the two commandments come to the same thing. The love of God can express itself in actual conduct only by the doing of God's will. If God wills nothing but the true good of man (and, as we might be inclined to add, all sentient beings), the conduct to which the love of God prompts will be the same as that enjoined by the second great commandment which, in the words of the Gospel, is " like unto " the first.[1] The performance of ritual ordinances, sacrifices, acts of worship,

[1] Matt. xxii. 39, probably an addition of the Evangelist; Mark (xii. 31) has simply " the second is this."

286

etc., will thus only be valuable in so far as they stimulate to the doing of God's will in the service of man. It is true that, if " on these commandments hang all the law and prophets," be treated as an addition of the Evangelist, Jesus does not explicitly recognize that there are no other commandments not included in the two, but in many passages He implies it : for the other commandments cease to be binding when they conflict with them, and they do conflict the moment they are not duly subordinated to the two. To spend time and money on sacrifices, except so far as to do so will make the sacrificer or others more willing to perform the two great commandments, would be to put the command to sacrifice above the command to love. The implication was fully developed by St. Paul and the Church.

Does this imply that the first commandment becomes superfluous, and that it may in practice be superseded by the second? Not at all. For, (1) it is of extreme importance to recognize that the service of man is the Will of God— that religious motives should be brought to bear upon and invoked to secure the performance of the duties prescribed by abstract morality. (2) In particular the love of ideal perfection is likely to be stimulated by the belief in an ideally perfect Being. Devotion to a Person is a stronger motive than devotion to an idea. (3) The insistence upon the love of God is particularly valuable in preventing " the enthusiasm of humanity " from degenerating into mere hedonistic Utilitarianism. It tends to emphasize the truth that the good of man which the Christian is to promote is not his mere pleasure but his true good—that ideal of Humanity which constitutes the true end for which his life was designed by God, and which is an expression of the character which belongs eternally to God. The love of God is love of the moral ideal considered not as a mere ideal, but an ideal realized in a personal Being.[1]

The teaching of Christ recognizes two motives for Morality which prompt to the same conduct—love of God and love of man. There is no trace in His teaching of the monstrous doctrine which I have heard preached by men who are regarded as typical (if rather old-fashioned) representatives of Anglican doctrine—that love of man is impossible without the love of God consciously present and recognized as such in the mind of the agent. This doctrine is, indeed, opposed to an explicit declaration of Jesus : " Inasmuch as ye did it unto one of these My brethren, even these least, ye did it unto Me."[2] (It is possible that " brethren" may mean merely " followers of Christ," but this is hardly likely if the words be a genuine utterance of Jesus.) This beautiful saying implies that there may be much true Christian morality in those who have not used the name of Christ, or been consciously inspired by the love of God. This is quite consistent with the assertion that ideally the love of God ought to be combined with the love of man, and that the first may be a most valuable mode of inspiring the second. Both, in fact, spring from the same root—the love of all that is worthy of love, love of what is good absolutely or universally. The later doctrine of the Church brought the two motives together by its insistence upon the love of Christ—the ideal Man in whom the perfection of God was most fully revealed and realized—at once the highest revelation of the divine character and the supreme example of human goodness. This union of the two ideal motives to Morality

---

[1] " Conscientiousness is the sum and substance of the love of God." Tyrrell, *Essays on Faith and Immortality*, p. 26. The saying may be accepted with the proviso mentioned above.

[2] Matt. xxv. 40.

has, no doubt, been one of the ideas to which the Christian Religion owes its strength. It still possesses enormous value ; but it should always be insisted on in such a way as (1) to keep prominent the idea that Christ is the Revealer of God, and not to substitute the Son for the Father or encourage the idea that the Father's character is unlike the Son's, or that the Father is too far off and impersonal a Being to be loved and prayed to ; (2) to treat the historic Christ as the symbol and embodiment of ideal Humanity, without resolving Him into a Christ who is ideal in the sense of being unhistorical. It is right to do good to man " for the sake of Christ " ; we cannot legitimately say " we will do good to man *only* for the sake of Christ : if it were not for Christ, we should do nothing of the kind." True Christian love, as has been finely said by Seeley, is " the love of the ideal Man in each man, or, as Christ Himself might have said, the love of God in each man " (*Ecce Homo*, chap. xviii). It is a love of the possible Christ in every man.

Further to discuss this subject would involve an examination of the whole question of the relation of Religion to Morality, which I have dealt with somewhat fully in *The Theory of Good and Evil*, Book III, chap. ii.

U

APPENDIX II. ON CHRIST'S TEACHING ABOUT FUTURE REWARD AND PUNISHMENT [1]

THE question of our Lord's teaching about the future life does not strictly belong to our subject, but it is so closely connected with it that it seems advisable to add a short discussion of it to these lectures. It is, indeed, scarcely possible to draw a strict line between the ethical teaching of any teacher and his attitude towards the future life. The teacher's ideal comes out in his conception of the future life itself and of the relation in which it stands to the life of action and aspiration here and now. We cannot help facing the question whether there is anything in our Lord's teaching upon this subject which prevents our accepting Him as our supreme moral Authority.

Attempts are sometimes made to disparage the moral teaching of Jesus Christ on the ground that He invited men to be good and to do good from hope of future reward and dread of future punishment. Sometimes it is even suggested that such hopes and fears are set before men as the sole motives for righteousness and the avoidance of sin. This suggestion can, I think, be definitely refuted. Christ did appreciate and teach the intrinsic value of goodness and the intrinsic evil of sin. The question was, of course, one which had never been presented to Him in the technical language of philosophy. But the idea that goodness is to be valued solely on account of its posthumous reward is in-

[1] This note is reprinted from the *Modern Churchman* by kind permission of the editor.

290

consistent with the whole tone of His teaching both about God and about human duty. He distinctly makes the love of God the supreme and ideal motive for goodness. You cannot love from hope of reward or fear of punishment. God was to Him a loving Father, intrinsically righteous and beneficent ; and that is quite inconsistent with the theory that the divine commands are wholly arbitrary, that virtue means merely the doing of what is commanded by God for the sake of reward and the avoidance of what is forbidden under penalties : and nothing less than this is implied in the theory that the mere hope of reward or fear of punishment are the sole motives for right conduct. But it is quite undeniable that He did also seek to encourage men to do right and to resist temptation by the thought of a future life, the character of which would depend upon the use they made of their wills in this life. If this is to be regarded as demoralizing " Eudaemonism," most of the Moralists who have seriously believed in Immortality will incur the same condemnation. There is nothing demoralizing in such teaching if it is not made the *sole* or the *chief* motive for virtue, and this most certainly our Lord never did. I deliberately exclude from this enquiry all other aspects of our Lord's " Eschatology "—the question what He meant by the Kingdom, when and how it was to come, etc. That question has already been discussed, so far as seemed necessary, in the second lecture. We must treat the Eschatology, for the present purpose, as a doctrine about the future life. Whether this life was to be lived " in Heaven " or on a regenerated earth, is a question of no ethical importance.

The hope of future blessedness has ethical value (1) educationally, as leading up to and preparing men for a more disinterested goodness ; (2) as affording help and encouragement to those who are indeed hungering and thirsting after righteousness, but are as yet far from being perfected Christians or from having (in Kantian phrase) perfectly " autonomous " wills. (3) In so far as the reward is thought of as itself consisting in a state of greater moral perfection or as a happiness which is the natural and necessary consequence of goodness, the doctrine of reward and punishment begins to assume a form in which it is not only consistent with the belief in the intrinsic value of goodness, but becomes hard to distinguish from it. It is, indeed, not the whole object of the good man to win peace of conscience or " inward harmony " whether in this life or the next ; but, in so far as he cares about goodness, he will not be able to win inward peace or happiness without it ; nobody can value goodness without valuing a good conscience. Thus the ethical value of the belief in a future life depends largely upon the character of the Heaven and the Hell which it encourages men to expect. That the Kingdom of Heaven which Christ invites men to qualify for was thought of in a spiritual and ethical manner I believe to be undeniable. There is no reason why this should not be admitted even by those who refuse to allow that our Lord's " Eschatology " in any way went beyond the level reached by the prophetic and apocalyptic teaching of Judaism. The " Kingdom of Heaven " was always to the Jew a " Kingdom of righteousness and peace," whatever else it may have been.

I confess I feel some indignation at the insincerity and superficiality with which these cant objections to any moral teaching which is connected with the hopes of a future life are often repeated. What Moralist, except perhaps an ultra-Kantian rigorist of a type which is not now much in fashion, objects to a teacher trying to keep boys and girls —or men and women—from yielding to temptations to drunkenness or impurity by telling them that they will be ruining their future happiness in this present life by so doing ? Why is happiness—whether we think of ordinary enjoyment or of higher æsthetic and intellectual pleasures, of human affections or of peace of conscience—any the less valuable or less noble because it is thought of as lasting for ever ? Undoubtedly the idea of " right for the sake of right "—of the *perseitas boni* (as the Schoolmen called it), of duty for duty's sake, of the autonomous will and the like —was not set forth by Jesus in the abstract way in which it has been taught by the best later philosophy, though not always by the philosophy of those who disparage Christian teaching on this head. In the insistence on this idea by later Christian teachers we may recognize a real development of the teaching of Jesus—a development which only brings out and emphasizes what is always implied in the teaching of the Master Himself. This is doubtless one of the truths which have been brought out into fuller light by the later work of the Spirit in the Church, but it is clearly implicit in His own teaching. If we ask ourselves how the relation between virtue and its " reward " presented itself to Jesus Himself, the following remarks of Mr. Montefiore probably get as near to His real conception as we shall succeed in doing :—

" It may also be observed that the ' eudaemonism ' of the beatitudes is of a special kind. They do not say, ' Do this, or be this, *because* you will gain a reward,' or, ' do not do this *because* you will be punished.' But they say, ' A certain line of action, a certain disposition of mind bring happiness now and hereafter.' The result follows necessarily from the cause. It is the law of God. ' Heaven ' and happiness follow as certainly from goodness as their opposites follow from wickedness. The one is not an arbitrarily added reward ; the other is not an arbitrarily added punishment. The result is contained in the premiss, as surely as the result of health-giving medicines or death-dealing drugs is already contained within them. The bliss of virtue, both ' now ' and ' hereafter,' is a continuous state, and not a something added *ab extra* to form a reward, and *mutatis mutandis*, the same may be said of vice. Thus the sting of the supposed ' eudaemonism ' is removed." [1]

It is not, indeed, and could not truthfully be asserted that peace of conscience or " the goodwill," is *all* that is necessary to happiness, and anyone who believes that the Power who rules the world is loving cannot but believe that the other things necessary to happiness will ultimately be added for those who already possess this its most essential element, and so much was certainly taught by our Lord.

Much more might very well be said upon this most important topic, but my special object in these pages is to ask : " What was the actual teaching of Jesus as to the duration of future punishment ? " Mr. Montefiore, who so admirably defends our Lord from the charge of eudaemonism, expresses great horror at what he supposes to be His teaching about everlasting punishment, a doctrine which even orthodox modern Judaism has repudiated. Upon this subject I would make the following remarks :—

(1) I should like to begin by stating quite definitely that the doctrine of everlasting punishment—in its ordinary, traditional acceptation—presents us with a view of the character of God so clearly revolting to the modern conscience, and so inconsistent with the general teaching of our Lord Himself about the Love of God, that we could not accept it in deference to any external authority whatever. I make this remark in order that I may not be

[1] *The Synoptic Gospels*, II, p. 485.

accused of approaching the subject with a fixed determination neither to accept the doctrine of everlasting punishment, nor to question the view usually accepted by Christians as to the moral authority of their Master. If Jesus did indeed teach the doctrine of everlasting punishment, and meant by it what the words naturally and obviously suggest, modern Christians would have to recognize in such an unquestioning acceptance of a traditional Jewish view another of those limitations of His knowledge which in some matters Orthodoxy itself has been compelled to acknowledge. It is not perhaps quite inconceivable—if we approach the subject without presuppositions—that He might have taught the traditional view in the traditional words without seeing how inconsistent it was with His own conception of the loving Father who is always ready to forgive the penitent ; but anyone who takes a high view of the ethical elevation of Christ's teaching—even apart from any theological or Christological theory about His divine nature [1]—is justified in approaching the subject with a strong indisposition to believe that He did so.

(2) All the teaching whether about future reward or future punishment is of a metaphorical character. If the Messianic banquet is not to be taken in a naïvely realistic sense (and even some Rabbis taught that the " eating and drinking " were not to be taken literally [2]), neither is the fate of those excluded to be so understood. They are shut

---

[1] It would be out of place to take such views into consideration, inasmuch as the moral impression created by the religious and ethical teaching of Jesus, and the character which they reveal, is the chief ground of the Church's teaching about His Person.

[2] We know that Jesus taught there was to be no marrying or giving in marriage, and that the righteous would be " as angels in heaven." The angels were never, I imagine, supposed to eat and drink.

out in the " outer darkness "—outside the brilliantly lighted banqueting hall—where there is " weeping and gnashing of teeth " (Matt. xxv. 30). Moreover, the metaphor here used is of a kind which vividly suggests the pains of remorse, though I am far from suggesting that these are the only pains which Jesus thought of, or which a truly ethical conception of punishment can approve. As to that other metaphor, " where their worm dieth not, and the fire is not quenched " (Mark ix. 48), it is probable that the primary thought is simply that of corruption— the corruption of the tomb—rather than of punishment, and of a fire which consumes what is corrupt. The words are vague, and they are derived from Isaiah lxvi. 24, where it is distinctly " the carcases of the men that have trans- gressed against me " which are to be consumed. Here the meaning of " unquenchable " is clearly " that which will not be quenched till it has consumed what is put into it."

(3) The only passages in the Synoptic Gospels which quite explicitly teach that the punishment will be " aeonian " are as follows :—

(*a*) It is good for thee to enter into life maimed or halt, rather than having two hands or two feet to be cast into the aeonian fire (Matt. xviii. 8).

(*b*) Depart from me, ye cursed, into the aeonian fire which is prepared for the devil and his angels (Matt. xxv. 41).

(*c*) And these shall go away into aeonian punishment, but the righteous into aeonian life (Matt. xxv. 46).

To these three passages may be added a fourth, which, *prima facie*, may be held to imply the doctrine of everlasting punishment :—

(*d*) " Whosoever shall speak against the Holy Spirit,

it shall not be forgiven him, neither in this world [aeon] nor in that which is to come " (Matt. xii. 32).

I will not here discuss at length the doubts which may be raised as to the meaning of this term " aeonian " [αἰώνιος] or the probable Aramaic original which it may represent. It is enough to say that it need not *necessarily* mean the same as ἀΐδιος, which is the ordinary Greek word for " everlasting "; and that over and over again in the LXX and elsewhere it is used of things which clearly are not endless. It *may* mean " agelong," " very long," or " belonging to the future aeon," and so be virtually equivalent to "future." It is pretty certain that for the Jew of our Lord's time it had acquired the more definite meaning " belonging to the Messianic age "; if so, the fire will be the fire connected with the Messianic Judgement, the punishment will be the Messianic punishment. Nothing will be determined as to its duration. It has, moreover, often been remarked that the word used for punishment (κόλασις) is one which distinctly suggests corrective, disciplinary, reformatory punishment. There were other Greek words for retributive punishment which the Evangelist might have employed if he had wished to do so. But such explanations will probably seem to some minds not very satisfying. After all, the term " aeonian " is applied also to the life of the blest, and there is no doubt that this was thought of as everlasting, though it may still be that the word does not *mean* " everlasting." Assuming that it does imply or include the idea of endless duration, it is fair to point out that these passages are all derived from the first Gospel; and, if there is a conclusion to which the general results of recent Gospel criticism point (no one insists upon it more strongly than Mr. Montefiore), it is that sayings in the first Gospel, unsupported by the other Synoptists, are very frequently coloured by the doctrinal beliefs or ecclesiastical arrangements of the Judaeo-Christian Church at the end of the first century A.D. These passages may well be " ecclesiastical additions " —like the authority to bind and loose, the committal of the keys of the Kingdom to St. Peter, the command to bring quarrels to be settled by the Church, etc. ; or at least they are in all probability very much modified by the unconscious influence of ecclesiastical tradition. And it is observable that the whole of the passage in which the second and third allusions to aeonian punishment occur (" I was a stranger and ye took me in," etc.) is one which on grounds quite unconnected with this question is by many critics suspected of being influenced by later tradition.

(4) I should say that this might be accepted as by far the most probable solution but for the fact that the last of the four Matthean passages has a parallel in St. Mark (iii. 29) :— " Whosoever shall blaspheme against the Holy Spirit hath never forgiveness, but is guilty of an aeonian sin,"[1] and is found in another form in St. Luke. Now in this passage I would observe (a) that the idea of " everlasting " or " eternal " sin (if it is to be so translated) is not necessarily the same as that of " eternal punishment " ; (b) it is not said that the sinner against the Holy Spirit has actually committed an " eternal sin," but only that he is " liable to it," " in danger of it." This does no doubt imply that a state of eternal sin is possible, but not necessarily that the sinner's doom is finally fixed at the moment of death. (c) The simplest and possibly the original form of this part of the saying is that found in Luke (xii. 10), which has nothing about an " eternal sin," but simply

[1] So the revised text for the textus receptus translated " in danger of eternal damnation " (more strictly " judgement ").

" it shall not be forgiven." Luke is here probably following Q (cf. Streeter in *Oxf. Studies in the Syn. Probl.*, p. 171). " Ecclesiastical additions " are certainly not peculiar to the first Gospel, though they are more frequent in that Gospel than elsewhere, and it is quite possible that Mark's " but is guilty of an eternal sin," and Matthew's " neither in this age nor in that which is to come," may be varying attempts to explain and emphasize the simple " it shall not be forgiven." (*d*) If Mark's " aeonian sin " be regarded as original, the meaning may be " a sin which will be condemned at the Judgement, which will exclude from the Messianic Kingdom." We may then suppose that both Matthew and Luke have attempted to explain in different ways a word not easily intelligible to Gentile readers. (*e*) If Luke's version be accepted as the original, it may still be contended that even the Lukan saying implies the severer doctrine. If there is a sin which cannot be forgiven, and if there is to be a punishment for unforgiven sin, does not this, it may be asked, imply an everlasting punishment? I should answer " Certainly not." It would be quite compatible with the belief in the extinction of unrepentant sinners at the Judgement or after an interval (and this was one of the recognized forms of Jewish opinion on the subject), or with a terminable punishment. One who has suffered the full punishment due to his sin has not, in the obvious sense of the word, been forgiven. There is the utmost uncertainty about the exact form and original import of this mysterious saying about "sinning against the Holy Ghost," and these doubts must cast a certain amount of suspicion upon the whole saying. Without asserting that the expression " Holy Ghost " was unknown to the religious vocabulary of Jesus, it is eminently characteristic of the Evangelists. It is, to say the least of it, quite possible that the whole passage, in spite of its high external attestation, may have grown out of some misunderstood saying of a much less definite character. But, if it is genuine, it says no more than this : " Other sins may be forgiven at the Judgement, this one will not be so forgiven." As to the consequence of condemnation, nothing is determined.

(5) There is one other passage in Mark which may be held *primâ facie* to imply the doctrine of everlasting punishment. " It is good for thee to enter into life maimed rather than having two hands to go into Gehenna, into the unquench-able fire," and the following verses ending " where their worm dieth not, and the fire is not quenched " (Mark ix. 43–48).

Now this passage is the equivalent in St. Mark of the passage cited above from the first Gospel (xviii. 8). If it is treated as the original form of the saying, then we get rid altogether of one of the Matthean passages in which the word aeonian is used, and the suspicion is strengthened that the word " aeonian " belongs to the ecclesiastical vocabu-lary of the two first Evangelists. In that case all the Matthean passages will be shown not to be exact reports of the Lord's saying. But it may be asked whether Mark's " unquenchable fire " does not imply the idea of an ever-lasting punishment no less explicitly and even in a more terrible form. I do not think so. To say that the fire is unquenchable does not necessarily imply that every one who is plunged into it will remain in it for ever. If I say that at a certain time somebody was suffering from " an unquenchable thirst," I do not say that he continued to suffer from it even for the rest of his life, still less for ever ; I only mean that he would like to have quenched his thirst, perhaps tried to quench it, but could not. The fire is one which those who find themselves in it have no power to quench. The same remark applies to the expression in a later verse, " where their worm dieth not, and the fire is not quenched" (Mark ix. 48), which is not found in Matthew. I do not, therefore, regard these passages as teaching or necessarily implying the doctrine of an ever-lasting punishment which no repentance can avail to end.

Moreover, in spite of the prejudice which is always excited by critical conjectures which may be branded as "convenient," I cannot help feeling a strong suspicion that "into the unquenchable fire" is a gloss of the Evangelist, and that the original saying had only "Gehenna" or "the Gehenna of fire" (as in Matt. xviii. 9 and v. 29, 30), for which the first Evangelist has substituted "the aeonian fire," while St. Mark has expanded it by an explanation— an explanation by no means superfluous for Gentile readers.[1] This is the version of the original saying which most easily explains both variants. I have already pointed out that all the expressions used by our Lord—Gehenna, unquenchable fire, "weeping and gnashing of teeth," etc., were traditional Jewish terms, which need not be sup-posed to imply "everlasting punishment" if they did not invariably do so in the current rabbinic teaching of the time.

(6) And this last remark brings us to the whole question of contemporary Jewish opinion on the subject. I admit that, if it could be shown that the belief in everlasting punishment was the established Jewish belief of the time (outside the conservative Sadducean circles), the *primâ facie* conclusion would be—for those who are unwilling to admit that the religious insight of Jesus rose far above the general level of His time—that Jesus shared that belief. But this is not the conclusion to which the best authorities on the

---

[1] Dalman pronounces that the Aramaic equivalent of Gehenna "is the one term whose use by Jesus is assured, since all three Synoptists record it among the words of Jesus" (*The Words of Jesus*, I, 161).

subject have actually come. There were many views current as to the future destiny of the wicked. And among them was certainly the view that the wicked were ultimately extinguished.[1] Our Lord cannot be definitely shown to have adopted the severest view. We are surely not called upon to believe that He adopted that one of the current opinions which was most difficult to reconcile with His own teaching about the Fatherhood of God, though it may well be that, in the depth of His stern indignation against sin, He may have used severe but vague prophetic language without expressly attempting to reconcile it with His other great conviction about the love of God.

(7) There are a few passages which, without explicitly teaching the doctrine of an everlasting Hell, have sometimes been regarded as pointing in that direction, e.g. the saying " broad is the way that leadeth to destruction " (Matt. vii. 13). This saying is Matthean only, but it has a fairly close Lukan parallel in " Many . . . shall seek to enter in, and shall not be able " (Luke xiii. 24). These words in Luke are followed by the passage beginning " When once the master of the house " and ending " Depart from me, all ye workers of iniquity. There shall be the weeping and gnashing of teeth, when ye shall see Abraham and Isaac and Jacob, and all the prophets, in the Kingdom of God, and yourselves cast forth without. And they shall come from the east and west," etc. (xiii. 25–28). Now here it may be observed that these last words are freely rejected by many critics (including Mr. Montefiore) for their Universalism,[2] and on that hypothesis the whole passage

---

[1] In the Ethiopic Enoch the Messiah will " destroy them from the face of the earth " (Sim. xlv. 6, cf. lxii. 2). I will not attempt to collect the views of other Apocalyptists, but will refer generally to Canon Charles's *Eschatology.* Cf. Thackeray, *The Relation of St. Paul to Contemporary Jewish Thought,* p. 116.

[2] But see above, p. 110.

might be considered doubtful. But I am not myself disposed to adopt this view, and apart from this I see no reason for doubting the genuineness of the passage except that xiii. 28 follows rather abruptly upon xiii. 27, and suggests a separate saying brought into this context. But to say that *some* of the consequences of persistent sin against the light are irreversible, is a very different thing from saying that its punishment shall be endless. All the sayings would be compatible with extinction; indeed, Matthew's " destruction " might naturally be understood as pointing to that view. But they need not imply anything so definite as that. There is, indeed, nothing about punishment at all, but only about an irreversible loss. To suppose that opportunities lost in this life may never recur is certainly not an immoral opinion, or one which implies a low conception of the divine character.[1] And if anyone feels bound to hold that in some sense that belief in everlasting punishment which eventually became the traditional tenet of the Church must be true, he can rationalize it by understanding it in this sense, and saying that the punishment is simply a " poena damni," which need not exclude the hope of much progress in goodness or of much happiness.

The parable of Dives and Lazarus, as reported by St. Luke (xvi. 24), is the only passage in his Gospel in which Hell (Hades) is actually spoken of as a place of torment, but here there is nothing to indicate whether the torment was to have an end or not. It was for the time being impossible for Lazarus to revisit the earth during the lifetime of his brethren, not necessarily for ever. That is all that the words need mean. It may even be suggested that

---

[1] Other passages sometimes appealed to are Matt. vii. 21–23, x. 33 ; Luke ix. 26. But they do not necessarily or even naturally imply anything more than condemnation at the Judgement.

our Lord's reply implies that it was still open to them to hear Moses and the prophets.

(8) On the other hand there are a few passages which certainly suggest that the punishment of the wicked is not endless. The most definite is, " But rather fear Him which is able to destroy both soul and body in Gehenna " (Matt. x. 28). Luke has simply " hath power to cast into Gehenna" (xii. 5). If the Matthean version be accepted, we shall have a distinct reason for supposing that our Lord did not think of punishment in Gehenna as involving everlasting torment. And, indeed, the inconsistency of this passage, taken in its literal and natural sense, with the doctrine of everlasting punishment will be additional evidence either for doubting the genuineness of the " aeonian " passages in Matthew or for supposing that our Lord did not regard " aeonian punishment " as implying everlasting continuance in suffering. But perhaps, after all, the probabilities are rather in favour of Luke's simpler version—" to cast into Gehenna."

Then there is the saying, " What doth it profit a man to gain the whole world and forfeit his life ? " (Mark viii. 36). If we must not modernize so far as to give the passage a meaning which has no reference at all to the question of future reward and punishment, the obvious implication certainly is that the wicked ultimately cease to live. Another passage which may be appealed to in this connexion is " many that are first shall be last " (Matt. xix. 30). To be last in entering the Kingdom (if this be the meaning of being " last ") is not the same thing as being shut out from it altogether. (But perhaps, as Dr. Moffat suggests, this was originally a quite uneschatological saying. Cf. Mark ix. 35.) " Thou shalt by no means come out thence till thou hast paid the uttermost farthing " (Matt. v. 26 ; Luke xii. 59) may be cited as suggesting that there is a possibility of coming out (cf. Matt. xii. 32). Still more noticeable is "resurrection *of the just*" in Luke xiv. 14. Cf. xx. 35.

If these passages are not sufficiently trustworthy or explicit to enable us definitely to attribute to our Lord the doctrine that the punishment of the wicked is not endless, we have at least some reason for suspecting or otherwise interpreting every passage which is used to defend the opposite doctrine. On the whole, the truth of the matter seems to be that the thoughts of Jesus about the future of human souls did not generally travel far beyond the moment of the Kingdom's coming. Unrepented sin would involve condemnation at the Judgement and exclusion from the Kingdom, which was thought of as in itself the direst of penalties, and doubtless as involving further penalties. What those penalties were, and whether after a period of suffering there would be further opportunities of repentance—these are questions which Jesus does not answer, perhaps did not put to Himself, still more probably did not feel to be revealed to Him—any more than the day and the hour of the Judgement were revealed to Him.

On the whole then we may say that from the most severely critical and objective point of view the answer to our question as to whether Jesus taught the doctrine of everlasting punishment must be *non liquet;* the evidence that He did is quite inadequate to prove that He did, if the suggestion cannot be decisively refuted. Those to whom, from their belief in the supreme depth of His moral and spiritual insight, there seems to be a great improbability in His having held a doctrine which strikes them as religiously shocking and inconsistent with the general tenor of His own teaching about God, will feel themselves justified in going a step further and saying, " It is probable that He did not teach it." The most that seems at all

x

likely is that He may have acquiesced in conventional representations of the punishment of sin which, without actually speaking of everlasting torments, did not explicitly contemplate a place for repentance after the Judgement or a termination of penal suffering.

The probability of this conclusion may be strengthened by the consideration that such a doctrine is conspicuously absent from St. Paul (this is evidence also against the general acceptance of it by contemporary Rabbinism), and by the fact that it was long before it became the settled belief of the Church.

INDEX OF PASSAGES IN THE GOSPELS
COMMENTED ON OR REFERRED TO

INDEX